BIA

Zambezi River

...R.

Deka R.

Lukosi R.

...ji R.

...nkie

Lukosi

...onatela camp
...dova Dam

matoa
Ruins.

Dett

Gwaai R.

Mzola R.

Kana R.

Shongokwe R.

Shangani R.

...ey
...al Boundaries
...k Boundaries
Main Roads
Secondary Roads
Railway Line
Game Fence
Rivers

Dom
main
camp
Nyamandlovu Pan
Guvalala Pan

Shapi Pan

...Tur Road

...Pan

Jambuli
Pan

Makalolo
Pans

Mahurli

Kennedy

Ngamo

WANKIE

...ring

Ngweshla
Pan

Linkwasha Valley

NATIONAL

PARK

Labuti
Pan

Newahai
Pan

...arika Pan

Guabusubuya

Sicheesha
Pan

Sihumi Valley

Limpandi
Dam

Sibunini
Pan

Natu R.

WANKIE

The Story of a great Game Reserve

WANKIE

The Story of a great Game Reserve

BY

TED DAVISON

Illustrated by Penny Miller

Ted. Davison

THORNTREE PRESS

1998

BOOKS OF AFRICA (PTY.) LTD.

1005 Cape of Good Hope Savings Bank Building
St. George's Street
Cape Town

©

E. DAVISON
1967

ISBN 0-7974-1608-0

First published in Zimbabwe in 1996 by

Thorntree Press (Pvt) Ltd, PO Box 9243 Hillside, Bulawayo, Zimbabwe

PRINTED BY R.C.P. BELMONT
AND BOUND BY BOOKSET.
BULAWAYO - ZIMBABWE

To
Connie, Rodney, Gerald and John
and all our memories
of Wankie

The author acknowledges with thanks the advice of
Dr G. Bond, Mr R. Smithers and Dr W. A. Wragg.

FOREWORD

BY THE HONOURABLE IAN DOUGLAS SMITH
PRIME MINISTER OF RHODESIA

Some forty years ago, the Wankie Game Reserve was proclaimed, and Ted Davison, the author of this book, was appointed its first warden. He remained at this post for 34 years and during this period probably did more than anyone else in Rhodesia for the preservation and development of our wild game and the promotion of Wankie as one of the great tourist attractions of this world.

His tasks over these years are vividly and truthfully portrayed in the pages that follow, but the over-riding theme throughout is his love and affection for creatures of all shapes and sizes.

Men cast in the mould of Ted Davison deserve the highest praise and thanks, for they have carried out the hard, relentless and often dangerous task of preserving the animals of the Wild Kingdom so that future generations of Rhodesians can enjoy their heritage.

PUBLISHER'S NOTE

The publishers wish to thank the various people – all with the common denominator being their love of Hwange National Park, and concern for its well-being – who assisted in the up-dating of this expanded third impression of *WANKIE – The Story of a Great Game Reserve.*

In particular our thanks go to Dr John Hanks for re-cementing his bond with Hwange and agreeing to write the Introduction, and to Mr Viv Wilson for his interest and input regarding past and present wildlife numbers. Further, our appreciation goes to Ted Davison's sons for their permission to publish a new updated edition of their father's book, the first impression of which was published in 1967.

Whilst Ted Davison's book has, deservedly, become a regional classic in its own right, chronicling the history of a Wankie of long ago, it is hoped that the additional material added, via new photographs, Dr Hanks' Introduction, and an Afterword by Keith Meadows that presents more recent history, will contribute towards a broader overview and appreciation of this flagship national park whose fortunes, of late, have been mixed.

The use of the words *Hwange* or *Wankie* variably in the Afterword is not a sign of editorial dereliction or preference for either name. The phraseology matches the time frame in use at that juncture.

INTRODUCTION

Hwange National Park has built up a deserved reputation as one of Africa's finest wildlife sanctuaries, a crown jewel in a mosaic of protected areas that have a vital role to play in drawing visitors to the continent in their thousands to earn desperately needed foreign currency. When Ted Davison started work in October 1928 in what was then called the Wankie Game Reserve, he would have found it very difficult to believe that 60 years later the beloved wilderness, which he worked so hard to establish and nurture, would have the potential to make a really significant contribution to the economic transformation of southern Africa.

I wonder how Ted would have reacted to the realities of Africa in the late 1990s. The problems facing Hwange National Park today, which Keith Meadows has so succinctly described in the AFTERWORD, are not unique to Zimbabwe. The perception of *"a lacklustre commitment by its managing body"* is a symptom of a much greater malaise facing the continent which goes far beyond an apparent indifference to conserving some of the world's greatest natural assets. Why have conservation budgets been cut in nearly every African country, and why have rhinos and other valuable species been subjected to such unrelenting pressure? The answer to these questions is fundamental to an understanding of the "conservation dilemma" facing all developing countries, namely the pressure from the developed world to preserve vast areas like Hwange in a state akin to those first encountered by the early pioneers like Ted Davison, along with the pressures on the governments of these countries to accommodate legitimate human demands for the basic necessities of food, fuel, shelter and water.

What has changed in the last 60 years since Ted Davison first

I

set foot in a magnificent part of Africa that so many have grown to love? For a start, the human population has grown at a rate that few would have anticipated. Africa today has the highest population growth rate of any major region in the world and the lowest prevalence of contraceptive use. This high rate of growth has resulted in unprecedented human demands on the continent's natural resources, together with a level of land transformation by pastoral, agricultural, industrial and urban development, and by alien plant encroachment that has destroyed or fragmented natural habitats. As a result, designated protected areas stand alone in splendid isolation, visible even from a satellite orbiting the earth. For those living in poverty in a degraded resource base, adjacent to an apparent abundance of grassland and woodland, with everything from additional grazing for livestock, to wild fruits, edible roots, medicinal plants, firewood, honey, fish and meat, the temptation to encroach is very great indeed.

There is a growing body of evidence to indicate the vulnerability of fragmented, small habitat islands which remain as designated protected areas. Even if all other factors which could impact on wildlife populations were brought under control, a combination of genetic and environmental changes, coupled with the susceptibility of isolated populations to various wildlife diseases, could well undermine the long-term viability of such isolated populations. Theories of island biogeography have recently become a major concern of Africa's wildlife managers. After all, they are managing "islands", surrounded by a "sea" of transformed and often degraded land, occupied by a species which resists invasion by others.

It is a regrettable reality that overpopulation and poverty go hand-in-hand. Of the world's 35 poorest countries, 29 of them are in Africa south of the Sahara. Some of these countries face a situation of absolute poverty. For example, right on Zimbabwe's border is Mozambique, whose economy since its independence from Portugal in June 1975 has suffered not only the damaging effects of nearly 17 years of war, but also drought, floods, famine, the displacement of millions of people and a scarcity of foreign exchange and of skilled workers. As a consequence, Mozambique became one of the poorest countries in the world, heavily reliant on foreign credits. The vast majority of Mozambicans live below the poverty line, and social indicators are among the lowest in Africa. In 1995, according to estimates from the World Bank, the country's gross national product (GNP) was US$1,513m, equivalent to only $88 per head. The developed world should not be surprised that conservation budgets are low or non-existent under such circumstances of such absolute poverty. The state is under great pressure to address the more immediate needs such as the provision of housing, health services, roads, education, and employment opportunities.

Consequently, it should come as no surprise that the majority of Africa's protected areas are inadequately funded and unable to maintain basic infrastructure and facilities at an acceptable standard for international tourism, the one industry that has more potential than any other to create the jobs that are so urgently needed. Furthermore, the chronic shortage of funds coupled with poorly motivated and inadequately trained staff has made it increasingly difficult, if not impossible, for protected area managers to safeguard valuable endangered species, or even in some cases to prevent human encroachment. Hwange National Park is not alone in the problems it is facing.

An added complication throughout Africa has been brought about by civil wars, some of which have been exacerbated by external interventions, and most of which have left many people dead, in exile, or exposed to famine. In southern Africa, Angola,

Mozambique and to a lesser extent Zimbabwe, Namibia and South Africa experienced several years of conflict, a guerilla war that had, and still has, a profound effect upon economic relations with bordering countries, and on internal post-independent economies. These realities cannot be ignored. There would clearly be great benefit in Zimbabwe taking advantage of much closer links with the well-developed economy and infrastructure within South Africa, yet the suspicions associated with the legacies of apartheid still persist, breeding an inherent and insidious reluctance to join hands with colleagues to the south in programmes of mutual benefit.

Protected areas will not look after themselves. Each and everyone in Africa is under threat, and pressures will increase as human numbers continue to grow. They require management on a day-to day basis, and this management is not cheap. The challenge for wildlife authorities is how to optimize financial return from the sanctuaries under their charge without destroying the ecological, territorial and aesthetic integrity of the areas concerned. It is no longer realistic to expect taxpayers in the African countries that house some of the world's finest national parks and game reserves to dig deeper into their pockets for the funds required. They have too many other immediate social problems requiring attention. Nor is it realistic to expect the international community to continue to provide annual running expenses for these areas. There is simply not enough money to go around. One source of funds that has not been exploited to its full potential is that of the tourism industry.

No other industry anywhere in the world has the same capacity for sustained and sustainable growth. In 1997, world tourism arrivals reached a total of 613 million. If present trends continue, 1,000 million tourism arrivals will be reached in the year 2010, bringing in receipts in excess of US$1,550 billion.

IIII

In 1998, tourism will create over 231 million jobs, and by the year 2010 this should have increased to 328 million. The relevant point of these statistics as far as Hwange National Park is concerned is that much of this growth is anticipated to be in nature based tourism. Southern Africa, with its splendid celebration of biological diversity, stunning landscapes and well-developed hotel and transport infrastructure, should be at the forefront of this remarkable new opportunity, developing a vision for marketing the region, quadrupling tourism revenue within the next five years, providing the jobs that are so urgently needed, and ensuring that the national parks and game reserves (one of the main draw cards of the industry), are adequately funded. Tourism must go right to the top of the political agenda. It must be embraced by national and local leaders, actively supported, encouraged and facilitated by them, and promoted as the premier sustainable industry that will lead the subcontinent into the next millennium.

Certainly, tourism of the wrong kind can be disruptive and destructive. There will inevitably be those who will oppose further development in and around Hwange. Such opponents should first of all be asked where the funds and the national commitment will come from to put the park back on track, and then be reminded of the four key guiding principles of responsible tourism, which are as follows:

Responsibility to the environment. Hwange National Park is a semi-arid part of Africa, with all the inherent sensitivities associated with excessive visitor usage. It is nevertheless underutilized as a tourism destination, both spatially and temporally. Existing facilities can be improved and new ones developed without compromising or threatening the quintessential essence of this special corner of Zimbabwe. What might be perceived by some as a threat to the very wildness of Hwange, has to be turned into an opportunity for its survival.

v

Involvement of local communities. For far too long, the managers of most of Africa's designated protected areas have ignored neighbouring communities. Given the task facing Ted Davison at the time, it is perfectly understandable that he referred to those living on the boundaries of the Wankie Game Reserve in 1928 as a "menace". The last 60 years has seen a remarkable change in attitude, and if Ted were still alive today I believe he would have accepted the necessity for this transformation. Human populations have grown, and it is totally unrealistic to expect wildlife sanctuaries to survive intact when they are surrounded by people living in poverty and in degraded environments, often moved out, fenced, and excluded, all too often receiving no benefit from tourism revenue. The genuine involvement of neighbouring communities is one of the greatest challenges facing the future of the continent's wildlife sanctuaries, not just by creating jobs for people, but also by creating ownership opportunities for people as equity partners in new business enterprises. Africa needs success stories in this field, and Hwange can show how it should be done.

Responsibility to respect, invest in and develop local cultures. Cultural tourism has been undervalued in the past, and is growing in popularity and demand. Such facilities can be accommodated in and around Hwange National Park to supplement and compliment nature based tourism. However, an invasion of foreign visitors could destroy local cultures and values, and thus careful attention will have to be given to maintaining the dignity and self-respect associated with traditions that go back for many generations.

Responsibility to visitors. For a tourism industry to thrive and grow there is no substitute for a satisfied customer. Those who have received excellent service, experienced the unrivalled pleasure of wildlife encounters, and enjoyed the high standard

VI

of hospitality that Zimbabwe can offer, will return, telling their friends to come too. Attention to the safety, security, and health of visitors is equally important in order to satisfy customer demands, all part of a "satisfaction index" which has to be recognized and actively promoted. The private sector, with its entrepreneurial expertise and wide knowledge of the hospitality industry, from computer based booking facilities to the running of tours and lodges, must be given more opportunities in developing Hwange National Park to its full potential. The challenge is to optimize the private sector potential through a careful process of commercialization without privatization.

Hwange National Park has one additional factor in its favour, and that is the exciting possibility of linking the park with protected areas in neighbouring countries to form an "Upper Zambezi Peace Park", a vision for the future which will link Hwange to the Chobe National Park, and to the Moremi Wildlife Reserve in the Okavango Delta of Botswana, north to Namibia to the Caprivi Game Park, and across the border into Zambia through the teak forests to the Kafue National Park. This will create a massive new conservation area or "peace park" centered on the Victoria Falls with a combination of habitats and wildlife species unequalled in Africa.

At the official opening of an international conference on Transboundary Protected Areas as a vehicle for International Co-operation held in Somerset West in September 1997, Dr Pallo Jordan, South Africa's Minister of Environmental Affairs and Tourism highlighted the significance of the tourism industry, particularly in southern Africa, and also noted that the nature tourism component of this industry is significant, and is likely to increase in the future. The Minister said: *"Peace parks are particularly appropriate for the southern African region which has been racked by wars and other forms of conflict for the past decade. Peace parks will be a token of a shared commitment by the peoples and governments of South Africa*

VII

to strive for peace and to pursue the option of peaceful resolution of conflict as an intrinsic condition for the welfare and development of our region". Hwange National Park can take the lead in making the dream of peace parks become a reality. Ted Davison would surely have championed such an initiative.

John Hanks, Somerset West, August 1998

AUTHOR'S PREFACE
TO THE SECOND EDITION

With the release of the second edition of the book "Wankie", which was first published in 1967, the author would like to stress that much has transpired since the book was written.

With the improvement of water supplies by the building of dams, the sinking of boreholes, and the installation of pumps, the Park has been able to carry a greatly increased game population.

As was predicted, some culling of elephant and buffalo has been necessary — this was done with a minimum of disturbance to other game animals; and the tourists were hardly aware that a very considerable number of animals had been removed. The fact that modern methods were employed — using helicopters and spotter planes, together with an adequate staff of efficient men — enabled whole family groups or whole herds to be removed at one time, leaving no stragglers or disturbed animals. The removal of a large number of the bigger animals undoubtedly reduced the pressure on the browsing and grazing, enabling the Park to survive two consecutive very dry seasons with very little, if any, mortality due to poverty. There was little indication that there was any migration to watering-places outside the Park.

How different the position would have been had an oil shortage occurred at the same time as the drought necessitating the closing down of most of the pumps. There is no denying the fact that Wankie National Park is now very dependent upon oil; and, had the Foot and Mouth fence been erected along the railway, and an oil shortage brought about a large scale migration of game towards the Gwaai tributaries, the mortality along the fences would have been catastrophic. As it is, the proposal to erect the fence along the railway as well as the South East boundary was hotly contested; and a compromise between the Veterinary Department and the National Parks resulted in the fence being placed North East of the railway, leaving open a corridor to the Gwaai river. This was a safeguard which happily has not become necessary up to now.

In the event of a serious water shortage, it is difficult to forecast just how the animals in the Park would react. Many of them have lived for generations within the Park boundaries and know no other water supplies outside their own limited feeding range. Would they be able to locate water outside the Park, or would they simply remain in the Park hoping for the onset of the rains? There is little doubt that many of them would perish whatever they did.

Game has been encouraged to use the corridor to the Gwaai and to cross the railway-line between Dett and Kennedy, establishing themselves in the Dett Vlei region. The new and very popular Wankie Safari Lodge is right in this corridor — should there ever be a big migration to this area, it would be, without doubt, the finest game viewing region in Africa.

The full effect of the game fence is only now becoming apparent, as, on a recent visit to the Park, it was surprising to note the almost total absence of wildebeest in the Sibanini area. This was the terrain which carried the main wildebeest population of the Park — quite apart from the large numbers which invaded the locality during water shortages in Botswana. Now, however, the Ngamo/Kennedy district carries the main wildebeest herds, while the Southern section is deserted. This is attributed to the fence cutting off the normal range in the Nata river basin.

The large numbers of elephant and buffalo in the Park cannot be solely attributed to natural increase. The disturbance created in Bechuanaland (now Botswana) by the establishment of the Colonial Development Corporation's million-acre Cattle Ranch and the anti-game policy of this concern probably caused many animals, previously only seasonal migrants into the Park, to become permanent residents. Fortunately the C.D.C. cattle ranch, like many other projects of this organisation, did not last long; and it, like the Ground Nuts Scheme in Tanganyika, and the Egg Scheme in Gambia, folded up.

Although the Wankie National Park is on a sound footing, well protected by legislation, it still faces the danger of expropriation. During its life, there have been two dangerous onslaughts when it was proposed by high-ranking government officials to deproclaim the Southern half of the Park on the grounds that the land was not being used and could be put to better use as part of the Gwaai Native Reserve. In the one case there was to be no compensating factor, but in the other the Park would have been extended Northwards to the Matetsi River. This would have been of little benefit to the game resident on the Kalahari sands, as few of them would have changed their habitat to that extent. It would have meant the destruction of all the game South of the demarcated line and breeding up a new population North of the Deka river. Being a totally different geological formation, the game of the two areas are entirely different, and the loss of the species in the Kalahari sands would not have been compensated for.

Today, the danger of deproclamation due to lack of development has not been removed altogether, but, now that there are roads and established water-points, perhaps the land is even more attractive to the agriculturalists who still see the Park as non-productive. The substantial foreign currency earned from the tourist trade in the Park means little to these land-hungry people. The Wankie National Park could accommodate thousands of African tribesmen with very little effort on anyone's part.

Before the writer retired from the Wankie National Park, the staff were culling about 200 elephant a year, all of them outside the Park, from herds which invaded the Tribal Trust Land adjoining the Park. Since then no less than 4 529 elephant, 2 442 buffalo, and 4 566 impala, have been removed from inside the Park. All of the meat accruing from these operations was sold for consumption by the lower-income group of the population and for pets' food. This is not the end — culling of elephant and buffalo must go on from time to time.

Surely the fact that all this protein is being produced will establish the Park as a production unit over and above the substantial revenue derived from the tourists.

These figures do not take into account the animals captured for translocation to other Parks and game reserves. These include: 243 zebra, 39 roan, 85 elephant, 39 buffalo, 11 sable.

T. D.

March, 1977.
Salisbury, Rhodesia.

CHAPTER ONE

ONE dark night in September 1928 I alighted from a train at Kennedy halt which lies about half-way between Bulawayo and the Victoria Falls. On the railway siding I was met by John Lundin, a game catcher in the area, who introduced me to two other residents of the neighbourhood. I was twenty-two years old and the reception committee (if we can call it that) peered at me curiously in the dark. We stood under a dripping railway water tank and chatted for a few minutes. The conversation went something like this: "So you are to become the game warden of this area? What do you know of this type of country? What do you know of the Bushmen? They will kill you or you will die of thirst trying to catch them."

This was the rather cynical welcome I received when I arrived to take over the Wankie Game Reserve. I had met John Lundin in Salisbury some days before I set out on this journey which was to be the great turning point of my life. It had been arranged that I was to stay with him at his camp at Kennedy where he had a number of animals which he had captured for zoos in Australia. Lundin and his partner Japie Herbst held permits to capture game animals for zoos and these permits were allowed to expire when the area was proclaimed a game reserve. Lundin, his partners, and some of his friends were about the only Europeans who knew anything of the vast, dry, semi-desert which it had been decided should be Rhodesia's first game reserve.

The only other people, apart from the local Bushmen, who had been into the country in recent times – in fact since Selous's days – were two police patrols who had been in quest of ivory poachers. One patrol under Trooper Heatley went into the northern part of the area to surprise European poachers believed to be at Shapi pan; on this occasion Heatley reached Shapi and named one of the pans in that group after himself; but in later years I was never able to decide which pan it had been. The other police patrol, under Trooper Yeoman, walked in to Ngwashla pan about fifteen miles from Kennedy, in their bare feet, in order not to identify themselves by their spoor to the Bushmen, who were sure to be watching the paths.

The only maps I had been able to acquire of the area showed Ngwashla, Shapi, and Heatley's pans but none of them had been accurately positioned. There was a track shown running from Dett on the railway to Shapi pan and this was about all the detail contained on the maps of those days.

Lundin had undertaken to take me by motor lorry into the area to see if there was still water in any of the pans and, if the pans were dry, whether there was any water under the surface.

After a quick visit to Wankie Colliery by train to make myself known to the N.C.O. in charge of the police as well as to the Native Commissioner, I returned to Dett, where it was decided I should establish my headquarters. My visit to the administrative officers had not produced any valuable information on the country over which I was now in charge, beyond the names of some of the local residents who might know something of the locality. I came away with the feeling that very little was known about the place, the game, or the people living in it.

The decision had been taken by the government of the day to make this stretch of some 5,000 square miles of uninhabited land into a game reserve as a result of a questionnaire sent out to all native commissioners, and other people who had some knowledge of the game of Rhodesia. From their recommendations this area in what was known as the Wankie Native District was chosen.

I knew nothing of the area when I arrived other than what I had been told, and the prospects of making a successful game sanctuary of it did not look very bright. There was, apparently, very little water in the area during the dry season and there was a threat of a tsetse fly invasion from the north-east, across the Gwaai river. Game was not very plentiful. Even in Selous's days (when this early hunter visited the dis-

6

trict) he preferred to hunt in the hilly country north of the proposed reserve and not in the reserve proper; even although the greater part of this flat Kalahari sand country was free of fly as was the case before the game was depleted by the Rinderpest of 1896. The fact that the Kalahari sand areas dried out almost completely in the dry season in years of poor rainfall no doubt caused game to move towards the Gwaai river and its tributaries where, in fact, Selous found his game.

All this area had been left out of the proposed reserve even though it was largely unoccupied. Selous in his day travelled as far as Linkwasha and Dopi vleis by ox-wagon and, for fear of encountering tsetse fly, left his wagons there; thereafter walking, to do his hunting further north. The fact that the fly did not penetrate into the Kalahari sands for many miles but limited its spread to the mupani country which lay north of the main watershed was something of a comfort, for it was an indication that at least not all of the reserve was threatened.

Soon after my arrival at Dett I was joined by Lundin and a Major Goad from the Irrigation Department. Together we loaded up Lundin's battered old Chevrolet three-ton lorry and prepared for our journey to Shapi and my first real glimpse of the Kalahari sand country. On to that old Chevrolet (which had no bonnet, cab, windscreen, or doors) we loaded our camp kit, consisting only of beds, bedding, food, pots and pans. We did not consider tents as there was absolutely no chance of rain or dew and we did not take a portable bath as we knew there would be insufficient water for such a luxury. Our main load consisted of 120 gallons of water and ten gallons of spare petrol.

Major Goad (a drilling expert) was a likeable sort of chap; a tall military type, not given to wasting his words but friendly enough. Lundin, by contrast, was a stocky, sunburnt Swede, as talkative as you please, with a rich fund of anecdotes from his hunting experiences. Wiry and strong and well versed in the ways of the veld, Lundin was a useful companion in the bush and a great raconteur around the camp fire at night.

It had been an exceptionally bad season. The rains had failed and the area into which we were going was believed to be almost waterless. Our job was to find out (before the rains did come) if any of the larger known pans still held water and to investigate a report that water could be obtained from dried-up pans by the simple process of digging for it in the very centre of such pans.

7

Our guide's hunting exploits (which had, of course, now come to an abrupt end with the proclamation of Wankie as a reserve) had never taken him far from the railway. It had always been necessary for him to get his captured animals to rail, by various means; for example, giraffe could not be transported by lorry or ox-wagon, but had to be walked. To carry his equipment Lundin had used a light ox-wagon and it was the tracks of this wagon we were now to follow from Dett to Shapi.

We set off shortly after sunrise, passing through the heavily wooded country, familiar to Rhodesian bush lovers; musasa, mupani, Rhodesian teak; a restricted horizon and the dirt track winding its way in and out endlessly.

All went well for the first three miles or so, then we struck our first stretch of Kalahari sand and the lorry at once began labouring and protesting. After half a mile the radiator was boiling furiously. Another mile farther we had to stop and refill the radiator; thereafter the routine was a stop every two miles to put in about two gallons of water. On the approximate basis of a gallon of water per mile for our thirsty Chevrolet, we began to wonder if the supply we had taken on board would be enough to complete the trip. However, we consoled ourselves with the thought that the more water we used the more we lightened the load; and thus, we hoped, the better the progress.

We toiled on and by nearly midday reached Tshebema, the first pan. It was only about fifteen miles from Dett. On subsequent patrols by horse and pack animals I was able to reach this pan from Dett in much the same time as our lorry had taken. Tshebema I was told was the Bushman name for a baobab tree, and the pan was named after a big one nearby, one of the very few I ever saw growing on Kalahari sand at a height of 3,200 feet above sea level.

The pan was dry – as we expected it to be. Well-worn elephant paths leading to it suggested that it had been used up to the time the water had given out, probably two or three months earlier. There were some old tracks of giraffe, eland, lion and hyena, but little else. The bottom comprised an area of about 750 square yards of hard-baked black mud. A small patch in the very centre was smooth and cracked, but the rest had been churned by elephant. The spoors were anything up to two feet deep and eighteen inches across and it was clear that the thirsty visitors included some very large bulls as well as small

8

calves. They must have used the pan right up to the very last drop of water, turning it eventually into a thick pool of mud. There were some dead birds in one of the larger, deeper elephant spoors – which told its own story. A little water had no doubt seeped into the hole soon after it had been made and for a day or so birds had been able to get a drink. After that drought had taken its agonising toll.

Major Goad went to work at once with a hand auger. This useful tool made a hole about nine inches in diameter. In less than an hour the hole was ten feet deep. Hopefully we watched – but there was not even a trickle of water. Nothing seeped through. The formation revealed by the auger was black silt to a depth of about four feet, then tough yelllow clay which became more and more sandy at depth. Clearly, the clay acted as a water-tight seal for water running into the pan from the surrounding country during the rains, but there was no seepage.

Up to this stage we had seen no game at all and very little spoor less than a month old. But soon after leaving Tshebema we saw three giraffe, the first I had encountered in the wild. They made off quickly and we saw little more than their necks above the stunted mangwe scrub.

We passed two more pans; both quite dry. At one of them I noticed where an elephant had been lying down in what must have been soft mud, leaving an almost complete imprint of its body, showing all the creases of its skin and the shape of its ears – indicating where the water level had been at the end of the rains. Later I learnt that the place was called Garagangwe (which means "rest a little"), being in the first piece of open grassland we had encountered.

Up to then the country had been high forest, some of it musasa and some Rhodesian teak with a little mupani near the pans. Most of it was leafless except for a welcome show of very new leaves on some of the musasa. At Tshebema I saw my first camel-thorn, a tree I was to learn to love in years to come. It was a very old specimen with much dead wood on it, but despite the baking dryness of the veld it was sending out a brave show of new leaves and yellow flowers.

I was surprised to see a herd of about twenty impala soon after we left Garagangwe. They were in good condition although they must have been without water for many weeks, if not months. There was no other game around. Had there been any water at all we would have been

9

sure to have seen some indication of game concentrating in the area. During the drought years that followed the proclamation of Wankie Game Reserve I found many other examples of impala surviving happily without water for months on end.

The hot day wore on. As we neared Shapi the going improved and we found ourselves moving out of the Kalahari sand on to harder ground. En route we passed an old camp at a big pan called Bembesi where a well had been sunk. Obviously the place had been used a good deal by both Africans and Europeans, but it was a desolate scene now. The thirty-foot well was dry, the huts deserted and collapsing and the bush taking over, as it always does at the first retreat of man. The place had clearly been a poacher's haunt, or at least used by someone trading with poachers.

As we neared Shapi the only living thing we saw was a single ostrich. Shapi pan was another disappointment; although we concluded it had not been dry for more than a month or so and Major Goad was of the opinion that water could be located at a depth of, perhaps, less than fifty feet.

We made camp that night at Shapi – to be remembered as my first camp, indeed as my first night in Wankie Game Reserve. After a hard day in the bush, there is a tremendous sense of peace and well-being as you lounge at the camp fire, maybe yarning awhile, or just lying relaxed as the embers glow redly in the night.

This was not a night without incident, however. Soon after dark a hyena visited the camp, frankly curious for a moment or so before hurriedly slinking off along an elephant path to the west. Later, after we had turned in, I heard a single elephant taking the same path.

The next morning I found the spoor and suggested to my companions that we follow the path to see if it led to water. Lundin and one of the Africans both assured me that there were no other big pans for at least fifteen miles (as far as either of them had ever been in that direction) and Lundin also thought that if there were any pans, even twenty-five miles away, he would have heard of them from the Bushmen hunters he had met during his hunting days in the area two years before.

Without breaking camp, we crossed a sandy ridge south of Shapi and down into another depression, where Lundin had once seen signs of a Bushmen camp and well. We found the place and soon had a hole down about seven feet. There was a little seepage of water but Major Goad thought the supply would be too limited to make it worth opening up for game. "Might be sufficient to serve a camp-site though," he added. Nearby was the carcass of a very big giraffe, and since we had at least found a little water we called the place Giraffe Spring. You will not find the name on many maps to-day!

Three punctures on the return journey to Dett did not help matters, but at least our ancient Chevrolet managed to struggle home. En route we spotted smoke from a veld fire to the north. All the grass along our route had been burned off months before and we were somewhat surprised that there should be any, not far away, left to burn. We had seen no sign of a veld fire the previous day. It was about fifteen miles from the railway at Inyantue siding and possibly had started on the railway, burned itself out, and then, after a lapse of two or three days, started up again – an occurrence which I was to find not uncommon.

We spent the night at Dett and then set off on the second leg of our trip to another well-known pan called Ngwashla. To get there we motored along the fire-guard flanking the railway to a point beyond Kennedy. On the way we called in at a farm (*Petties Farm*) which was one of two within the area proclaimed as a game reserve. I remember as we drove up to the house there was a tiny garden with one fine grapefruit tree in it. (Incidentally, the tree is still there.) The owner of the place, a certain Mr Going, came out and I recognised him as a man I had met at Kennedy siding a few nights earlier when I arrived by train to take up my appointment as game warden. He had not been very cordial then, and he was far less now. In fact there was downright hostility in his whole attitude.

"You're the So-and-so I met at Kennedy siding, eh?" (after Lundin had introduced us properly) "and what do you think you're doing in a place like this?"

He was about sixty years old and obviously considered me to be an infant.

"You don't know the place," he went on, "you'll die of this or that or the other, or the Bushmen will shoot you."

I told him I would take a chance on all that and I thought I would get to know the country well enough. Eventually he invited us inside for some refreshment, and there followed one of the strangest afternoon tea sessions. To keep the place cool, the owner had every window shut and the blinds drawn, which gave the room almost a funereal effect. Mrs Going, a very pleasant woman, provided us with tea and, in semi-darkness, we sat sipping it while Going talked of the hardships of his life and what he thought of the government and game reserves any-way. I may add that Going was an Irishman and, therefore, automatically "agin the government".

At heart he was a good fellow, no doubt, but after half an hour or so we were not sorry to leave his darkened house and push on to the next farm, *Sunnyside*. Here they were catching game for zoos and the farmer had a giraffe and about a dozen sable in a pen. This was per-fectly legal, for it was the last consignment in terms of the old licence, but thereafter no more permits were issued.

The way to Ngwashla was sandy but the country was much more open and there were many picturesque patches of vegetable ivory palms. Game was more plentiful since the animals had access to water along with the cattle at *Sunnyside*, and this actually had been en-couraged in order to make game catching easier on the farm.

The pan at Ngwashla was not quite as dry as those at Tshebema and Shapi. Black silt in the bottom had a hard crust about a foot thick and below that there was thick mud for four or five feet. A couple of sable had ventured on to the dry crust, broken through and been trap-ped. Unable to extricate themselves they had died a lingering death. The thick mud would not permit a hole of more than six feet, but we did establish the fact that at that depth there was hard clay. For my part, I would have liked to have camped the night at Ngwashla, for I was anxious to see what went on after dark in this new world opening up for me. But we returned and camped at Kennedy, where we expec-ted to find game coming to drink the waste water from the railway tanks when there were no trains about. A good deal of water was escaping from leaking taps, but it lured only a hyena and birds. The birds came in large numbers and it was fascinating to watch them helping themselves from dripping taps and actually fluttering into the open tanks and clinging to the struts inside so that they could drink direct.

Between Kennedy and Dett we noticed many elephant spoors across our tracks of the day before. The elephant were evidently making their way to the tributaries of the Gwaai river – probably the Sikumi swamp seven miles from the railway outside the reserve. We never sighted the herd; all we knew was that somewhere out in the drought-stricken bush it was engaged on much the same mission as we were ourselves – the search for water; but to them it meant life or death.

This was my first introduction to the Kalahari sand veld which I was later to learn covered about two-thirds of the area which had been set aside as Rhodesia's game reserve.

The boundaries of the reserve which had been decided upon were fairly well defined on the maps but not on the ground. In the north the reserve was bounded by privately-owned farms starting at *Deka* farm on the boundary of Botswana and by the boundaries of the Wankie Coal Concession. Only at one point for a short distance did the boundary reach the Deka river. In the north-east the boundary was the railway between Lukosi and Ngamo; the stretch between Dett and Ngamo, a distance of fifty miles being dead straight. It is not quite true to say that the railway was the boundary as the railway company owned a series of farms, three miles square and three miles apart, lying on the west side of the line. These were unoccupied. There were also two privately-owned farms which were occupied, *Balcarres* and *Petties* farms, to-gether owned by Mr Going, and *Sunnyside*, half of one of the railway farms owned by Mr Venter.

The south-east boundary marched along the border of the Gwaai Native Reserve, being formed by the Sihumi Vlei, a depression which began at the railway at the Ngamo pans and continued southwards for some fifty miles to its junction with another valley. At this point both valleys opened out and almost disappeared.

From here, the boundary of the Reserve lay along a line (which had never been cut or surveyed), between two points about thirty-five miles apart. One point was the junction of two valleys, which we could never find, the other a point on the Tswana border where the old Mpande Mutenga (or Panda-ma-tenga) road forming the boundary between the countries crossed the Nata river. The boundary of the Reserve then followed the territorial boundary northwards along the old road as far as Deka farm, which was on the Deka river.

The natural boundaries of this vast expanse of unoccupied land from an ecological point of view were the Deka river in the north, the Gwaai river to the east and the Nata river to the south. But all these rivers had been denied to the reserve for political reasons and even in those early days I could see trouble when game increased as eventually it would if

13

my work was to be successful and animals started drifting to the bigger natural water supplies during the dry season.

For two months, until the wet season started, I would be unable to get into the reserve to find out what was there and what was going on. I occupied myself getting some quarters built at Dett, but as Dett in those days depended enirely on water brought by rail from Kennedy, twenty-three miles away, there was little prospect of my being able to establish a home in the little village. However, I was fortunate enough to find an old well at a quarry site about a mile from the station and here I set about building my home, consisting of two pole and dagga huts, which were meant to serve until more permanent structures could be afforded.

I acquired the services of two Bushmen and four other local Africans as well as an Angoni cook, a great character who served me for many years. Two horses and two pack mules arrived in due course and I started teaching myself to ride.

I was by no means a greenhorn in the veld. I had spent two happy years in the bush as a tsetse fly ranger in the Lomagundi district at Doma where I had learned a great deal about the veld and the game animals there. In addition to this I was born at Hartley and spent my boyhood days roaming the country in between bouts of boarding school. There were, however, no elephant in the Doma area in those days and all I was to learn about the great animals would be new to me.

The two Bushmen I engaged were a disappointing pair. One was tall and lanky and so riddled with tuberculosis that he could not walk more than two miles without stopping for a smoke and a rest; but he was a wonderful tracker, and knew his way about parts of the reserve. His name was Nhalabati. The other was called Nari. He, too, had T.B. and was very little use to me as he did not know the country inside the reserve but he had two sons who, although very young, promised to be useful in later years.

The true Bushmen who knew the reserve well and were good hunters were reluctant to work for me. Most of them lived along the Nata river or in Botswana. They were not interested in working for anyone who was not hunting game as they were afraid that they might be instrumental in the arrest of their friends or relatives – resulting in reprisals for having guided the "policeman" into their territory, revealing to him their secret watering places.

I spent the first wet season patrolling the country within about twenty

14

miles of the railway, where there was little danger of getting lost and, during the rains, there were hundreds of small pans and water was easy to find.

In addition to the two occupied farms already mentioned there was a timber concession operating inside the reserve which was cutting many thousands of cubic feet of Rhodesian teak, which is the mkusi or *Baikiaea plurijuga*. This concern was based on the railway but had mills twenty miles out in the reserve in the Linkwasha valley. They used donkeys to drag the logs to their temporary wooden railways for transport to the mills, where they were sawn up. This concession was allowed to expire and was not renewed once the area had been cut over.

There had been another concern established to grow wheat at Bembesi pan (near Shapi) at the foot of White Hill, the only hill in the reserve south of the main watershed. This concern had folded up before I arrived, fortunately, for I do not believe that a single grain of wheat was ever planted and the show was just a trading post for poachers under the guise of a farm. Ivory was a very saleable commodity in those days.

During these early patrols I did not see much game. The little I did see I had to hunt for by picking up the spoor and following it to where the animals were resting during the day. Occasionally a giraffe or eland would be seen but mostly the game came out into the open to feed and drink only at night. It was evident, however, that there were a great many lions in the reserve. Their tracks could be found at almost every water-hole and they could be heard nearly every night. Their kills were frequently found and this was a source of supply for most of our meat, I seldom had to shoot for meat for my gang of labourers. We could rely on finding at least one fresh kill a week. For myself I shot wild duck for the pot as they were plentiful.

It was decided as a matter of policy to reduce the lion population and give the game a chance to increase. There was a good nucleus of giraffe, eland, sable, roan, kudu, impala, elephant and lion, but other varieties were scarce. During my early patrols I never saw a sign of wildebeest, or buffalo and very few zebra.

CHAPTER TWO

WHEN the rains were almost over and my horses and pack mules had become used to patrol work and would not bolt for home the moment they were turned out to graze – or buck off their packs the moment they saw or smelt a wild animal – I prepared for my first long patrol. This was to take me to the western boundary of the reserve and into the south where I believed the country was different, being mupani and not true Kalahari sand. The route planned would take me right through the heart of the reserve and I had no idea what I would find there. Few Europeans had ever been into this part and written records of their journeys were almost non-existent. I had, in the meantime, acquired the services of a Bushman called Vumandaba, a tall, quietly spoken man who had been as far west as a pan called Nehimba. Vumandaba and I travelled many long miles together and became a very good team in the bush.

The only records of this area were scanty descriptions by people such as Selous, Baines and others, of journeys through the bush or along the old Mpande Mutenga road. Bushmen who knew the area kept their secrets, refusing to divulge any information at all – probably because they felt this might lead to the arrest of relatives engaged in poaching. The few maps that existed showed little more than a blank space with a few pans dotted in the extreme south. The Mpande Mutenga road running along the western flank of the reserve was also the western border of Rhodesia. No one could tell me much about it for it was no longer used as in the early days when it was the main road to the Victoria Falls.

Vumandaba was, in fact, a treasure. He was one of the few Bushmen prepared to co-operate with the authorities, knew enough "kitchen kaffir" to make communication between us reasonable enough, and he had the bush wisdom of his race. Since he himself had been no farther than Nehimba, he secured detailed instructions from his father on how to get from there to a place called Shakawanki, thence to Domtchetchi; the latter being a well-known halt on the border road in the early days before the advent of the railway line.

My patrol pushed out from Dett early one morning in April 1929 with all the pack animals well loaded with foodstuffs (mainly mealie meal for the Africans and crushed mealies for the horses), bedding, and one small bucksail. It was a patrol of exploration into the unknown, for in those days there were parts of the reserve about which no one knew anything at all. We had to find out what poaching was going on, too, and put an end to it.

We travelled as far as Shapi pan along the same wagon track as Lundin had used on my first reconnaisance in September. But how different the country looked now. Where only some eight months ago the whole area had been in the relentless grip of drought, there was now an abundance of verdant grass and thick foliage on all the trees and shrubs. There was water in every little depression and on many of the pools were wild duck, some with clutches of young. Although we did not see much game the signs were far more apparent than on my previous visit. We spotted a good deal of elephant and giraffe spoor; there was evidence of lions, too.

We reached Shapi on the second day, camping a prudent distance from the pan – prudent because we had learnt on our first night out how maddening mosquitoes can be. I had a mosquito net, but the horses and mules were so pestered by these creatures that their stamping and shaking kept me awake most of the night. It was, of course, necessary to sleep close to the animals to protect them from possible attack by lions.

As we were starting off the next day we had our first accident. One of the mules took fright at the sudden, explosive emergence of a warthog from a hole just off the path, and promptly bolted. On end of the pack-bag came loose and sixty lbs. of mealie meal was strewn along the veld in a long white trail. Only when the pack became unbalanced and the saddle slipped, did the mule come to a trembling halt.

The whole incident looked ridiculously funny, but we didn't smile when we realised its seriousness. We now had insufficient food for the Africans; the trip was due to last some three weeks, and we now calculated that we had lost rations for six days.

We decided to camp where we were and send a couple of the Africans back with a mule to Dett for some more meal. Our mules turned out to be infuriatingly gregarious creatures; one would not go without its companion and they both wanted to remain in company with the horses. In the end the Africans decided to go without pack animals, and carry the extra meal themselves. It took them three days to get there and back, bringing with them fifty lbs. of meal. In the meantime, the four Africans who were with me, plus two dogs, had consumed about twenty lbs. of meal; so we were still only thirty lbs. to the good. I was learning veld housekeeping the hard way; calculating patrol food was ever a difficulty. However, we set off again and soon reached Nehimba.

During my enforced stop at Shapi I explored the surrounding country with Vumandaba. He led me to a number of pans in the vicinity, none of which had names. A herd of elephant had just left one of these as we arrived, leaving behind a smell very reminiscent of a cattle kraal, so I called this pan *Danga*, which is the Shona name for a cattle kraal. The pan is still known by this name to-day.

From Nehimba we travelled south-west along a well-worn elephant path which went on for mile after mile, touching at a number of good water points. At about half past two that afternoon we met a herd of elephant using the same path but travelling in the opposite direction; this was the first herd I had seen out in the open during the middle of the day. In order not to disturb them we left the path, travelling down wind for about 200 yards, before resuming our original course parallel to the path.

This proved to be a mistake, for when the elephants reached the point on the path where we had left it, they got our scent and they, too, made off down wind, coming on to our scent again and veering away from it – which brought them directly at us. By shouting and banging on a dead tree with the back of an axe we were able to reveal our exact position to the bewildered beasts. They turned again, re-crossed the path and made off up wind. This was one of my first lessons in dealing with my charges.

We camped that night at a big pan which Vumandaba assured me he recognised as one called *Shakawanki* (from the description given to him by his father) because it was shaped like a human ear and that was the Bushman name for an ear.

There was little game about, but I spotted, for the first time in Wankie, zebra and roan. Numbers of wild duck were disporting themselves on the pan. I did a little shooting, just enough for us to have one each. To my surprise I found that the dogs would not touch the wild duck.

The next day we went on to Domtchetchi. We very nearly crossed the Mpande Mutenga road without realising it, since it had become so overgrown with disuse. As soon as man retreats, it does not take the bush long to eradicate all traces of his work. Generally speaking, the road was no more than an elephant path with rather less bush and trees along it than elsewhere. The only sign of recent traffic was some old donkey spoor and droppings at a camp site, suggesting that a party of Africans had used the route about a month previously. In all our exploring so far this was the first evidence of human beings since we left Dett seventy-five miles away.

We had little difficulty in following the road south-east towards the Nata river, until we reached a pan which Vumandaba thought was called Tamasanka. From this pan, however, we could not even find the track marking the border. We set off along an elephant track running roughly in the direction we wanted to go – south-east. It led us into a big depression where the type of country changed, becoming predominantly mupani. Here we came upon clear evidence of human occupation. We could see where branches had recently been cut and where someone had been digging for roots and bulbs. We came upon two donkeys and as soon as they saw us they galloped off along a well-worn path.

"Follow them," hissed Vumandaba and, knowing what he meant, I dug my heels into Santoy and followed at a brisk trot. Sure enough, the two donkeys led me to a Bushman encampment. I galloped round the little settlement of absurdly small grass huts to cut off the retreat of anyone who might seek to escape. All I saw were some small children who stared in frank amazement. I then rode into the camp and found, to my astonishment, a little group of females squatting round a middle-aged woman who was giving birth to a child. There were no men in the village, and there was no privacy about the operation. Two of the older women were chewing some herbs, taking mouthfuls of water, so that they could spray the juice from the herbs over the labouring woman. I never found out what the herbs were or what these primitive midwives were supposed to achieve with their strange magic. This was something outside my ken and I left the village and returned to my men realising this was primitive life as I had never seen it before.

In the village there was ample evidence of poaching with portions of giraffe and eland skin lying about and fresh meat from a sable hanging over a bush to dry. I found that I was unable to converse with these people at all.

That night we camped near the poachers' village and at dusk three men came in from hunting. They were armed with spears and accompanied by three dogs. Vumandaba was able to talk to them. He learned that they had been camped there for a month, having no idea that they were doing anything wrong. They claimed to have no firearms and all the meat they were living on was from lion kills which they had found.

I warned the men that the area was now a game reserve and that they were not allowed to live there. By sunrise the next morning the entire village was on the move – men, women, children, donkeys, goats and dogs. The woman who had given birth to a son had her new-born babe on her back, and in a large basket on her head she carried two newly born goat kids. She stepped out briskly with the rest.

We followed the Bushmen for a little way, but as they were heading for the south-west into Botswana we again turned south-east. Fortunately Vumandaba had obtained a description from the Bushmen of what the Sibaninni river looked like or we might not have found it. It proved to be a wide shallow watercourse just like a string of pans, the distinction being that the main watercourse had freshwater mussel shells lying about. There was nothing to suggest that it was a river.

Once on the watercourse we followed it until we again reached the border. Here, as we expected, we found quite a large native settlement at a big pan on the border which is called Sibaninni. One of the chiefs, a retired Botswana policeman, came to visit my camp, mounted on a horse and carrying a good 7·9 Mauser rifle. We were pleased to be able to buy some mealies to replenish our dwindling rations. These the village women pounded into meal for us with their wooden mortars.

At Sibaninni I met an old Bushman named Makaraba, a wizened old chap who looked about ninety, although he may not have been a day over sixty. The old Bushman and Vumandaba had a long conference and he gave my guide a detailed description of the route we were to follow and the names of some of the pans we would pass on the way. On the day we struck camp and left, Makaraba accompanied us to a watercourse which he said we were to follow as this would lead us to the railway line, which was about one hundred miles away.

It seemed incredible that such a small watercourse could persist for such a long way, as we were to be travelling upstream. In fact, we found that we could not follow the stream bed for more than thirty miles and it was only by coming on the spoor of some Bushmen with donkeys that we were able to get back on the right track.

We tracked the Bushmen to their camp, which was much the same as the other we had visited. But the occupants of this camp obviously had firearms, for we found empty Martini-Henry cartridge cases as well as a small bag of black powder, although there was no trace of any gun. We put the senior member of the group under arrest for being in possession of firearms. We had no intention of holding him, however. "See that he – er – escapes during the night," I told Vumandaba. The prisoner duly (and no doubt thankfully) "escaped" and we were thus relieved of the burden of keeping him under arrest and feeding him. Since he "escaped" we could be quite sure he would not be found again in the reserve!

These Bushmen, in fact, evoked a degree of sympathy. They were not really poachers in the worst sense. Just like a pride of lions, they killed only for their own needs, amounting to not much more than an animal a week. However, the law had come to Wankie Game Reserve and it had to be implemented. As time went on, I came to know these little people and learnt a great deal from them. They were full of humour and really likeable old rascals, most of them. Now the best of those I knew have gone to the happy hunting grounds.

This particular party were camped at a pan which they told me was called Labuti, where they could obtain water all the year round by digging wells some five feet deep. I calculated that it was very near the boundary of the reserve.

With the help of the Bushmen we got back to the right watercourse and, thereafter, it proved easy enough to follow. Eventually we landed up at Ngwashla in country well known to Vumandaba.

We rested the animals here for a day. On the second night prowling lions stalked the camp. The first indication we had of imminent attack came from the dogs who rushed through the camp barking madly. The mules began pulling wildly on their tether ropes. We quietened them as best we could and I positioned myself ready to shoot. But the lurking terror out in the darkness called off the attack. We did not see the lions, but the spoor next morning showed clearly their intention. One of a pride of three had crept up to within ten yards of the mules.

Surprisingly, this was the only occasion on the whole patrol when we had any trouble at night. We had, in fact, seen lion spoor at nearly every pan at which we had camped and twice found fresh kills, actually seeing the lion responsible.

From Ngwashla we took the forty-five miles to Dett in easy stages, although most of my provisions had run out. The commodities I missed most were salt and fat. For days I had lived on boiled rice and boiled duck without salt.

Eventually we got back to base. Perhaps the highlight of the whole patrol was when I sat down at a table again, saying, "I'll have some fried steak and potatoes please," and Samuel my cook rose to the occasion.

Having done a patrol of the southern half of the reserve I was soon off on another trip to the northern half. This was a very different matter; the country was largely hilly and stony, the horses and mules soon developed sore feet and we had to try and keep to the softer ground. This part of the reserve bordered on occupied farms. One of these was run by a Greek farmer named Garos. He had in his storeroom a worm-eaten rhino horn which he had found on the farm some years previously. Rhino spoor had not been seen on the farm for some years but at one time he estimated that there were at least four of these animals about. Garos also told me about some ancient ruins near a pan called Mtoa. His description of them was quite exciting, with walls six feet high and a chevron pattern in them with monoliths on the top. Garos had visited them once searching for gold ornaments in the floor of the main ruin; but he did not, he told me, find anything.

My next point of call was on an old man, H. G. Robins, who owned some farms called *Toms Farms*. These were named after two small streams, tributaries of the Deka river, *Big Toms* and *Little Toms*. The streams I was told were named after Tom Saddler, a friend of Selous who used to hunt in that area around 1875, camping between the two streams.

Robins took up the two farms, *Big* and *Little Toms*, in 1914 and ranched cattle, later taking a lease on an extension to the south of the two farms. On this extension there was a salt pan which was a great attraction to game. Old man Robins told me that at one time he had a hide built at the pan and the range marked off all round and, using a telescopic sight (a rare thing in those days), he used to shoot from the hide. He said he had given it up as the price paid for game skins had fallen off so badly; he could only get 5s. for a giraffe hide and less for other game skins.

The old chap had given up shooting and had intensified his efforts to keep off poachers. He had sold all or most of his cattle and bought an annuity, on which he was living in a quaint old pole-and-dagga house surrounded by a high wire fence – inside which he kept some of the biggest great danes I have ever seen. At the gate there was a notice "beware of the dogs" and an old ox bell. On the bell being rung, a servant would run out of the kitchen and tie up the dogs. So used had the animals become to this routine that when the bell sounded, the dogs (there were five of them) would each run to its own post to be tied up, taking no notice of the visitor at the gate.

The Great North Road at that time passed through *Toms Farms* and Robins had many visitors who would call on the old man and, accompanied by a guide supplied by him, would motor over the roads connecting his cattle kraals to see game. Naturally the old man took up the attitude that he was the premier game protectionist and that I would do well to listen to him and fall in with his ideas. He was obsessed with the notion that the country to the south was infested with poachers, all of whom were concentrating their efforts on the game on his land. He knew very little of the country which had been declared a game reserve and seemed to have no conception of what 5,000 square miles was like. He had a grand idea that the reserve should be the "warehouse" where the game should breed and be protected while his farms should be "the shopwindow" where game could be on view.

By the end of this patrol it was clear that poaching in the reserve was actually not nearly as serious as I had been led to believe. There were Bushmen nomad families wandering about armed with muzzle loaders but they did not seem to be using poisoned arrows or wire snares. There was little sign of recent poaching by Europeans except near the timber concessions. Not poachers, but water (or lack of it) was obviously going to be the big problem in establishing the reserve.

By July, in all but exceptionally wet seasons, practically all the water in the reserve would have gone and game which needed water at short intervals would have to find it outside the reserve. In the north, where the Deka river provided the main water supply, nearly all the land was owned by private individuals who were fortunately nearly all favourably disposed towards game and had no objection to the animals congregating on their land during the dry season. (One farm did eventually become a shooting box in later years). There seemed no future for the northern half of the reserve unless land was acquired to give the game access to the Deka river. In all but one place the boundaries of the private land were five to ten miles from the river, the exception being a narrow strip of land just west of *Toms Farms*.

H. J. ROBINS

CHAPTER THREE

I HAD not been in my post at Wankie Game Reserve much more than a year when I was ordered to capture a young giraffe for Pretoria zoo, where the only male of the species had died. "Catching 'em alive" was something of which I had no experience; however, orders were orders (especially when they came from a cabinet minister) and as the man on the spot I had to get on with the job.

Obviously the first thing to do was to find out how to set about the task from someone with experience. The man I turned to was John Lundin, who had been catching giraffe for sale to Australian zoos until Wankie had been proclaimed a game reserve. John gave me some useful advice on handling giraffe after capture, but insofar as the actual capture was concerned it was clear I would have to learn the hard way. (I did. The thorns I collected in the course of the enterprise still show in the form of scars on my back today!).

John was selling out his outfit since no more permits were being issued to private firms for game capture in the reserve. I was lucky enough to get his hunting horse, a big dark roan called Turk, which Lundin had ridden for most, if not all, of his giraffe-catching exploits. Turk was getting on in years, but what he lacked in staying power he certainly made up for in his almost uncanny ability to manoeuvre through the bush, hurtling in and out of trees and shrubs at top speed.

I had very little experience of horses, having by no means mastered the art of riding, much less of going at speed through the bush. Nevertheless, I lost no time in getting out on Turk and trying him on animals

25

such as eland and fully grown giraffe. It was a great thrill to feel him virtually take over once he realised what was expected of him. When he saw the animal I was chasing galloping at full speed just ahead of him, he would fix his attention on the quarry and follow, gaining on it until he was only some ten or twelve yards behind it. He made no effort to overtake the animal, however, until he got some encouragement from me, when he would then spurt forward, ranging alongside and almost touching the animal's flank. He was a little apprehensive of fully grown giraffe, keeping well clear of the wildly swinging hind legs.

After a few weeks of practice in this way I started to train a Bushman who could ride to accompany me on Santoy, another horse which I had at the time. His job was to be on hand (when the giraffe was caught) with the ropes to secure it. I, for my part, started practising with a "Rhodesian lasso," the tool which I hoped would eventually make the catch.

A "Rhodesian lasso" is a length of soft rope attached to a light stick, about eight feet long, in such a way that the loop of the lasso swings free at the end rather like a flag. The idea is to pass the loop over the animal's head once it is close enough, then pull the loop tight and let the stick go.

At last all was ready and we were soon to start hunting for a suitable animal in a convenient place. This was important as the capture had to be made close enough to the railway to get the giraffe on to a train for the journey to Pretoria.

At this point we had an extraordinary stroke of luck. Lions killed a giraffe about ten miles from Dett and as lions were too numerous (taking a heavy toll of the ungulates) for a new and poorly-stocked reserve such as Wankie, I decided to try and trap the lions. Traps were set at the kill, and on visiting the place next day I found that a lion had gone off with one of the traps. Following up was no problem and we soon came up with the lion, and despatched it. On the way back to the kill to re-set the trap in the hope of killing more lions, we came across the fresh spoor of a young giraffe. It was not accompanied by any adults and we concluded that it was an orphan calf belonging to the giraffe killed by the lions. We had no idea of the sex of the baby giraffe but, as it was an orphan and stood little chance of survival if left in the bush, I decided to try and catch it.

We hurried back to my camp at Dett, returning with both horses and three Africans on foot, together with ropes and tools for building a pen for the giraffe, in the event of our catching it before the lions did. We soon picked up the spoor and followed. It was about 3 p.m. when we spotted the little giraffe (I say "little" as it was quite young, but stood about eight feet high).

I rode quietly towards it, followed by Tickey the Bushman on the other horse. When we got within 50 yards it started to gallop off. Up to then Turk had not seen it, but as soon as it moved off he spotted it, immediately giving chase as I dug in my heels.

At first the chase took us through some rather heavy timber at a moderate pace. Turk was picking the way and I had to duck low to avoid some overhanging branches, nearly losing my catching stick. After some 300 yards the giraffe led us out into more open ground, covered with shrubs four feet high with an occasional tree. Turk quickened the pace of his own accord and was soon close behind the animal. We galloped on in this way for perhaps another 200 yards, then I gave Turk a nudge and he raced alongside. As I reached forward to place the noose around the neck, the giraffe shied off to the right and Turk over-shot it. As he turned to follow I all but came off. By the time I had regained my seat firmly the giraffe was a good fifty yards away. Turk soon made up this gap and, before the giraffe could make the cover of more heavy timber, I was able to have another shot at getting the rope around his neck.

This time I succeeded but it took me some while before I could pull Turk up sufficiently to get any strain on the rope, thus bringing the giraffe to a stop. While pulling up I had difficulty in keeping Turk on the same side of the tall bushes and small trees as the giraffe, thus avoid-ing getting the rope tangled. If this had happened it would not only have pulled me from the saddle, but could have brought the giraffe to a sudden stop, which might have dislocated its neck. Once I slowed the giraffe down to a little more than walking pace I jumped off Turk and brought it to a standstill; no doubt just then it was the most surprised giraffe in the world.

After what seemed an age Tickey came into view. I had been holding the giraffe which did little but walk around and around me. But when Tickey rode up the animal again took fright and almost pulled me off my feet. Fortunately I was able to hold it. The next move was to draw the giraffe up to a clean boled tree, and, holding it close to the trunk, throw a saddle blanket (which we took off Turk) over its head. Once blindfolded it stopped struggling and kicking, while we set to work putting a number of coils of rope loosely around its neck. These we bound together to form a sort of thick collar. We did the same thing around its girth just behind the shoulders, then bound these two collars together on either side like a crude harness. We then passed a loop of rope around the tree and secured it in such a way that the animal could walk around the tree with about a foot of slack rope. At this stage we removed the blanket.

By this time the other Africans had come up. It was too late to build a pen so we cut branches and erected a rough screen around the giraffe, keeping it tied to the tree for the night.

With all the excitement of the chase we had completely forgotten to take note of the sex of our captive, but when I did remember I was delighted to find that it was a male.

During the night the giraffe ate some of the leaves from the branches around him and I was able to induce him to take a small drink of water from a dish held up to his mouth. Soon after nightfall the lions could be heard feeding on the carcass of the mother giraffe which was only about half a mile away. Towards midnight they came nearer to us, roaring. This frightened the captured giraffe into making frantic efforts to escape. It seemed far more afraid of the lions than of us, its human captors.

Next morning we decided not to erect a pen around the animal as planned, but to take it straight to my camp at Dett. We sent Tickey off with both horses to bring some more Africans and something to eat, none of us having had anything since breakfast the previous day.

When all was set for the trek back to Dett we attached a rope to either side of the girth we had fitted the previous day and, with one rope on each side and one forward (like the guy ropes on a flag mast), we started to lead "Dandi" – as I decided to call our giraffe – back to my camp. Leading was rather difficult in the bush but after about an hour we came on to the Dett–Shapi road and from there the going was easier. We had to take the trek in easy stages as every now and then the giraffe would begin to struggle, tiring itself, and we would have to rest and calm it. The ten miles took us just on eight hours. On arrival at my camp, the procedure of the night before was repeated, the giraffe being tied to a tree for the night.

By nine o'clock the next morning Dandi was safely in a pen which we constructed of poles and we were glad to remove the rope harness which by this time had begun to chafe him a little.

For the next six weeks Dandi was kept in his pen, learning to eat sweet potato tops, a commodity which would be obtainable for him on the train journey south and for his early days in the zoo. At the end of this period the harness was again fitted and Dandi was walked between guy ropes from his pen to another pen, this time built inside a railway truck.

After twenty-four hours in this pen, when I hoped he would be used to the passing of engines and trains, the journey south started. Dandi's pen was in one end of the truck and mine in the other end, for I had to travel with him all the way.

Before the pen for Dandi had been built we had ascertained the maximum possible height – thirteen feet from the rails. With a foot to spare above his head, the pen was twelve feet six inches high and it seemed to tower above all the other trucks on the train. We had been assured that the height was all right so far as possible overhead obstructions went, but many times as the train approached overhead bridges and telephone lines, my heart was just about in my mouth. Sometimes on that long haul south, I wondered if Dandi – looking at me speculatively with his liquid brown eyes under the long lashes – was ever aware of the concern I felt for him. I like to think he knew.

The journey lasted four days and nights, and was most uncomfortable for both of us, but at last we arrived in a siding in Pretoria where the zoo authorities were waiting to take Dandi away. They used the same harness as I had done and so, for Dandi, the wild was ended for ever, as he walked the last mile to his future home through the busy streets of Pretoria, guided by the same "guy" ropes that had led him out of Wankie. People stopped and stared in amazement. Almost sedately perhaps with just the slightest touch of disdain – Dandi trod his way through the Pretoria city to the zoo.

Thereafter I could write in my log "mission complete," but my heart had not been in the business. I had grown to love the creatures of the wild too much ever to take any pleasure in shutting them up in zoos, and I was very glad, indeed, when the authorities decided some time later that there would be no more catching of game for this purpose.

And Dandi? Somehow I never quite lost an awareness of the bond of companionship and even affection that had grown up between us. I visited him several times after that, and during subsequent leaves to South Africa.

These holidays and visits to South Africa became frequent events, and in a way it happened that Dandi had his own back on me, for if I had robbed him of his liberty he was instrumental in relieving me of mine. After I delivered him to the zoo I went to Johannesburg to stay with a friend and there met a fair-haired post office telephone operator, Constance Burnside. We were married in Bulawayo in November 1932. Thenceforth I had a companion in my pole-and-dagga shack built near Dett railway station. Later we found a better site for a home in the shade of a huge "giraffe" acacia tree on Pettie's farm. The house we built there became the nucleus of the present main camp of the Wankie National Park. In all our years in the park we had much happiness and contentment in that little house which still stands in the shade of the same tree today.

Connie

CHAPTER FOUR

As mentioned previously, the policy of lion destruction had to be implemented in the interest of the game stocks generally. I used traps, trap guns, and hunted the lions with dogs. For this purpose I acquired a pack of a dozen dogs from the pound in Bulawayo, and after trying them out I selected half as useful for the job. The best was a half-breed border collie, with a lot of sheep dog in him. He was obedient and courageous. He would not actually come to grips with a lion, but could bring one to bay by running ahead and worrying it. I called him Ranger because of his habit, which he had before I got him, of ranging round and round me at a distance of about one hundred yards.

Another member of my dog pack was a half-breed pointer who was a coward in that he kept at a safe distance when the lion was at bay, and had the nasty habit of running back to me if the lion rushed at him. But he could pick up the spoor and follow it when the other dogs could not find it. Little fox terriers were the best at bringing the quarry to bay and keeping it there, while their incessant barking guided me to the scene. One of these terriers, a half-breed named Tiny, would leave the bayed-up lion and come back to me as I was trying to follow up, then she would run back again to rejoin the hunt; thus giving me a lead as to the direction I should take.

These hunts usually started at a kill made the night before. The lions would seldom be found near the kill which was either located by spotting vultures dropping down to feed or by noticing the direction of the roar of the lions during the night. Once the spoor had been picked up my Bushmen would follow it until the lions were flushed and then the dogs would take over. I seldom used a horse for these hunts as either Santoy or Turk would bolt once I dismounted to shoot. If this happened it usually meant sending back to Dett to recover the horses as they would not go back to my temporary camp, returning always to their home and stable. When they ran off there was a very real danger that lions would get one of them on these long runs back to Dett with the reins trailing. On such occasions, however, I always sent two Africans to follow after the horses just in case the reins got caught up or they did not return to Dett. Sometimes we were able to overtake the runaways after the hunt but this was so worrying that I soon abandoned horseback as a method of hunting and preferred to walk – and run when necessary – to keep up with the pack.

On one occasion I was hunting a lioness and two cubs. We followed them without seeing anything of them, with the dogs going on ahead. I heard the dogs start barking as they flushed the lions a second time and a little later I could hear that the lions were at bay, or so I thought. When I came up with the dogs they were all around the base of a big tree but I could see no sign of the lions and there was no growling from them. I approached cautiously while Ranger went up to the tree and stood on his hind legs. I realised then that the lions had taken to the tree. It was some time before I located one of the cubs high up in the tree hidden by leaves; when I first saw it I thought it was a baboon. It turned out that the cubs, which were a little less than half grown, were in the tree but not their mother; she had got away.

When we were successful in finding a kill but could not find the lions, I set traps around the carcass. These consisted of powerful bear traps, laid in shallow holes and covered with dry leaves and grass. I did not anchor the traps to a log but attached a six- or eight-foot length of heavy chain. It was possible to follow the lion with the trap on its paw and it would keep company with the rest of the pride. When we came up with them it was very often easy to despatch one or two members of the pride before shooting the trapped animal. It was amazing how far away the clanking of the chain could be heard before the dogs came up with the lions.

Of course, a lion with a trap on a foot would be in a foul temper and would not hesitate to charge if it saw any of my party before I had managed to get in a shot. Even with a trap to hamper it a big lion could move at a surprising rate and somehow seemed more difficult to hit than a free running lion.

Lions have been known to get out of traps. This happened to me on two occasions. The first time a nice young lion was caught by a front paw. It was in open country where I could see it well. The animal was thoroughly exhausted so I tried to sneak up to it and get a photograph. It was sitting with its hindquarters in a bush, in the shade of which one of my fox terriers had dug a hole where she was resting. When I was about fifty yards from the lion it lay down with the trap and captured paw underneath its chest. To my horror it jerked its paw a couple of times and then withdrew its foot, minus the trap, and lay with both front paws stretched out in front of it. Evidently, when it lay on the trap it had compressed the spring sufficiently to open the jaws a little, just enough to get its paw free; but it did not realise what had happened. A trap's most effective grip is when the lion is caught by the toe. In that position the jaws are completely closed but if the whole foot is in the trap, the jaws are still half open and a sharp jerk may dislodge the foot.

Hyena sometimes got caught in traps set for lions with nothing but a chain as an anchor. They proved much more tenacious, dragging the trap for miles and miles and, when they were overtaken, refusing to be bayed up by the dogs. Although I never lost a trap in this way there were times when it looked as if I were going to do so, because the dogs, tired and thirsty after a long walk in the hot sun, lost interest in the spoor and would no longer hunt. It then took some perseverance to catch up.

In conjunction with my lion control work there was still much to be done in exploring the reserve and finding out what was in the country – game, water supplies, and so forth. I started mapping some of the confusing conglomeration of watercourses that existed in the Kalahari sand area. "Watercourse" is the wrong expression for most of them, as they were merely long straight depressions with a string of small pans in the lowest parts. There was no watercourse as such in the flat country, and if water had ever run in these valleys, which way had it flowed?

There were some of these valleys, which were quite distinct, such as the Sumamalesha, which started in a glade at Kennedy on the railway and ran south-west, and the Linkwasha which also started in open poorly-drained country on the railway. These two valleys joined up but, strangely enough, they both diminished the further they were followed until the watercourse eventually petered out altogether. Other valleys with no watercourses just seemed to disappear; in fact, in many cases they could only be followed by keeping to an elephant path connecting up a series of small pans, divided from another similar valley by a ridge of high timber, which was mostly teak forest.

My early mapping was done with an "army" prismatic oil immersion compass and a cyclometer mounted on a cycle-wheel in a pair of forks with handlebars. It was pushed or pulled by an African on whom I had to keep a sharp watch. If the going became a bit heavy due to thick bush or grass he could see nothing wrong in putting the contraption over his shoulder and carrying it. On plotting my figures on to paper I found that I had the unique position where two watercourses crossed each other but I had not noticed anything of the sort on the ground. I concluded that my primitive mapping was at fault and, to my sorrow, I tore up the papers.

Some of the valleys I mapped were almost dead straight, only the elephant path zig-zagged about a bit. The true position only became clear to me when, many years later, I flew over the country and had a look at it all from the air. Then I discovered that in many places there were in fact two depressions crossing each other, but one was a drainage system and the other was not. It was, in fact, a depression between long low sand dunes covered with forest. Strangely, these two phenomena represented two bygone ages, one when the country was less densely wooded than it is today, when the moving sand had been blown into these long ridges; and the other by a period when water in considerable quantities flowed down the watercourses cutting across the sand dunes.

Much later on the country was photographed from the air. These long straight depressions showed up very well on the prints. Elephant paths, too, showed up clearly, giving a map of a vast network of parallel paths. The general direction of the sand dunes is east and west, while the main elephant paths travel in the same direction. The map produced by cyclometer and compass showed only four main drainage valleys and I ignored dozens of smaller valleys which I had come across.

The main pans in the reserve do not lie in these depressions but are, for the most part, situated on the crests of the watersheds. When I first visited Nehimba I was amazed to find that we left the Triga vlei and went up a gentle rise for a couple of miles and then on the top came upon this open sandy place with a depression at one side, where there was a lovely clear pool of water. The sides of the pool were sandy, with water oozing out of the sand and trickling down into the pool. There was not much game about just then as it was early in the dry season but, towards the end of the season, when all the water in the pool had dried up, the seepage continued and elephant were digging big holes into the sides of the pan and getting water from them.

These buried pans, for that is what they are, form important links with the past. There are several of them of which Nehimba is the best known, but Shakawanki (which is also the name given to me by the Bushmen) is the largest. Others are ShabiShabi, Lememba, Labuti, Tamasanka, Nqwasha and, lastly, Domtchetchi. There are also several small ones which the game do not frequent as the water is too deep down, one of which is near the Dom pan on the ten mile drive. This supply has been opened up by a bulldozer.

This source of water, the buried pans, all have one thing in common – they are surrounded by a stretch of loose sand which supports very little vegetation, being almost devoid of trees and shrubs, while even the grass is of a tufty coarse type which is only found around these pans.

The depressions in which the water collects is in sand and not clay as in all the other pans, but four or five feet below there is the clay seal, just the same. What we really have is a natural pan covered with loose sand. How did these pans form? Are they the result of heavy game concentrations at big pans in some bygone time, which resulted in the soil being blown away or drunk with the muddy water of the pan, or carried away by elephant mud-bathing, leaving only the coarse sand crystals. With the destruction of the vegetation this sand had drifted down the slope into the pan, covering it over.

The Bushmen know these small buried pans, as it is not difficult to detect them by the particular type of grass which grows around them. The Bushmen used to dig wells for themselves. When they moved on they filled in the wells, re-opening them when they again visited the area. At the bottom they would place a large quantity of grass covered with strips of bark which collected the moisture and made it easy to obtain water on their next visit.

Newahari (which lies at the top of a ridge to the south-west of Labuti) is a famous Bushmen well which was used for many years after I went to Wankie, although we did not find it until 1950. There are also signs of old Bushmen wells at Shumba. These little people keep their secrets, even from people who feel they know them well and are in their confidence.

When Wankie was going through one of the dry spells and water was very scarce, I made an attempt to increase the amount of water available at Nehimba by scooping out some of the sand at the bottom of the depression. This was quite an undertaking. My wife and'I camped at the pan along with about a dozen Africans and a span of sixteen oxen. In the morning the oxen worked, scooping out the sand with dam scoops. In the afternoon they grazed, tended by six or seven Africans as there were a number of lions about as well as the danger of elephant stampeding them. At night the oxen had to be very carefully kraaled. In addition, each animal was tied to a tree in the kraal and some of the Africans slept in the enclosure with them. Lions (which were attracted in the first place by the water) made repeated attempts on the cattle but they never got any, although we were there for nearly three weeks.

Our labours were heartened by the sight of game standing patiently on the outskirts of the vlei waiting for a drink. They came down very cautiously when work ceased at mid-day and everyone was taking a rest. During this work my wife and I were surprised by the arrival of a solitary old baboon, although we never saw a troop anywhere about. The old boy sat among some short shrubs and watched the work, much to the amusement of our African labourers. My wife put out food and a dish of water for the animal, who accepted it while watching everyone very closely. We never found out his reason for joining us but we concluded it was old age. On completing the work we left him with a good supply of food and, of course, we never saw him again.

When the cleaning out of the pan got down to the clay line we started unearthing numerous knobkerrie heads. They had evidently been there for a long time; fifty years perhaps. They were kerries which had been used by Bushmen to kill sandgrouse as the birds came in to drink at the pan in the evenings.

My Bushmen used to tell me interesting things during our wanderings. It was at Nehimba that one of my Bushmen guides told me that he first saw a European woman, when he was a very small boy. My wife and I were very amused at his description of this good lady of long ago. She was without doubt a very large specimen of the typical Voortrekker wife, complete with kappie and large brood of children, who stayed with

36

her at the wagon while her husband hunted the area with members of my Bushmen's clan.

We also unearthed a pair of elephant tusks at a depth of nearly four feet. They had evidently been quite a nice pair, weighing about sixty pounds each but as they dried out they crumbled and flaked away, being quite valueless, while knobkerries at the same depth were in an excellent state of preservation. There were also a number of flints – lost, no doubt, by Bushmen who used them to make their fires as they did not possess matches in those days.

There was a plant growing in Nehimba pan which the Bushmen used in their tinder boxes. This was a very pithy hemp-like shrub. When dry, Bushmen collected and burnt it, but before the combustion was quite completed they crushed it into the container (usually a piece of antelope horn) and extinguished the fire. This left a kind of very fine charcoal which would start to smoulder at the slightest contact with a spark. Many is the time I have had to rely on my Bushmen to make a fire for me in this way as, being a non-smoker, I was frequently without a match. Of course, I always had a camera with me and, on occasions when I needed a fire and no Bushmen were about with their tinder boxes, I would make fire by using the lens of the camera or binoculars. By concentrating the sun's rays on to a piece of elephant dung, which would start smouldering and by gentle blowing I soon fanned it into a flame.

Dry elephant dung was wonderful stuff for catching and staying alight. Sometimes when the whole party were short of matches a piece of smouldering dung would be carried along and when this burnt out another piece would be picked up, and so on to the next camp. So inflammable is dry elephant dung that I have seen a pile of it start smouldering fifty yards ahead of quite a slow-moving veld fire, merely from the tiny sparks that are carried forward by the wind. How often smouldering dung had been responsible for a veld fire starting up the day after it had burned out at night I cannot say, but I suspect it often occurs.

CHAPTER FIVE

THE take-over of Balcarres and Petties farms by the government in exchange for land of equal value in another part of the district was a heartening move. I was able to move from my pole-and-dagga huts at Dett to a small cottage built for us on the site of the old farmhouse. It was very small indeed, just one bedroom, and one living room with a tiny veranda. There was a bathroom but no lavatory or basin. We purloined a lavatory from the railways, transporting it out to the farm on a small ox-wagon. We had no running water and had to bucket all water from a well, which was shared by the Africans, in the front garden. In spite of these disadvantages my wife and I made ourselves comfortable and had, for the Kalahari sand country, a very nice garden. Over the years we received many hundreds of visitors in our small home – to which the government added a little more accommodation when our sons arrived. It remained, however, quite inadequate for the amount of entertaining which was required of us.

Soon after this the government also purchased three farms on the northern boundary and added them to the reserve, thus giving a frontage on to the Deka river of some fifteen miles in addition to the frontage on Toms farms. This was a big step forward, as it meant that we – or rather the game – were no longer beholden to private farmers for a dry season watering place. These additions did not affect the game in the main part of the reserve which was the Kalahari sand area lying south of the main watershed. The only open water to them here was the

Gwaai river and its tributaries, the Dett and the Sikumi. The latter was a favourite drinking place of the elephants. It consisted of a big swamp about two miles long and 200 yards wide. There was water over the entire area, which was covered by a floating mass of reeds and ferns. No game, other than reedbuck, dared to venture on to this sudd; it was a death trap to unwary game which got caught in it while trying to get at the green grass which was always present. Occasionally, elephant got bogged; I saw one which was quite unable to extricate itself even although less than ten yards from the edge. The poor beast was quite exhausted and had to be shot. All trace of it disappeared in about two years. I wonder how many more lay concealed below the sudd.

The tsetse fly menace was growing worse and "fly" was creeping up the Dett vlei encouraged by game from the reserve watering on the Dett and the Gwaai. In 1936 I actually caught a fly in the reserve at the homestead and my dear old horse, Turk, as well as my milk cows became fly struck and died.

As a counter measure the area between the reserve boundary (the railway line) and the Gwaai river was opened to free shooting and shooting by paid African hunters. This was a terrific drain on the reserve and some very fine herds of eland, some giraffe, as well as sable, were destroyed. A number of elephant were shot but they were wise enough to learn that they were safe when west of the railway. It was not long before elephant would make an excursion to the Sikumi for a drink at night and be back home in the reserve before daylight. This commonsense in my charges led to some very lurid comments by the free shooting types, who were after ivory. I took a hand in this and hunted herds which stayed east of the line during the daytime and would disturb them in an endeavour to drive them back to the reserve.

In those days I could not afford to lose even one member of my large, wild family; they were all precious breeding stock. I took the opportunity, too, of learning something about shooting elephant. I shot a few bulls to teach the others that the area was dangerous. This was very effective and the herds soon kept to the right side of the line.

My first elephant was shot in a patch of very dense thorn bush, known as Synanga, at the head of the Dett valley. I picked up the spoor of a small herd on a path leading from the Sikumi into this patch of cover, following it to the edge of the thick stuff. There I tethered the horse and walked on the spoor, but not far, as I soon came to a bunch of big camel-thorn trees, where the elephant had evidently been resting. The dung was fresh and covered with tiny flies.

Under the next group of shady trees I came up with the herd. There were three young bulls standing with their hindquarters against a big tree and just beyond them were several others. I had no difficulty in sneaking quietly up to within twenty yards and putting in a brain shot. The great animal threw up its head and collapsed on its chest, then rolled over on its side. All the others raised their heads, making off slowly, but seemingly not the least bit alarmed.

After about ten minutes spent examining the fallen animal – the first dead elephant I had examined – I followed up the herd to see what they had done. The herd had moved farther into the thick bush but it was not long before I came up with them again. I was wondering what to do when there was a shout from the Bushman I had with me and I looked round to see a huge elephant coming towards me from down-wind on my left. The animal was screened by a dense patch of thorn but was very close and getting closer. I dashed off to the right to try and get clear of the bush and the elephant did the same. Before I had gone more than a couple of yards the animal was alongside me. I fired at its head but have no recollection of where I aimed. It went crashing down in the bush and small trees went with it. The elephant fell on its left side which, for me, was fortunate indeed as, had it fallen the other way, it would have fallen on top of me.

The elephant lay on its side for a few seconds, then tried to regain its feet. Its great head would rear up and, just as it was about to reach a vertical position, it would crash back on to the ground again. I tried to get in a brain shot as the head came up, but missed twice. I ran around to the other side and, as the head lay on the ground, I put a bullet into the back of the head between the ears. The animal's back legs went up into the air, stiffening out and quivering. My second elephant lay dead. At the time I was sure the elephant had been charging me but later when I got to know elephant better I came to think it was merely running away from the Bushman.

All the shooting had really frightened the rest of the herd; they could be heard clearing off at a great pace with much splintering of trees and trumpeting. I did not follow them again but I do not think they left the safety of the Synanga until after dark for, when we got back to the horse over an hour later, we heard an elephant rumble in the cover and it was most likely one of the same herd.

It is interesting to note that in later years the road to the reserve passed close to this dense bush and elephant were nearly always about there, standing in the shade making visitors welcome without a sign of fear. They were, in fact, the welcome party at the gate and a great thrill for people arriving at main camp.

At this time (it was in June) there was still water in the reserve and there was no real necessity for elephant herds to leave in search of water. The game population east of the railway on the fringe of the "fly" belt was being reduced and it was my aim to keep as much game as possible away from this area.

Just how much game there was in the reserve we still did not know but, now that I was getting to know my way about and where water was to be found, I set about finding out. Stock-taking, in fact, had to be done, but not with a sale of mark-down prices as in the city. I was fast becoming a miser about my animals and would give nothing away, not even a hare!

Giraffe could be found on most outings in twos and threes, but elephant and lion could be located only if they were actually hunted; or, at least, if hunting methods were used to seek them. So to find out where the elephant hid themselves during the day, how big the herds were, and so on, I developed a system of wandering, with a couple of trackers, from pan to pan until we came across the spoor of a herd. We would estimate the time of day the spoor had been made – by the condition of the droppings, state of leaves and branches broken off by feeding animals, and the way in which grass and shrubs had been trampled – thus working out how long it would take us to come up with the herd and whether or not we could catch them if we followed them.

On one such occasion we started out at about six a.m. on a day in April, following a fortnight's spell of dry weather. There had been a heavy dew that night and at the first pan we found the spoor of a single elephant, probably a bull. He must have passed that way in the early hours of the morning as the dewdrops had fallen from the grass where he had touched and very little more had formed. We followed for a short distance but, as the spoor did not join up with any other,

4–W

we gave up. It was the herds we wanted to check, not merely single animals.

At about nine o'clock we cut the spoor of a herd of about ten elephant as we were nearing a small pan. They had been spread out, with little indication of feeding. The spoor led away from the pan and, before deciding to follow it, we checked to see if they had been drinking. They had. The water had been made very muddy and there was a fair amount of spoor around. On the bare ground around the water were fifteen piles of dung, so we concluded that there had been more than that number of elephant. In addition, there was the spoor of at least two very young baby elephant. Since we had seen no baby spoor with the first lot, it followed that two herds must have been at the water during the night.

Dung beetles (large black members of Scarabaeidae family which feed on dung) had broken down the heaps, making it difficult to estimate the time the elephant had been there. So we looked for other clues. On a patch of dry sand we found marks where large drops of water had fallen, almost certainly dewdrops knocked from the grass. This, in turn, meant that the animals had been there after the dew had formed, probably between midnight and sun-up.

We went back to the original trail since the imprints in the sand seemed to be fresher than those at the pan. After we had followed it for about a mile it joined up with the spoor of another herd which had two babies in it.

The picture began to form more clearly now. Almost certainly the group we had followed and the one it had now linked up with, both belonged to the same herd which had been at the pan. Up to this point, the group we had been following had been travelling more or less in single file without feeding much but, from the point where the spoors joined, it had spread out and was feeding more. In other words, "our" group had probably loitered at the pan and subsequently had hurried to catch up with the main herd again. With the whole herd spread out we could not count the spoors and we estimated that there were between forty and fifty elephant with three small calves. So far as we could judge, there was no mature bull with them.

A steady breeze was blowing from the south-east and the spoor led to the north. Vumandaba, my Bushman tracker, wisely chose to keep well to the side that would not give our scent away to the herd if they happened to turn down-wind, and at times he deliberately moved off the spoor altogether. It was heavily wooded country; even at a hundred yards I would not have been able to see any elephant. Nevertheless, the state of the droppings and the ever-active dung beetles told us clearly enough that we were still a long way behind.

There is a fascination about tracking. Such little clues often mean so much. I noticed, for example, that leaves which had been torn from trees seemed to have dried up more than those I had seen an hour earlier. Vumandaba explained that until the sun had got on to them, they would not have dried at all, so that those we were now finding could have been torn off trees before sunrise.

Where there had been digging for roots the newly-turned earth looked older than any we had found previously. It was now about eleven o'clock. To me it was somewhat depressing to see the spoor apparently getting older instead of fresher, but in another hour things began to change: the dung beetles were more in evidence and the droppings were attracting more flies.

Soon the spoor led into open country, the direction changing slightly right. Ahead of us was a belt of heavy green thorn trees and here Vumandaba thought the herd might possibly be resting. We made a cautious detour to the left down-wind, gradually working our way in towards the belt of trees. We went into the trees for about 100 yards and then turned into the wind. Every now and then we would stop and listen, but there was no sound. After another 300 yards we came on the spoor again. True enough, the herd had stopped for a rest; we could see where they had bunched together in the shade of big trees surrounded by thick bush; but I doubt if I could have seen them at more than twenty-five yards' range. The trail led on out of the belt of timber and followed the belt up-wind. The dung looked fresher; it was lighter green and had not yet been broken down by the beetles; although they were certainly doing their active best.

Progress was now much slower, with frequent stops to listen. Still there was no sound, even though the increased evidence of flies on the droppings told us clearly enough that we were not too far behind. We carried on like this for over a mile, the trail leading in and out of the timber which consisted of thick thorn trees, even thicker now than at first. Vumandaba reckoned that the herd was moving at about the same pace as we were and that we would come up with it when it next stopped to rest. At last, on one of our "listening" stops we heard a faint rumble like a distant motor car. It lasted only three or four seconds but it was enough; the herd was about a quarter of a mile away.

We moved about 100 yards to the left, down-wind. There were some big shady trees ahead where we thought the animals might be resting. And we were right. As we moved cautiously we could see that the "undergrowth" about the trees had a much more solid appearance than that on either side; in fact here was the herd.

Moving closer we could see the backs of some of the larger elephant, but when we got to within fifty yards the animals were completely concealed by the bush. We could see nothing of them, but there was plenty of noise. Every now and then we could hear the hard dry skin of an elephant rubbing against another. Occasionally one would blow through its trunk, and there was also the sound of droppings falling. There we were within fifty yards of them after a long hunt, and yet I could not see one of them.

We withdrew to the shade of a big tree in the open, where we sat down to see what would happen. The noises continued, but there were intervals of complete silence. I climbed into the branches of a tree, but even then could see only the top of one head. We rested for an hour. All was very quiet. Then we became aware of elephant noises half a mile away. On investigating we discovered that the whole lot we had been waiting to see had quietly given us the slip. They had done it in two moves. The herd had split up, the first group moving off, subsequently followed by the second group – while all the time we thought we had the lot under observation.

However, we picked up the spoor again and soon located the herd sheltering under even bigger trees but with less undergrowth. I was able to get up to one family and watch them from a range of thirty yards; it comprised three old cows, four adolescents and one baby calf. Not far away was another bunch including two lying on their sides.

From a secure position behind a large tree I watched what was going on. The three old cows seemed to be asleep on their feet, only moving their ears now and again, or shifting their weight from one leg to the other. The adolescents were more restless, turning round and brushing against each other from time to time. They would dig in the sand using the toe of a front foot with a forward motion and pushing a lump of sand on to the end of the trunk; the trunk being laid on the ground in

44

a sharp curve, and then by a swift curl of the tip – up would go the "handful" of sand over the creature's back. As they shifted their weight from side to side the sand ran in streams off their backs.

The baby seemed much more awake than any of them. It would move from one old cow to another and then back to its mother. On one occasion it knelt down and put its forehead into one of the shallow holes dug by the others, and pushed up a small amount of sand. Talk about playing sand castles! It certainly was enjoying the game, every now and then shaking its little head. When thirsty it would walk up to its mother in a most determined way and the old girl would move her front leg to expose her breast and the little chap would reach up for a drink.

After about half an hour, the whole group woke up and, led by one of the old cows, moved off, passing the next group. Only the little calf took any notice of the "neighbours," cocking its little ears and running past them in front of its mother as though afraid.

I moved my position to observe better the next group, in which there were five, including a youngster out of the calf stage. A young bull was lying down, apparently fast asleep, the tip of his trunk curled like a giant shell. He was breathing heavily, almost snoring and sending up spurts of sand with every breath. Another elephant had its hind-quarters wedged between two trees and was leaning back, its trunk was resting on the one lying down and it, too, was seemingly fast asleep – out on its feet, if you like.

After about twenty minutes the group started to move off, the sleeping pair being most reluctant. The one lying down made a great fuss of getting to his feet. First, he threw his head sideways and rolled on to his chest, then the front feet were pushed forward and the forepart of the great body raised. Finally, with a great effort, up came the hindquarters, the head shaking, the ears clattering. The whole herd was now on the move. They soon came out into the open and I was able to count up to thirty-six. There were more in the thick scrub ahead. I continued to follow until all had entered a dense, scrubby thicket and then, as the afternoon was now well advanced, I decided to make tracks for my camp before darkness.

This method of actually hunting up the herd and counting them or their spoor gave a very good idea of what was present but it was very much a hit-or-miss method. It was possible, for instance, to get to know a herd and to recognise it again even by the spoor. One of the indications we looked for was the number of very small calves in each herd, as few herds had the same number of young. The proportion of bulls to cows was not such a good guide as the bulls would frequently leave the herds and wander off on their own.

Naturally, I kept a tally of all the game I saw on patrols but this was not enough. As early as 1933 I started keeping a tally of the number of animals against the number of miles travelled. There was little point in recording one hundred head of game unless some indication as to what area they were dispersed over was also noted. To see one hundred head in 200 miles of travel is a very different thing from seeing one hundred in twenty miles. This sort of information I found better than actually hunting up the game and counting them. It soon became evident that I would have to record not only the distance I was covering but the area as well; so I began to estimate the area I could see from the saddle of a horse at any one time.

A quarter of a mile on either side was about the average visibility, which meant that on a patrol I was covering a frontage of about half a mile or one square mile for each two miles travelled. It was a little less during the wet season when the foliage was thickest. As these figures mounted up over the years it was possible to see what the population trend was and right from the start this showed encouraging results.

As it was not possible to see very small animals such as duiker and stembuck except in open country, I only kept figures of animals of warthog-size and bigger, ignoring also creatures such as baboons, monkeys, jackals, and so on.

The figures at the start revealed that there was less than one animal to the square mile that could be seen. It was not the true figure of the number of animals present but it was a minimum; at least the animals recorded were there. As time went on these figures revealed more and more of what was happening in the animal world. There was a noticeable rise in the number of animals seen each year about September or October, but to what extent this was due merely to better visibility it was too soon to decide. Visibility seemed to be at its best in August after the leaves had fallen and before the new leaves came out.

There was little doubt that there was some migration into the reserve from Botswana each year early in the dry season and a reverse migra-

46

tion after the rains had set in. It was very evident, too, that game concentrated on the bigger water supplies as the dry season wore on and the smaller pans dried up. The game was more readily seen but this was offset by the drop in the numbers seen in the areas remote from water supplies.

From information I had been able to gather from Bushmen when I did patrols of the Botswana border it was clear that there was a big annual migration of wildebeest up the Nata and Sibaninni rivers about September each year. I determined to see this area when the game was in the reserve and with that object in view my wife and I set off on a patrol to this area late in September 1936.

We set off from Ngamo very early one morning carrying as much water as we could in water-bags, water-bottles and two-gallon screw-top tins. Our outfit consisted of my wife and myself mounted; she on our one and only horse, Ginger, and me on a mule Old Jock, who was a great character, full of tricks. We had one other mule, Sandy (who carried a pack), three donkeys and five dogs; five Africans (of which two were Bushmen, Vumandaba and another called Tickey). None of us had ever been to Sibaninni by this route before but we chose it because it was along the boundary and there was a chance of coming in contact with poachers and getting some water from them.

All the first day we travelled along the Sihumi valley which marked the boundary, but we did not make contact with any of the local population or find any sign of water. In the evening I watched the direction in which doves were travelling but there were very few of these. There was no sign of game beyond an occasional giraffe spoor and it was evident that there was no water about. We had enough water for our own requirements but the animals had none all day; in fact, they had had none since about 3 p.m. the previous day, for one and all refused to drink in the early morning.

We were on the move again early the next day. The country was drier and more devoid of game than the day before. There was little shade, as there were few big trees in the bottom of the valley where the elephant path was, but we kept on doggedly until well after sunset. We estimated that we must be nearing Labuti but the country was not familiar. We thought it better to stop before it got too dark in case we missed the Bushman path which leads to Labuti, which we had seen the year before.

47

That night the horse and mules were very restless. They would not eat their rations of crushed mealies. We had to be particularly careful to keep them well tied up for fear they would bolt in search of water. The donkeys did not seem to be troubled but they, like the horse and mules, ate grapefruit with great relish when we offered them. It was very funny indeed to see them crunching up the fruit with the juice running down their jaws. They all made clear to us that this was fine and they wanted more. We gave the dogs a drink, carefully rationing them. By the time we had finished our evening meal there was no water left at all.

We started out next day, a rather worried party, for if we failed to find Labuti or if there was no water there we would have a long trek to find any. We worried about our animals most. My wife and I had tinned food and fruit but we could do nothing to help Ginger and his pals. They walked along heads hanging, very weary and looking at us in that sad way animals do when things go wrong.

It was not until about eleven o'clock that we began to recognise the country and our chances of finding Labuti improved. Even then Vumandaba was not at all happy, for he said there were no signs of Bushmen or game. He was afraid the pan had dried up.

During the morning I realised we were one dog short; it was old Shangan, one of my lion-hunting pack and an elderly girl. My wife had our two fox terrier house-dogs, Spottie and Tiny up on the saddle with her some of the time. The other dogs had a habit of digging a hole in the shade of a bush and lying down to rest and then catching up the patrol in the cool of the evening. Because of this we had not missed Shangan. But during this patrol I had noticed that these resting periods grew longer and longer; sometimes I would not see the dogs for half an hour or so and in the end Shangan did not catch up with us at all.

By about 2 p.m. we were sure we would reach Labuti, but still there was no sign of Bushmen and when we arrived at the pan there was no sign of life and no water in the "well" the Bushmen had used. Bees were, however, passing in and out, no doubt drinking from the damp sand at the bottom.

We began to unsaddle and make camp, while one of the boys began digging in the bottom of the well. In half an hour he had a hole about four feet deep with just a trickle of water oozing into it. But it was water and deeper there must be more. Yet was it there? The bottom of

(photo courtesy National Archives of Zimbabwe)

The early writings of the hunter-explorer F.C.Selous (above) covering his wanderings in Mashonaland and Matabeleland, including the region today known as Hwange National Park, gave Ted Davison some history of the region he was tasked to develop as a game sanctuary. His only other information came from resident bushmen and tribespeople (below) who lived in the inhospitable reaches of the Kalahari sandveld.

(photo courtesy Davison Family collection)

Office work tended to take up less time in the early days.

Game Reserve staff on morning parade.

Ted Davison, circa 1929, Wankie Game Reserve.

Game viewing in the early days.

Early semi permanent 'fly-camp'.

Newly weds.... Connie and Ted Davison,
married in Bulawayo in 1932.

Sable and patrol members keeping an eye on each other.

Wildebeest photographed by Ted Davison at Sibaninni Pan in the south of the Reserve, 1933.

Brown hyena, photographed in 1933 by the author.

Preparation for field patrol. Ted and Connie Davison with two of their sons.

The author with famous pre-historian Neville Jones examining ancient rock engravings at Bumbusi.

Nyamandhlovu Platform circa 1940 (above) and
in March 1998 (below).

Fence repair. The wire fence on the southern boundary of Wankie after a considerable stretch had been flattened by elephants.

(photos courtesy Davison Family collection)

The same fence was the cause of the deaths of several giraffe which became entangled in the wires.

Operation Rhino, August 1962. Led by Ted Davison, a combined team of
National Parks and Wildlife Conservation personnel brought eight white
rhino from Natal, South Africa to Southern Rhodesia - thereby
re-introducing to the region a species that had become locally extinct.

Giraffe capture in Wankie.

No. 124]   [24th February, 1928.

ESTABLISHMENT OF GAME SANCTUARY,
WANKIE NATIVE DISTRICT

IT is hereby notified that His Excellency the
Governor-in-Council has been pleased, in terms of section
4, sub-section (1), of the "Game Law Consolidation
Ordinance, 1906," to declare that the following animals,
namely-

Elephant	Giraffe	Tsessabe
Rhinoceros	Eland	Wildebeest
Hippopotamus	Kudu	Waterbuck
Warthog	Bushbuck	Reedbuck
Buffalo	Gemsbuck	Impala
Sable antelope	Duiker	Steinbuck
Roan antelope	Zebra	Sharpe's steinbuck
Ostrich		

shall be protected in the area in the Wankie native
district defined hereunder, and shall not be hunted or
destroyed for a period of five years from the date hereof;
provided that holders of special permits to capture game
in the area referred to shall be allowed to continue
their operations during the currency of the permits
held by them.

Description of Area

All Crown lands in the Wankie native district
lying west of the railway line and south of the following
line:- From the beacon No. 153 on the western border of
the Wankie native district, eastwards following the
boundaries on the southern side of the following farms,
namely: Deka, Mahohoma, Nantwich South, Tom's
Extension and Deka Ranch to the easternmost beacon of
the latter; thence in a direct line to the north-west
beacon of Sinamatela Ranch; thence southward
following the boundaries of that ranch to the
Sinamatela River; thence down the Sinamatela River to
the south-west boundary of the Wankie Concession,
thence southward along the boundaries of that
concession and Railway Farm 47 to the railway line.

(photo courtesy Davison Family collection)

The birth of Wankie Game Reserve, proclaimed in the Government Gazette
in February 1928.

Ted Davison and some of his merry men.
Staff 1961
Tony Boyce, Chris Brits, Bruce Austin, Henry Cantle
Tim Braybrooke, the author, Jordie Jordaan, Fred Starkey, Ron Thomson.

The Warden watching elephants watering.

Chief Game Warden Davison, Wankie Game Reserve.

(photo courtesy Davison Family collection)

A rare picture of white and black rhino together, clearly showing different facial and mouth characteristics.

(photo courtesy Davison Family collection)

Drought takes a
yearly toll.

(photos courtesy Clem Coetsee)

(photo courtesy Mark McAdam)

Giant killers and giants. As the dry seasons progress, so the vegetation and water sources come under increasing pressure.

(photo Keith Meadows)

the hole became hard-packed sand and clay and all the water which seeped in did so from the sides and not the bottom. Then the sides began to fall in as well as the water oozing in. Our poor old mokes were not very helpful as they kept pushing the boys aside trying to get at the water and we had to tie all the animals up in order to get on with the work. By sinking a one-gallon tin into the bottom we were able to catch a little very dirty water but this would rise only so far and no further. We soon learned that we could get one gallon of water in twenty minutes, and that it was useless waiting longer before bailing it out. At times when the tin was emptied it floated on the loose sand and would not stay down; this meant the hole had to be cleared out again.

By nightfall we had all had enough water except the horse and mules, so we kept on drawing the small supply right on through the night, going back to the hole every twenty minutes, until all the animals were satisfied. I found that it was better to give the beasts their water mixed with bran as they were hungry as well as thirsty and the wife and I mixed their ration and fed them each in turn from a dish. It was cheering to see them begin to pick up their heads and look like our usual happy pets. Donkeys, especially, can be most amusing and are very human in their ways. Ours were, of course, great pets as well as very good workmen. We were distressed when the missing Shangan did not turn up (but, happily, we found her back at home when we returned from the patrol).

We left Labuti about midday the next day and that evening came on a small pan with a little muddy water in it, just enough for the animals. Here there were more signs of game and we had seen the spoor of quite a big herd of wildebeest as well as some elephant. This was hopeful and we were sure of finding more water – which we did on reaching Leasha pan the next day. From there to the Sibaninni river was only half a day's trek, where there was plenty of water in big but dirty pools.

It was good to see so much water as well as to find that there were some fish in the pools. I had a couple of small hooks and a length of line with which I soon had a rod rigged up and a couple of barbel on the bank. Up to then we had lived on tinned food only, while the boys had dry meat and mealie meal. We were all glad of the change. There were some bream in the pan, too, but all I could catch were very small. The barbel went up to about two lbs. Nothing fresh comes amiss on a patrol like ours and we cooked even the smallest fish.

While we made camp and settled in for a good rest, our pack animals had a wonderful time. They rolled and drank and fed, for there was a fair amount of grass around the pans. I was very relieved indeed to see their condition picking up. In those days our animals were very precious and the loss of even an old moke was a serious matter.

Around the pans there were a number of pelicans, and we were delighted to see them fishing in a very orderly manner. The flock would take off from a mud bank where they had been resting, line up across a pool and move in line towards the end of it, stabbing into the water with their great beaks all at the same time. As the pool narrowed the line of birds would contract, eventually from two deep to three deep. Driven into the shallows the fish would be seen darting about, jumping into the air and disappearing into the pelicans. As the first line of birds reached the shore they walked up the bank making room for the next line, all of them well filled and looking smug.

After preening themselves the birds began the whole process over again. When the evening shadows fell the flock took off down the river towards Botswana, going no doubt to their home at Lake Makari-kari. Our Bushmen made some caustic remarks about birds who came and ate our fish and then pushed off elsewhere. Their way of expressing themselves on matters like this was always a source of amusement to my wife and me. Each morning our pelican flock returned and provided us with hours of interest.

In Sibaninni pan we found a very lovely water lily, not known to me. It was pale cream in colour and with much larger leaves than the usual blue and pink water lily of the pans nearer home. The sight of these beautiful flowers did much to make our camp attractive. We tried to grow them at our homestead garden from the seed, which we found was contained in a jelly-like substance after the flowers had died. But although we had an established fish pond with ordinary lilies in it we had no success with the Sibaninni type.

Although there were some nice big herds of wildebeest about there were not as many as I had expected, but as we moved farther down the river towards the border they became more numerous. The Bush-men at Sibaninni came to visit us at our camp on the border. For many of them (particularly the women) my wife was the first white woman they had ever seen. Old Makaraba, whom I had met before on my first patrol, turned up in his best clothes, consisting of a white pique dress waistcoat, a loin cloth, and a battered old felt hat. With our Bushmen to interpret for me I learned a great deal about the country around them and, as was customary, we exchanged presents. Any little item thrown out of our camp, from a tin to a box or bottle, was eagerly taken off. They brought us eggs, tiny little ones which we tested for freshness before using. We liked the Bushmen and found their humour delightful. In the reserve area today there are few of them left, at least few of those pure-bred Bushmen we used to meet on patrol.

We spent about two weeks on the Sibaninni and did one short patrol south along the border to the Nata river. On that day it rained nearly all the time and was bitterly cold. In this area there was not as much game as at Sibaninni but we were pleased to see a number of reedbuck which did not seem to be present at Sibaninni.

Before we left I was sure there had been a big increase in the wildebeest population. We saw large herds coming to the water in the middle of the day. They would approach the water at the gallop, raising as they came great clouds of dust which could be seen long before the animals themselves. On reaching the pan the first line would soon be pushed farther out into the water until some were forced to swim to the far bank. The herd would spread out, occupying more and more of the bank until the whole of the pool was covered.

It was obvious from the state of the grazing along the river that these big herds had not been in the locality very long. Old Makaraba and other Bushmen told me that the first herds had only recently arrived. There was little else beside wildebeest and elephant but we did see seven Cape hartebeest and a few single roan. On our return home we wanted to impress on our patrol boys the necessity of recording such game as hartebeest (which are rare) and showing them pictures of these animals in books was an eye opener to them. They just could not make head or tail of pictures. Vumandaba, however, was able to get the idea into their thick skulls.

We made the return trip along the Mpande Mutenga road as far as Domtchetchi, then across the middle of the reserve back home. It had been a hot dry trip and we were both burned as brown as red Indians, but it had been very interesting and well worth while. I had been glad to see few signs of poaching.

A very amusing aftermath of this trip was my wife's famous yeast story. She made yeast from potatoes and raisins somewhere along the road after one of the donkeys had eaten her dried yeast from a pack bag. When we got home there was the usual clean out of all tins, boxes, and so on, as well as the storing of field kit ready for our next trip. Neither of us gave a thought to the yeast bottle until one afternoon our old garden boy, Longone, let out a yell as if fifty devils were after him. When I got to the back door there he was covered in white foam. Our cook had put the yeast bottle away corked and in the hot cupboard it had worked, and when Longone opened the cupboard to put his daily quota of eggs inside it burst all over him. Bits of bottle had to be carefully removed from his person and his ruffled feelings smoothed down. The laughter of all and sundry caused by the "Missus's" muti, did not make Longone feel any better.

CHAPTER SIX

IT was about this time, 1936, that a start was made on getting roads cut into the inaccessible parts of the reserve. There were rough tracks leading to an old cattle post at Dom pan on *Balcarres,* so we set about extending them towards Shapi and beyond, and the "beyond" was a very long way away. It took years to make the roads in Wankie.

We had no tools other than mattocks, axes, and shovels but with these a gang of fifteen Africans were set to work. We camped with our workers on the job and had a scotch cart and a team of oxen to move our kit along. Wives, of course, have a special load of their own, and mine was no different to other women. She took her basket with knitting, sewing and goodness knows what else in it; including a few hens and even one of our milk cows. Camping together did make "home" for me and she was not lonely, as she would have been if left at the homestead.

It was amazing how quickly each camp came to have its own features. Birds became tame and fed from our bush table, small animals arrived and settled down. Luckily for me, my wife does not mind mice, rats, and such creatures. Her only real hate is spiders, and these she can cope with when no one is about to cope for her. She woke one night with something tickling her face and discovered a jerbil sitting beside her looking very surprised (in fact they were both surprised) but when we chased the little chap away, all was well.

After the track had been cut the oxen were used to drag a thorn tree over the ground several times to remove or beat down the grass and smooth out the bumps. As we moved along, the road was measured

53

and mapped and a metal tag erected every mile. Before we reached Shapi, however, a distance of thirty miles, more than seventy-five per cent of the pegs had been torn down by elephant. At first I thought they could smell them but some were only removed after they had been in position several weeks. It was evident that they could see them although they were only about two inches square and in most cases nailed to a tree. This was my first introduction to the elephant's destructive habits. I was to encounter it again when I started putting up sign posts. We were not amused by our elephants just then. My wife and I spent long evening hours cutting tin, stencilling numbers and making our mile pegs, which we thought rather smart, only to have them tossed away like so much rubbish.

One morning, just as we were moving camp from Guvalalla pan, a gemsbuck came into view walking towards the pan. I signed to everyone to sit down and keep quiet while I sneaked down to the water's edge in the hope of getting a photograph. To our great amazement the animal walked past the pan without stopping and right into the camp where it mingled with the oxen and donkeys, taking no notice of the dogs that rushed out at it, nor taking any notice of us. It was almost as if the creature (a fine bull) had at some time been in captivity and had no fear of humans. It hung about the camp about fifty yards from the people who had by now continued with the packing of the camp, and the loading of the scotch cart. For most of the time it was with the donkeys, continuing to graze as if it were one of them.

When everything was ready we moved off along the new road and, more amazing still, our new friend came with us. The dogs had, by this time, got used to him, no longer barking, while the gemsbuck, for its part, took no further notice of them.

As we moved along the road we must have looked quite a cavalcade. My wife was on the scotch cart in the lead; I followed on the horse; the gemsbuck followed me only some ten paces behind; followed in turn by the dogs and an African carrying my rifle and water-bag.

Our next camp was pitched at White Hill pan, a trek of about ten miles on which the gemsbuck accompanied us all the way. That night after everything had settled down for the night, after a kraal had been built for the oxen – who were tied up inside to stop them breaking out should lions attack – one of the Africans who was walking about in the dark almost stepped on to the gemsbuck lying in the grass. The creature had got as close to the domestic animals as it could. When disturbed it spun round on the African, presenting its sabre-like horns, almost touching the terrified man; yet the creature did him no harm. In the morning it had gone and we saw no more of it for some months, when it came down to Nehimba pan while I was camped there, joining the donkeys for about an hour, then again it walked quietly away. This was the last I saw of our friendly gemsbuck.

As we pushed on with the road the ration problem became difficult. I refused to shoot game for rations and we did not get enough from lion kills to satisfy the gang. In any case, I had to stop Africans walking off the job just because they saw vultures dropping down. By depriving the lions of the whole of their kill we were merely forcing them to kill again, when I might just as well have the animals myself. Fortunately, we had a couple of good walkers in the gang. They walked out to the camp every week with forty pounds of meat including two pounds of salt beef for my wife and me. There were no fish in the pans here but we did vary our diet with a chicken now and then with, of course, as much variation in tinned food as we could manage.

When the road got beyond the Shumba vlei into the mupani country we had to resort to shooting and, as impala were plentiful, I felt we could afford one a week. Fresh venison cooked in various ways proved a very welcome change. My wife was becoming quite a good veld cook with our old Samuel to teach her. Her most important lesson was in using the correct wood for the camp fire. This, according to Samuel, was something she had to learn. He got annoyed with her if she put anything on the fire without his permission. Between them they made excellent bread and scones and without any home comfort we lived very well and were very happy in the bush. "Do it yourself" became our motto and it's surprising how much we accomplished with an axe and the materials found in the veld, for making kitchen tables, seats, and so on.

It was my hope that we could link up with the roads on *Toms Farms*, thus making a through road leaving the main Victoria Falls road at Dett and rejoining it at *Toms Farms*; but Old Man Robins would not hear of it. He would not consider having a road giving access to his farm which could be used by the "noisy, badly behaved" tourists from the game reserve. Even when Robins in his effort to get government help in developing his "game sanctuary," as he called it, made over his land by deed of gift to the government in exchange for two boreholes and windmills together with a new house built to his own design, he would not permit of the roads being linked up. Only after his death was this accomplished.

By this time I had acquired an assistant, Jim Till, who did much of the early work on the roads. He got on better with Robins than I did, but still he could get no concessions out of the cantankerous old boy.

The government were reluctant to vote money for development in Wankie Game Reserve until it became clear how the tsetse fly operations were going. But when it seemed clear that the advance of the "fly" had been arrested, some money for development of water supplies was made available.

A drilling machine moved into the reserve from the Gwaai Native Reserve, putting down the first borehole at Ngwashla. The drill then moved to Toms Farms where it put down two boreholes.

To save time and money Robins was forced to agree to the cutting of a road linking the two road systems, to allow the drill to pass off his land into the game reserve. This road he closed immediately afterwards and I discovered after his death in 1939 that a trench had been dug across the road and covered with sticks and grass like a game pit. Anyone who crossed this track would surely have come to grief. I felt fortunate that it was not me, for on the first occasion I used the road I had one of the old man's Africans on the truck. As we approached the boundary he started tapping on the cab. I thought he had seen some game but when his tapping became more violent I stopped to find out what was the matter. Immediately the boy jumped off the truck and ran a few yards along the road ahead of us and uncovered the trap. Needless to say I was not amused. I could easily have been seriously injured or even killed and my African staff as well.

Robins was not the benign old gentleman that his friends made him out to be. The dear old man was "like a gnome," as one good lady author expressed it in her book. Robins was not amused at this description of himself. Once when I visited him he asked what a gnome was. He pronounced the "g" hard which reduced me to silent laughter. My explanation of the word did not please him one bit. He earned himself the gnome title by wearing a knitted jelly bag cap like an old-time sailor, together with a pyjama jacket which he put on to receive visitors.

56

The introduction of engines to supplement the windmills for pumping water into the pans changed the whole Wankie picture. Funds were naturally very short during the Second World War when the reserve was officially closed to visitors because of petrol rationing. We did, nevertheless, try to help servicemen on their short leaves, if they could get enough petrol for the trip out to us. I was away, off and on, in connection with military duties, but on the whole, my work of developing Wankie proceeded fairly well.

With the additional engines, troughs were no longer allowed to dry up and the pans, too, were kept at a satisfactory level. In a few years we had no less than six boreholes with engines scattered over a wide area. This was enough to keep the game on the sandveld satisfied even should a drought be experienced. But it could not rest at that, for as the game increased so it was essential that the water supply be built up as well.

The permanency of the water supplies soon began to have its effect on game migration. Those animals which had previously been present in small numbers now appeared in greater numbers. Some wildebeest came through from the Sibaninni area after a severe water shortage in the southern section. They settled in at Ngamo. These numbered fourteen only at the start but they were joined in subsequent years by new herds, and the population spread to Kennedy and Nymandhlovu, increasing as time went on to several thousand.

Buffalo, too, soon discovered the improved conditions. Up to 1940 I had only seen small troops of bulls at Shumba and there was one small herd of about fifty on the Deteema river in the Deka basin. There were indications that some came in from Botswana during the dry season and returned when the rains set in. In time these buffalo stopped the return migration to the west and were joined by more and more from outside the reserve. It became evident by 1945 that the buffalo population, as much as the elephant, were one day going to present an over-stocking problem.

The pumps were a very marked success but it became obvious that some waters were more popular than others. This was because the water being brought to the surface was in some cases highly mineralised, being very attractive to game. In fact, the pans became not only a source of water but of mineral salts as well. This was particularly noticeable at Nyamandhlovu where giraffe (who only normally require

57

a drink once a week or even less) would come to the pan day after day. A neighbouring pan, Dom, only some two miles away, was not nearly as popular a drinking place for all kinds of game.

The salts which the game seek and which occur in the natural salt licks – a common feature on all the glades or near the pans, in the sand veld areas, but not so common in the mupani country – are sodium and lime. It is usual for salt licks to form where, for some reason, the subsoil has been brought to the surface by some agent such as termites or antbears. Even small mounds of subsoil which are pushed up by harvester ants or mole rats are often eaten. It is undoubtedly sodium and lime which provide the attraction as on analysis these licks show a percentage of from ·09 per cent to ·25 per cent of sodium and ·33 per cent to 1·02 per cent of lime. The water from Nyamandhlovu borehole contains a high percentage of both these as well as an iron content. On the other hand, some boreholes produce water with little lime or soda in it; Jambili is one of these. The water from this borehole is almost pure and contains practically no salts at all. This is no doubt why this watering point has never become a popular game spot, despite the assured water supply.

Browsing animals seem more attracted to salt licks than do the grazers. The most frequent visitors are elephant, giraffe, eland, gemsbuck, kudu. Even ostriches frequently use salt licks.

The high concentrations of game which continued right through the year accelerated the destruction of vegetation around the pans and in only a few years the trees in the vicinity began to disappear.

As time went on it became more and more obvious that water was the key to the Wankie Game Reserve's future. With the sinking of a borehole at Ngwashla a new era had been opened up. The greater part of the reserve is flat and sandy, with little run-off during the rains, consequently there are no rivers or streams and very few small watercourses. Yet the country is studded with pans, the vast majority of them only some twenty or thirty yards across, and when full about two feet deep. These pans have been, to a very large extent, formed by game animals themselves. Most varieties of game, particularly elephant, have a great liking (it might almost be called a craving) for minerals, which they eat with the soil where it contains these ingredients.

Ant-heaps as we have seen, were the main source of supply. Ants brought the subsoil to the surface exposing these salts, and game would obtain their need from these anthills. This, in time, formed a slight depression in which water collected. With the soil being eaten and the muddy water being drunk together with the dust (formed by the continued trampling and digging by game) being blown away, these depressions grew rapidly and with the continued puddling remained quite watertight. It probably takes many thousands of years for a pan capable of holding a million gallons of water to form, but there has been game in the Wankie area for a very long time.

In many places along the main watershed there are big deposits of lime just below the surface, and these have formed big open glades where there are few trees and not much grass. The best known of these are at the Main Camp, Kennedy, Ngwashla and Ngamo. These areas are much favoured by game and it is here that the largest pans have formed. When the water in them is getting low and is much puddled by game, samples have shown that well over ten per cent of it was matter in suspension; so that an elephant drinking fifty gallons of water would be carrying away in its stomach fifty pounds of soil. In the course of only one year a single elephant might remove from pans some five tons of soil in this manner alone; quite apart from the quantity carried away on its feet and body after a mud bath. The dust raised around a pan by a big herd of elephant or buffalo is quite appreciable. In windy weather – particularly those wind storms which precede the first thunderstorms – when game is concentrated at the highest level, the amount blown away must amount to many tons.

In the absence of watercourses upon which dams could be built, it was the pans which offered the best possibilities of improving the water supplies. In the bottom of each pan there was a considerable layer of silt which went into suspension readily when the pan was full of water and game churned up this soluble matter. When the pan became low the material in suspension became so concentrated that the water in it was no longer available to game, resulting in a great deal of loss. In an effort to make the pans last longer, an attempt was made to remove thick mud with ox-drawn dam scoops, as in those days there were no tractors available. We had little success, as by the time the material in the pans became workable there was no water for the oxen. The small amount of work done in this way, however, made a great deal of difference to the water supplies.

Our attention turned, therefore, to the underground water supplies, and a scheme was evolved for sinking boreholes near pans. The idea was to replace at least some of the evaporation by erecting windmills on the boreholes and pumping into the pans. By this means it was hoped to build up a sufficient supply during the rains and early dry season – when game pressure on the main pans was not very high – to carry the pan over into the next rainy season.

This scheme, unfortunately, did not work out very well. The silt in the bottom of the pans was such that with continual trampling the water still became too dirty for game to drink before the rains commenced. However, with the boreholes providing fresh water, it became possible to clean the pans out with the oxen and dam scoops. This was successfully done at pans such as Nyamandhlovu, Dom, Shapi, and Ngwashla. It was found that the main formation of the pan should not be disturbed as the seal formed by the mud was not very thick. The removal of only a few inches caused the pan to leak, as this watertight seal was like a saucer with porous sand underneath. This is, possibly, how these places derived the name of "pan." The main clay seal formation of the pan is quite distinct from the silt which forms on the bottom.

This method of pumping into a cleaned pan was an improvement but it was still not enough as game were able to break up the actual formation of the pan and the water became as dirty as ever.

I then hit upon the idea of running the water into some sort of trough which was strong enough to withstand elephant and other heavy game. I knew from visiting the timber concessions' watering points that it had to be a strong trough because thirsty donkeys and cattle broke down most troughs in time.

I knew, too, that some game were reluctant to drink from a raised trough, preferring to drink in the natural way from little puddles formed by the overflow. So I devised a concrete trough which was very simple to construct and was quite effective. It consisted of a circular trench about twenty feet in diameter, a foot wide and four feet deep, filled with a strong concrete mixture with a pipe let in at the pump side. When the concrete was thoroughly set the centre of the circle was excavated to a depth of about two feet and that was all. There was no concrete bottom to the trough, mainly because this was too expensive in those days, when we had no lorries and all cement, sand and stone had to be carted to the site.

These troughs were built close to the edge of the pan where there was clay to build upon, while the overflow from the trough could run down into the pan.

Game was slow to take to these troughs, preferring to drink from the pan. Even if the pan was empty or very dirty the animals walked past the trough full of clean water, taking no notice of it. To them the right place to look for a drink was at the bottom of the pan and not halfway up the slope. Elephant were the first to take to them, guiding the other game to the trough.

This worked very well as long as the windmill kept the trough full or nearly full, but if the wind failed, as it often did for days at a stretch in September and October, game would dig in the bottom of the trough in an effort to get a drink. They would even eat up the saturated soil deepening the inside of the trough so that small animals like warthog had difficulty in getting out. To stop this, big stones were placed inside the troughs and embedded in the bottom.

Windmills, however, did not provide the ideal set-up as they did not pump sufficient water to keep game satisfied. During windy weather the mills could pump only about 5,000 gallons a day; while towards the end of the dry season when water was most needed, I doubt if some of them pumped more than fifty gallons a day. A herd of a hundred elephant (and there were several herds of that number as early as 1940) would consume 5,000 gallons in one drink. If they visited a pan and did not get sufficient water they would change their routine, moving to some other watering point, often outside the reserve, where they would remain until the rains had started.

By this time Wankie Game Reserve had become more firmly established and funds for water were more readily available, making it possible to switch over to diesel engines to pump water for game. The set-up was to have the windmill pumping all through the rains and switch over to engines in the dry season.

It was not long before the elephant learned that the troughs contained clean water and on their visits to the pan they would spend all their time drinking from the trough and only go into the pan to bath. It was not long before they associated the throbbing of the engine with clean water and if, for any reason, the pump was not running and the trough empty, they would stand about in a most expectant manner. Sometimes they would wander off, standing under the shade of trees for hours, even days, and then within twenty minutes of the pump being started they would be back at the trough. Yet this actually only happened in the case of individuals or small herds. Big herds, when not satisfied, would hang about for an hour or two, returning every now and then to the trough, then move on either to another pump or some other water supply. Of course, it was imperative that the windmills and engines had to be protected from inquisitive elephant. I had learnt when I put up mile pegs and signposts along the roads that anything strange in the form of metal attracted their attention and was likely to be pulled down. A windmill was particularly vulnerable and easily wrecked. I could imagine the look of satisfaction on an elephant's face as it brought one crashing to the ground. Soon after our arrival at our cottage at Main Camp a very old windmill on the farm was pushed sideways by elephant. I was taking a stroll one evening when I noticed the old mill looking rather odd, and called my wife to have a look. We decided that it was definitely off centre. We walked the quarter mile over to an old water tank and found the spoor of a couple of bulls who had been drinking there. Thereafter I knew that everything I introduced to the reserve in the development line would have to be protected from my large family. Labourers working on the roads who left their tools overnight had many a time a long walk looking for them after they had been carried away in the dark. Lions, too, were guilty of this offence, chewing the handles of shovels and other implements, and carting them off along the paths.

Protection was provided by a circular trench some thirty feet from the windmill, dug to a depth of six feet and tapered from about six feet wide at the top to six inches at the bottom. This was too wide for an elephant to step over and too narrow for him to climb down into and up the other side. The trenches, of course, did not last many years as during the rains the sides washed in and the trench became wider and more shallow; but by that time game had accepted the structure and it no longer attracted their attention.

The pipeline from the pump to the trough was another problem as elephant would frequently dig it up and twist it into all sorts of shapes. Even when it was buried two feet underground, they would find it and pull it up. The fact that the pipeline had been laid for some time did not seem to make much difference; perhaps they could hear or feel the water running in the pipe.

CHAPTER SEVEN

To the north of the main watershed in the reserve the country is hilly, composed of sandstone and gneiss with a great many watercourses, nearly all of which dry up soon after the rains. At three places there were small springs which dried up only in the worst years. Dams have been built at all of these sites. The earth dam on the Deteema river was no sooner completed than a good rain storm put a few feet of water into it, but when the next storm came, before the dam had filled, it burst, leaving a great gap right at the highest part of the wall. Nothing daunted, we repaired the breach, only to have it burst again with the first flood of another rainy season. There was a lapse of time, some years in fact, before any further repair work was done, the breached dam wall being an eyesore to my staff and self. The third time the whole wall was rebuilt and again it stood for only a short time after filling, when it gave way.

The next time we dealt with this "hoodoo" dam of ours we repaired it with the addition of concrete and, after that, it held and is today one of the best game spots in the area. No sooner had this dam held back some water, even before it burst the first time, than quite a big crocodile put in an appearance. This was strange as the nearest water where crocodiles were known was the Deka river not less than ten miles away. I was not aware until then that crocodiles wandered so far from perma-

63

nent water and so early in the wet season, but more surprises were to come.

The next dam was built on the Mandavu river which was on *Sinamatela* ranch, one of the blocks of land bought in and added to the reserve. This dam, also an earth dam, burst before it was full, leaving a small pool instead of what should have been a nice big stretch of water. Much to my surprise there was a crocodile in the pool. Where the creature came from heaven only knows. The Mandavu river flowed into the Lukosi river, which in turn flowed into the Gwaai river. Except for one small pool about fifteen miles below the dam there was no water all the way to the Gwaai, which was at least thirty miles away.

When repair work was begun on the breach we found a hole in the wall which had evidently been made by a crocodile. The sides were worn smooth where the creature's body had scraped along the hole, while its spoor was clearly seen on the muddy bottom of the hole. Here, then, was the answer to our dam failures, in every case a crocodile had obviously bored a hole into the soft earth bank below water level, thus causing a burst when the dam filled finally.

The Deteema dam had burst three times and now that it was full again and we were confident that crocodiles had been responsible for the breaching of the wall, we decided to try and rid this dam of these creatures before they damaged the wall again.

Accompanied by my two sons, Rodney (age twelve) and Gerald (age ten), I camped at the dam and after dark set out in a small home-made metal rowing boat, armed with a shotgun and torch. Knowing that there were at least two crocodiles, we soon located one of them, Rod having no difficulty in putting a shot into its head at quite close range. The body floated and we hauled it into the boat. We then rowed slowly up the dam in search of the other croc, when suddenly the one we had in the boat showed obvious signs of life. We could not put another shot into it as that would have put a hole in the bottom of the boat. The crocodile, seven feet six inches in size, became rather too lively for our liking and I abandoned the rowing seat and we all took up positions in the prow and stern of the boat with our legs dangling over the side.

In this position we started to paddle for the bank of the dam, the side of which nearest us had a steep bank with deep water right up to the shore line which was heavily wooded. Gerrie kept a torch shining on the croc while Rod and I paddled up to what we knew was a bare gravelly beach. Just as the boat was about to ground we were greeted by a deep growl. Gerrie flicked up the torch and revealed four lions within twenty yards of us. For a moment we did not know what to do; however, we decided to try and drive the lions away, so we shouted at them and they made off into a patch of thick long grass. But they did not go farther; we could still see their eyes reflecting the light of our torch.

I was out-voted when I suggested that we land and get rid of our croc, so I tried to despatch it by jabbing it on the head with a paddle, but this served only to bring it to instant life. It started thrashing about and uttering a low snarling sound. This seemed to attract the lions who came back on to the gravel verge, approaching to within fifty yards of us. Shouting had no effect on them this time and Rod fired a shot over their heads. The shot startled them but they did not make off, they merely lay down.

Faced with a crocodile if we took to the water and the lions if we took to the shore, we were debating the position when the matter was decided for us by two of the lions starting up a full-throated roar. We began paddling madly for the opposite bank. Our croc lay still for a time and we made good progress but then the beast started crawling about the bottom of the boat, which upset our balance as at one time all its weight was on one side and then on the other. In our precarious position we were unable to shift our weight to counterbalance the croc's change in position and it looked at times as if our boat would capsize. If the crocodile had tried to climb out over the side I am sure we would have capsized.

All this time the lions were indulging in full-throated roars at intervals of about five minutes, but they were at least getting a little farther away each time. At last we reached the bank and had to turn the boat stern first. With both Gerrie and me on the stern with our legs over the side and the crocodile at our end, we would have foundered if Rod had been the first out, leaving all the weight at the back of the boat. We managed to make the shore while Rod walked tight-rope-wise along the side of the boat to safety.

After a breather, during which time the lions roared again, we dragged the boat and the crocodile out of the water, then pitched the boat over, landing our croc on the bank. Rod then gave it another shot which put "paid" to it. That ended our crocodile hunting for the night and we rowed back to camp. The next day we managed to bag the other crocodile and hoped we had cleared the dam. It was some time before another – much smaller one – put in an appearance, but by then we hoped the dam wall had consolidated sufficiently to stand up to its digging activities.

I am doubtful now if the crocodiles did, in fact, come from downstream. In each case, there was a small spring near the site of these dams with plenty of water during the rains and, although it has never been proved, we are now inclined to believe that these creatures lived in these areas and aestivated in some concealed spot during the dry season. Possibly they had a hole excavated by themselves in damp soil near the spring. The entrance to such a hole would soon be trampled in by elephant and become quite invisible.

One year a crocodile about six feet long found its way into the pan at Shumba. Where it came from no one knows and where it went to is equally mysterious for it just disappeared during the wet season, and never appeared at any of the other pans in these parts. This is all the more remarkable because there was usually no water at Shumba during the dry season, until a borehole was sunk there.

Although crocodiles were far more widespread in this waterless country than one would expect, it is a strange fact that there are none in the Nata or Makarakari drainage system. There is enough water and fish for them to live happily in this river system but I never saw a sign of them there and the Africans in the locality were emphatic that they did not occur.

One crocodile, which is known to have lived in the Wankie Game Reserve since August 1937, is still there. It was caught on the Shangani river in 1936 living for its first year in a goldfish pond at the home of Mrs Beadle, wife of Mr Justice Beadle who later became Sir Hugh Beadle. Due to its habit of wandering off into neighbouring gardens where it caused consternation among the poultry it was presented to me, being railed to me at Dett in a fruit box. The creature then measured twenty-six and a half inches, and was about twenty months old. That was in August 1937. From newly-hatched crocodiles which I have measured, it is estimated that this one would have been about twelve inches when hatched. Its growth had been recorded at intervals since we got it.

Growth rate of Beadle, the crocodile: Caught December 1935.

		Length	
	1935	12	inches
	1936	16	,,
November	1936	22	,,
March	1937	26½	,,
August	1937	26½	,,
December	1937	30	,,
March	1938	34	,,
June	1938	37	,,
October	1938	42	,,
December	1938	45	,,
April	1939	48	,,
July	1939	50	,,
November	1939	51	,,
March	1940	53	,,
		(Weight 35 lb.)	
October	1941	71	inches
December	1941	72	,,
December	1942	84	,,
May	1945	88	,,
December	1945	88	,,
December	1946	90	,,
December	1949	93	,,
December	1950	94	,,
December	1960	105	,,
August	1966	110	,,

The rate of growth seems to have been fairly regular up to about thirteen years when there was a marked slowing up. Possibly this is due to the animal having reached maturity. We have no indication as to the sex of the crocodile but have always assumed that it is a male and it has always been known as Beadle. He is probably one of the most photographed crocodiles in Africa and has always been obliging, lying for

67

hours at a pan on the ten-mile drive. Latterly, stern warnings were posted to visitors when he attained a really good size. Because he was known to be tame, visitors were inclined to take liberties with him, and those with small children were specially warned to keep the youngsters in the car when taking Beadle's picture.

For the first eighteen months that we had him, Beadle lived in a fish pond in our garden. It was quite a big pond as fish ponds go, being about eight feet in diameter and about three feet deep with an island in the middle. Goldfish had recently been introduced, a dozen only. We used to count them from time to time to see if Beadle had eaten any, but he never did. He fed on insects which fell into the pond. We encouraged this by hanging a lamp over the pool at night. The insects he seemed to like most were moths. We dropped king crickets in from time to time and, although he would take them, he did not always eat them. He took no notice of live mice which dropped into the water, and would not take meat, dead birds, or mice we put down for him. Frogs (not toads) released into the pond soon disappeared, but I never actually saw him eat one.

Birds used to drink at the pool in large numbers and they never took any notice of Beadle, while he, for his part, took no notice of them, even though he could have caught them with ease.

When he was about two years old, one day I noticed him lying on the side of the pool with something in his mouth. On examination this proved to be a blue breasted waxbill. Two hours later it was still there but at evening it had gone. I have no doubt he swallowed it. He had made his first kill. Not long after this we saw him again in the act of swallowing another small bird. He did it this time in the water with his feet braced against the side of the pool while he kept dipping his head under water as if to wash it down. We decided then that Beadle must go to a bigger pan; our garden birds were one of our main hobbies.

The Kalahari sands are not the most suitable for gardening. We were building up an attractive garden under the most difficult conditions, water shortage, long dry summers and so forth. Beadle was now three years old and we moved him to a small pan about a mile from the house, which was kept full by a pump. Here he had to fend for himself but we did on occasions give him a dead bird or mouse. For a time he would not take these, but eventually he did. There were fish in the pan, introduced some time before and he may have caught some of them. He seemed quite happy in his new home but became very shy and would not allow us to approach close.

In June he dug a hole in the bank of the pool just above the water line, and some ten feet into the side, but not more than two feet below the surface. During the cold weather he lived most of the time in this cavity. In April some catfish (barbel) were introduced to the pool, all about ten inches long. These soon disappeared; Beadle evidently had eaten them. In July 1939 a half-grown wild cat was found dead in the pool, with extensive injuries to a front leg and its head. We concluded that Beadle had killed the animal but it floated for days and was not eaten. I think it was taken, eventually, by a hyena.

One night, in November 1940, I was awakened by our dogs barking furiously at something in the backyard. From the frightened tone of their barking I thought it was a snake which was disturbing them but when I went out with a torch it was a crocodile and not a snake revealed in the torch light. Beadle had come home. By this time he was quite formidable, being four years old and fifty-three inches long.

I called Samuel, our cookboy, and between us we managed to drive Beadle into the meal store and lock him up for the night. The next day we measured and weighed him and found he was thirty-five pounds. It seemed best to take him to another pan four miles from the house where we hoped he would stop wandering home at night. There were fish in this pan, too, and we soon learned that he had taken to eating them for, on one occasion when we were fishing there, leaving a barbel on the bank, Beadle came out and took the fish. He did not eat it immediately but went back into the water and swam across the pool with it in his mouth. When in the shallow water, he proceeded to crunch it in his jaws while standing erect on his forelegs with his tail held up. When he had crunched the fish a number of times he turned it around so that the head went down first and swallowed it. It was not a big fish, only some twelve inches long, but he seemed to have difficulty in getting it down.

During the wet season, when all the small pans in the area contained water, Beadle would wander from pan to pan, and we were never very sure where he would be found. Once, just after the first heavy storm, we found him in a small pan where he was eating toads, and from the distended look of his stomach, I judged he had eaten a large number of them.

Even at this age Beadle's diet consisted of small creatures. We often saw him catch doves which came to drink, while once he caught a pelican, leaving only the large beak as a record. We never saw him catch wild duck but it was quite noticeable that duck did not alight on the water at the pan he was in, or if they did they soon walked up the bank getting well away from the water's edge. Jacanas and blacksmith plovers used to mob him when he came out of the pan to bask in the sun, the jacanas by screaming and running around him at a safe distance with their wings open and the blacksmiths by diving over him uttering their clicking call.

Here, too, Beadle dug a hole and this was again just above the waterline, but as fast as he dug it out it was trampled in by game, and he gave up the effort when it was only some six feet long. He then dug another hole in an antheap in and around the roots of a tree. The water used to lap this hole. When he first occupied it he used to lie in a couple of inches of water. It was not a long hole; we could look into it and see him and he was usually – although not always – lying facing the entrance.

Our crocodile continued to live on the ten-mile-drive where he was a popular exhibit for visitors. When he was eighteen years old we tried to give him a mate. She was a small crocodile captured on the Deka river. There were a number of little crocodiles about and I went to look over the pools with the intention of going back at night with a torch to catch one in the dark, as I knew how easy it is to approach a crocodile in the water when it is dazzled by a strong light. But I came on one about four feet long in a shallow pool where it went down to the bottom and, beyond stirring up some mud, took no further evasive action. I waited for the mud to drift away into the stream and could see the small crocodile lying on the bottom in only about two feet of water. This was a chance not to be missed. I waded in quietly and grabbed her by the nose with both hands and quickly lifted her clear of the water.

She lashed about a good deal, spinning around and around, with tail lashing against my legs. I held on and carried my captive back to the truck and popped it into a meal sack. Next day, it was released into the pan while Beadle lay on the bank watching the proceedings.

The new crocodile immediately dashed into the water while Beadle came swimming up to the spot where the newcomer had disappeared. We did not know if his intentions were honourable or not, and actually waited for an hour to see if anything happened. The newcomer came up once but Beadle either did not see her or took no notice and we left it at that. But that was the last we saw of our new crocodile and we have a feeling that the poor creature was eaten by our Beadle, not a gentlemanly act, you will admit.

Another opportunity occurred three years later. We were netting a pool on the Chingahobi river to catch fish for transfer to the new Mandavu dam, when a small crocodile came up in the net. It was about five feet long and just what we wanted. This, too, was kept in a bag and released next day. Almost from the time it was caught it shammed dead and when turned out of the bag lay on its back for a minute or more without moving. Then when it realised that we were no longer standing over it, the crocodile got up slowly and made for the water, quickening its pace as it reached the edge of the pool. That was the last we saw of that crocodile, too.

The next opportunity to find a wife for Beadle occurred on a small tributary of the Zambezi river near Binga, when a crocodile about six feet long got entangled in a net set to catch fish specimens for the museum. The museum authorities lashed this one to a log with soft insulated wire and presented me with their captive the same day. (As it happened, I was camping with them). This time we released the crocodile into another pan not far from the one where Beadle was living at the time, hoping that it would get over the shock of its journey before they met and have a better chance of defending itself. This worked, for the newcomer settled down very well and was often seen on the bank.

Some six months later, towards the end of the wet season the two were seen in the same pan. It was easy to tell the difference as Beadle was about eight feet long and much thicker in build. He was by this time twenty-two years old. But, alas, one afternoon a tourist sitting at Nyamandhlovu pan watching for game coming to drink was amazed to see a great commotion in the water and two crocodiles fighting. After about ten minutes things quietened down but a little later Beadle came out into the shallow water and swallowed something which looked like the end of the smaller crocodile's tail.

71

Soon after that the new crocodile emerged from the water with about half of its tail missing. It wandered off into the bush with the white sinews from the wound trailing in the sand. No more was seen of the creature for about three months, when it appeared in Ballaballa pan a good four miles from the scene of the fight. Both crocodiles continued to live in their respective pans and, as far as we know, have not met up again. So despite all our efforts we have no definite proof of Beadle's sex, but evidently the other one is the same sex, whatever it might be. Beadle has developed a very rugged profile which is an indication that the creature is a male, the profile of the female crocodile is longer by comparison and not so ridged. The only way to be sure would be to have him side by side with another crocodile of equal age and size and compare the contours of the heads.

Beadle is now thirty years old and it is high time some breeding took place, but perhaps there are no females in this little community of crocodiles. All the crocodiles I have shot and opened up have had stones in their stomachs. If Beadle has any it will be a mystery where they came from as there are no stones on the Kalahari sands and none in any of the pans he frequents. Just what is the function of these stones is not clear. I am of the opinion that they are ballast, designed to keep the density of the crocodile about equal or a little above that of the water. I have often seen Beadle swimming with his body under water and his tail on the surface swinging slowly from side to side as if trying to keep himself under. This only occurs when the pan is low and very muddy. Evidently the density of the water has risen due to the amount of matter in suspension and Beadle's buoyancy changed from negative to positive.

Crocodiles seem to have some method of changing their buoyancy from negative to positive for I have seen Beadle lying on the bottom of the pan, quite still, then suddenly begin to rise, without any movement, to the surface, and only when he was clear of the bottom would he move his tail slightly. Once his head had broken the surface he would remain quite still and float. This change of buoyancy is evidently brought about by flexing the muscles, thus slightly altering the volume.

Bernhard Grzimek tells us that seals carry stones around in their stomach in much the same way as crocodiles and I have no doubt it will be for the same reason.

The weight of stones in crocodiles I have shot have been:

Length of croc. 9′ 7″	Weight 236 lb.	Stones 1 lb.
„ „ „ 10′	„ 300 lb.	„ 1½ lb.
„ „ „ 10′ 10½″	„ 300 lb.	„ ½ lb.
„ „ „ 7′ 9″	„ 203 lb.	„ 9 oz.
„ „ „ Tail missing	„ 260 lb.	„ 9 oz.
„ „ „ 6′ 2″	„ ?	„ 11 oz.

The length of time Beadle would remain submerged when merely resting was from fifteen to eighteen minutes but if trying to hide he could remain under for an hour. The periods when he would remain submerged longest were in the cold weather when he was sluggish and possibly the metabolism of his body was at a low ebb. At that time his supply of oxygen would not be used up so fast.

Just how Beadle manages to catch fish is not clear as his eyesight under water is very poor, due possibly to the muddy state of the pans. We very often threw a dead bird on to the water and the crocodile would come for it right away. He would swim towards it and when some forty or fifty feet away would submerge and, as often as not, swim right past the bird, directly under it. He would surface again to have a look around, sometimes within a couple of feet of his target and would have to turn round before taking it.

When in the pan near the house where the water was clear it was evident that Beadle could see objects on the surface when he was lying on the bottom but I doubt if he sees objects above the surface. I have seen him rising from the bottom to take a breath of air and despite my waving my hand over him he would continue to rise until he broke surface and only then did he see me and dive immediately. There are, without doubt, certain angles at which a crocodile under water is unable to see objects which are above water, and directly above is one of them.

Although Beadle is now thirty years old and over nine feet long there is no record of his having eaten any mammal larger than a wild cat. There is ample opportunity for him to do so, as hundreds of animals about the size he would be expected to take drink regularly at his pan. He may, of course, have taken animals which he could swallow right away, such as young warthog which frequently mud-bathe

73

on the water's edge, positively asking to be caught. We do, on occasions, give him dead animals, such as springhares, and he makes short work of these, swallowing them within a few minutes. A bigger animal, such as a wild dog, he will tear to pieces by getting a grip of a small portion and then giving a violent shake of his head, thereby tearing the piece of flesh out. Although he has no molar teeth as such he would masticate his food to a certain extent by passing it to and fro at the back of his mouth, crunching it as he did so. Sometimes this crunching went on for long periods with rest breaks in between.

One of Beadle's favourite dodges when given a big piece of meat was to lie beside it in the shallow water and catch barbel when these fish came to feed on the meat. As he caught the fish he would crunch the barbel several times and then give an extra crunch or two just behind the fish's head. Then passing it to the front of his mouth, he would give a violent shake which invariably breaks off the fish head. He would then swallow the body, ignoring the head.

This method of shaking his head was carried out by a slow swing to one side and then a very fast whipcrack movement to the other side and back again. I have no doubt that this would put an end to any struggles of an animal he had caught; in fact, it may be a way of overcoming resistance. Another method he sometimes used to tear a carcass to pieces was to take a grip and then spin over and over. The leverage obtained by this method is terrific.

Crocodiles we have caught either in our hands or in a net seem to use this twisting habit to extricate themselves. I once saw two buffalo which had been killed by crocodiles on the Deka river being torn to pieces by this twisting method. There were seven crocodiles in attendance. They cruised about for hours not touching the carcasses, and then one would swim up slowly and, with the tip of its snout, would push the body for a while, then take a grip. It would lash out with its tail, spin over and over and, once a piece of flesh or skin had been torn loose, the crocodile would move into shallow water. There, with its feet on the bottom, it would raise its head and throw the morsel to the back of its mouth, lower its head slowly and take a gulp of water and swallow.

I have also seen this twisting technique used by crocodiles when caught on a line. The way to catch crocodiles on a hook and line is to have two hooks on the line, about two feet apart, each baited and laid on the bank. The crocodile will then swallow the first bait it picks up in order to be able to take the second bait. If only one bait is laid it will usually carry it off into the water where, while masticating or pulling on the line, it will dislodge the hook.

Over the years I have made several attempts to hatch crocodile eggs. On each occasion a nest was found on the Deka river in September. One was very fresh, the eggs having just been laid, on 20th September 1942. They were carefully transported to my garden, keeping them the same way up as they were in the nest, where they were buried in circumstances as similar as I could get to those pertaining on the Deka. There were 42 eggs in all. At the end of a month I opened one of the eggs, and made notes on the size of the embryo. On 13th November the young crocodile was four and a half inches long and the coloration was fairly well advanced. By 28th November the egg I opened showed that the length had increased to six and a half inches and the little chap was quite active. The eyes were open and very bright. There were no teeth but the creature would try to bite. There was a bare patch on the head and the yolk sac had not been absorbed into the stomach. In one egg I opened on 10th December, the embryo was only six inches long, but further advanced. The bare patch on the head had not completely closed over, while the yolk sac had become much smaller and harder. On 18th December the one I opened had a crocodile nine inches long in it with the head patch closed and the yolk completely absorbed. All the eggs in the nest were cracked. The claw on the tip of the nose for piercing the egg was well developed.

On 22nd December the eggs were attacked by red ants and several of the young crocodiles were killed just as they were emerging from the shells. I took the rest into the office and put them in a cupboard where we could hear the babies croaking inside the eggs. Only when I picked up an egg to examine it did the young make an effort to get out. They had difficulty in splitting the skin of the egg with the snout claw but once they had made a small hole, they soon squirmed their way out. They all died soon after hatching, and before the umbilical cord had broken to release them from the shell.

Although incubation conditions were not ideal the eggs did hatch in about ninety days and I am of the opinion that the baby crocodiles were left in the eggs too long, and that under natural conditions the mother would have unearthed them earlier than I did. The average length of the young at the time they hatched was twelve and a half inches, varying from thirteen to ten inches.

Crocodiles on the Deka river seem to protect their eggs more than they do on the Gwaai river. It was not difficult to find a nest on the Deka as the spoor left by the female about the nest site was easy to see and often the parent would be seen sliding into the water if disturbed.

We used to spend a great deal of time fishing on the Gwaai and only once did I find a crocodile's nest. This was at a spot where we often fished. We had fished there when the eggs were buried beneath our feet. On the day I discovered the nest there were unmistakable signs of a crocodile digging which, on closer examination, revealed half a dozen eggs just ready to hatch as well as a further twenty baby crocodiles in the water nearby, one swimming with the eggshell still attached to it. This was on the 18th December.

Crocodiles are not happy in the cold weather. Even on the Zambezi where it is never really cold (the temperature does not drop much below 35 degrees F.) crocodiles become noticeably lethargic, ignoring bait put out for them during June and July. On a fishing expedition near the junction of the Deka and Zambezi, I tried to catch a crocodile on a line. With this object in view the body of a monkey (shot on crop protection) cut in two halves, was laid on a sandbank where a big crocodile had been seen basking several times. The crocodile came out of the water and lay for hours beside the bait but did not take it. After a couple of days we moved the bait to another spot where several crocodiles basked in the sun on the sand, with the same result. We then put out fish just to see if any would be taken but, except for one filched by a fish eagle, these baits were ignored.

The next trip to this area in September was very different: anything we left out in the way of fish or meat was taken during the night. On this occasion we set a bear trap baited with a baboon carcass and caught a monster of a crocodile eighteen feet long. The trap was attached to fifty yards of wire rope but the crocodile only took out a little over half of it, becoming so entangled that when we came to examine the trap next morning the creature was dead. From this animal, however, I was able to gain a great deal of information, about weight, and so on.

We noticed the same thing with Beadle. He seldom took and ate anything we offered him during the cold weather, and it can be really cold in the pans where he lives! Frost in July is common, sometimes severe; the meteorological department, who have a station at main camp, have recorded seventeen and a half degrees of frost. I have seen ice on the fringes of the water in the Dett vlei at six a.m. and when on patrol during the winter months I often found water-bags frozen solid.

There are no fish indigenous to the Kalahari pan country in the game reserve. I found no fish of any sort except in the Sibaninni and the Deka river catchment areas.

Bushmen used to come from Botswana during the dry season when the pans were drying out in the Deka basin to collect barbel. Some years there were no fish at all, depending upon the amount of rain during the previous season. If pans overflowed into the river system then the fish would get into them but, if not, there were no fish to be had. I never saw bream in these pans, but I did record a small scaled fish of the barbus family; they were not very numerous but the barbel (Clarias) were very common.

Fish were introduced to the pans round about main camp from the Gwaai river. At first they did very well, bred and grew rapidly; but this was to be expected as the pans were alive with insect life, which included a shrimp-like creature about an inch long which looked as if it would be very palatable to fish. My interest in fish had a number of angles, one of which was the number of leeches in the pans, which attacked my horses and pack animals when they waded in to drink and feed on the lush grass growing in the pans. In another way I also wanted to improve the protein available to my African staff on patrol.

In addition to the insect life in pans, the dung deposited in the water encouraged a very considerable growth of plankton which, of course, was acceptable to fish. But the muddy state of the water caused by game towards the end of the dry season proved too much for the Talapita mossambica, which disappeared, although the barbel (Clarias) continued to thrive. They bred rapidly, and their spawn as well as one-inch-long fish could be found in the shallow water among the grass in January, soon after the pans had flooded. There did not seem to be as much spawn in the main pans where the fish had survived as there was in the smaller pans which had become linked to the main pans when they overflowed.

77

It required only a very shallow stream of water to enable the fish to travel from one pan to another. We never found, however, that barbel were able to travel from one pan to another unless there was a water connection. They would wander a long way from the pan provided there was just enough water to keep them wet. They did not swim but walked, using their pectoral fins as legs. It only needed a couple of pairs to find their way into a small pan to provide many hundreds of young fish which, by the time the pan dried up, would be four to six inches long. Incidentally, this walking by the barbel – which more often than not occurred in the roadways when flooded – gave a number of wet-season visitors something to talk about. They reported it to me as something they would not believe if they had not seen it themselves.

Carnivora such as lions, leopards, and hyena soon learned to catch and eat these little barbel when they were almost stranded. Young lions, in particular, had great fun scooping the fish on to the bank and eating them. After these frolics the lions would come away covered in mud from nose to tail.

On one occasion a leopard was seen at Nyamandhlovu pan in broad daylight, with obviously something wrong with it. Closer examination showed it to be just a bag of bones. Fearing that it was rabid (the first time we had cause to suspect this at Wankie) the animal was killed.

On cutting the leopard open to see what it had in its stomach it was found that the whole carcass was infested with worms and parasites. Specimens sent in for identification revealed that these parasites were derived from eating fish. Here was a clear case of a parasite being introduced to an area where the hosts had no resistance and the infection proving fatal.

We found on our fishing escapades to the Gwaai that the squeakers (*Synodontis zambesencis*) were great eaters of the bilharzia snails. We drew the attention of the authorities in Salisbury to this fact, as there was a possible control measure here. Dr Moseley, who was in charge of bilharzia research at that time, requested that some stomach contents be sent to him for examination and he sent me the necessary preservative for this purpose. To catch a few fish to provide this material we laid ground bait in the form of M'sess (the dregs left after making kaffir beer) and fished over this. About a dozen fish were caught and their complete stomachs removed and placed in screw-

78

topped jars of preservative. All went well as there were a number of snails as well as the ground bait in the stomachs.

A couple of days later, as I was preparing to parcel up the jars for posting, I noted bubbles escaping from under the lids and when I unscrewed the top of the jar it blew off with considerable force. Evidently the preservative which was pure alcohol, had preserved the snails, but not arrested the fermentation process of *M'sess*. What, in fact, we were preparing was a rather unique form of time bomb which could have exploded in the post.

Following this we did release some squeakers into a small pan to see if they would eat up the bilharzia snails, but the fish did not survive the cold winter.

CHAPTER EIGHT

POACHERS were not difficult to deal with when the reserve was first proclaimed but, as time went on and game became more plentiful, so the
poachers became bolder. In the early days, all we had to control were
wandering families of Bushmen; all the European ivory hunters had
pulled out before I arrived and they did not come back. The Bushmen
changed from the homeless nomad type to the more commercially
minded man who hunted, not only for his own requirements, but to
cart the dry meat away on pack donkeys to be sold in the native reserves or in the mine compounds.

The first policing of the reserve (in addition to our own patrols)
was done by native rangers who were posted at strategic points where
they built huts for themselves and had their wives and families. They
were issued with a Martini-Henri rifle and five rounds of ammunition for protection, together with two pairs of handcuffs. The rifle
and handcuffs added greatly to their prestige. Each native ranger was
allotted an area around which he had to patrol and he was to arrest
anyone found hunting or in possession of a firearm. We could not, at
that stage, arrest people for trespass as the Ordinance merely provided
for the protection of certain animals and birds which were listed. We,
for our part, visited the ranger posts from time to time and each
ranger had to report to headquarters once a month for pay and rations,
and give an account of his month's work.

This system did not work for long as these uneducated and rather simple Africans soon got themselves involved with the local inhabitants and found the temptation to do a little poaching on their own account beyond resisting. After a year's trial the system was altered and patrols consisting of one native ranger and one guide, who was a local African, were sent off with a definite duty to carry out. They returned to headquarters at the end of each patrol. These trips varied in length from three hundred miles to fifty miles and were supplemented by mounted patrols carried out by my staff and myself, one of whom was out most of the time. This was a marked improvement on the old system and these patrols brought the rangers into contact with poachers.

The poachers did not always suffer most; one of our patrols got on to the spoor of a party of three or four poachers, following them well into the reserve. The poachers were heading towards a pan known as *Magotshanutshe* (burned the honey). It became dark before the rangers reached the pan, so they camped down for the night, and, before first light they set out in search of the poachers' camp, which they found without trouble as the gang had a big fire going. After sneaking up to the camp the ranger and his guide rushed the camp and seized one of the poachers before he could escape. The others all fled into the dark taking their firearms with them. After a search of the camp for evidence of poaching, the party were standing near the fire as it was a cold morning. Suddenly a shot rang out and the ranger guide collapsed into the fire, shot through the head.

One of the poachers had sneaked back in the dark and shot him. The ranger gave chase but failed to catch the culprit, while the poacher he had arrested escaped with handcuffs on him. None of these poachers were known to the ranger but the ranger guide had said, just after the arrest, that he knew all of them but had not had time to disclose their names before he was shot.

The escaped prisoner was soon recaptured after the C.I.D., together with some more rangers and I, had made a search of the native reserve from which the poachers had come. It was not difficult to back-spoor them to the native reserve, where we captured the escaped prisoner with the handcuffs on. The murderer was tried and hanged.

We had another scare when a patrol came in from the border area reporting that one ranger was missing, together with a prisoner who had escaped. The story was that a party of Bushmen poachers who had

81

killed a giraffe, had been contacted, and three of them in possession of arms had been arrested. The same night, the leader of the Bushmen gang, Batani, had escaped in the dark. When this was discovered the ranger set off to where the women and children of the poaching gang would have gone. After waiting two days, when the ranger failed to return to them, the patrol concluded that something was wrong and returned to headquarters to report. It was then five days since Batani had cleared off and it really looked as if my ranger had run into trouble. The story was rife in our compound among the Africans that he had been murdered by the Bushmen.

It was known that Batani was a Masarwa Bushman from the Nata river. I set off for this area in a Land Rover with four native rangers and one Bushman guide. We arrived on the Nata late one evening and found the spoor of goats and donkeys across the road, indicating that there were Bushmen settlements nearby. We camped there and soon located the few little grass shelters which formed the camp. No one there knew where Batani was and did not know of his arrest. It was about fifty miles from this kraal to the place where Batani had escaped, so it was not surprising that the Bushmen had not heard anything.

My rangers told the occupants of the kraal what had happened and that it was believed that the ranger, who had now been missing for a week, must have been murdered. The menfolk in the kraal were very upset at the news. They told us that there were several other Bushmen settlements further down the river but they were sure Batani was not in any of them; he was most likely in Botswana.

All was quiet at the kraal until about 10 p.m. when I was awakened by much talking among the Bushmen just across the river. Soon it became evident that a party of six or seven men were coming towards our camp. Everyone was alerted. The party advanced to just within the ring of light cast by my pressure lamp, when one of them came forward and said that they had brought Batani. He stepped into the circle of light and immediately professed to know nothing about the murder of my ranger. He said he knew the ranger was after him and he had been moving from kraal to kraal at night, keeping ahead of him, having just arrived at this kraal and being told of the murder of the ranger. He wished to give himself up to prove that he had nothing to do with the murder.

After a lot of talking, we again formally arrested Batani for killing a giraffe in the game reserve, then went back to bed. We were up early and decided to go on to the other villages and see what news we could pick up. It was still too early to call in the police, although it looked as if we would have to do so. (These same Bushmen along the Nata had been responsible for the murder of two R.A.F. airmen whose plane had been forced to land near the Nata in Botswana during the war).

Just as we were almost packed up and ready to move on, a lot more talking was heard in the Bushmen village, and I decided to find out what it was all about. On going towards the kraal, I was greatly relieved to meet my missing ranger accompanied by all the people from the kraal. He had been following the rascal Batani from village to village for over a week and had just about given up hope of catching up with him.

It was a great relief to me as I had no illusions about these Bushmen along the border and I think my staff, too, never felt very safe while patrolling in the area. It was evident that stronger patrols would have to be sent out into these remote parts. This was done, the number of rangers being increased to three or four, and all armed.

Native rangers were always subject to the temptation to poach and from time to time we caught one of them in the act. One ranger in particular, who was a good police boy, was caught so often that we had to get rid of him. Later we arrested him poaching in a big way, using wire snares. He did a long term in gaol but had not been out long before we caught him again in the same area up to the same tricks. This time he went inside for a longer spell.

It is perhaps remarkable that very few accidents occurred among the native rangers due to encounters with game and there has never been a fatality. One ranger, who was a bit of a "townie" but a conscientious worker for all that, was plodding along a game path, his rifle slung over his back, his bundle of blankets propped over his shoulder, his eyes glued to the path only a few feet ahead of him and his mind, no doubt, miles away at a beer drink. Suddenly he found himself face to face with a buffalo bull standing directly in the path, some five or six yards away. Instinctively the ranger threw his blankets at the buffalo, hitting the animal in the face. Instantly the buffalo charged the ranger, hitting him amidships and carrying him on its horns several yards before depositing him in some mupani scrub; it then jumped over him and ran off, leaving the ranger alone.

83

The ranger's companion who witnessed the whole episode from farther back along the path, dashed forward and assisted the terrified fellow to his feet. They then continued their journey. Mulenga, the police boy, had sustained a couple of fractured ribs and when he reported to headquarters a few days later – very stiff and sore – he was rushed off to hospital.

Who would blame him when on his discharge from hospital he tendered his resignation?

CHAPTER NINE

WITH the steady increase of the game population our problems began to loom ahead. The elephant and buffalo herds were increasing at a greater rate than other animals, not all from natural increase within the reserve, but by an influx from outside. Clearly, the day would come when our water supplies would be so strongly patronised by big herds of these two species that the browsing and grazing in the country surrounding the permanent water supplies would become devastated and game animals would not be able to live there. That time was a long way ahead but until then the answer lay in the creation of more, and still more, watering points. There was, however, a limit to doing this, and sooner or later we would have to face up to the fact that as long as the elephant population went on increasing at the rate they were, either a drastic culling operation or an increased migration out of the reserve was inevitable.

As long as we could go on augmenting the watering points by one or two new boreholes or dams each year the position could be kept stable even in the event of a drought. It was clear that eventually we would have to face the time when either all the available space was used up, or the organisation required to keep the considerable number of pumps working would become too cumbersome and too expensive.

The policy adopted, therefore, was to keep on increasing water supplies each year and at the same time to cull out elephant or buffalo which left the reserve in search of feeding areas elsewhere.

As early as 1935 complaints began to come in of elephant raiding crops in the Lukosi area. This was the start of what was to be a long-drawn-out fight against elephant crop raiders. After visiting the area on horseback and finding out what the position was, I decided to try and scare the raiders, all of whom were bulls. My assistant at that time, Jim Till, as well as my wife and I, moved to the Lukosi area and set up camp on the banks of the river.

The plan was to wait until the herd of elephant raided the lands and scare them off by firing a number of shots over their heads. The Africans were instructed to carry on with their beating of tins and drums in the normal way, but to let me know as soon as any elephant were in the lands. An inspection of the lands showed that damage was not nearly as great as the reports had indicated, but nevertheless, if it continued the Africans might well lose half of their crop.

The first night nothing happened. No elephants raided the lands, but our camp was invaded by hundreds of mice. They clambered over our beds and into our food boxes. Even our mosquito nets did not keep them from scampering impudently over our faces. The next night we moved our sleeping kit out on to the bare dry sand of the river bed. Alas, this did not help much; as soon as it became dark the mice were back. We could see them clearly in the light of the camp fire, scampering over the loose sand to take shelter behind a box or bed. That night our sleep was just as disturbed as the night before.

Two elephants visited the area. We did not hear them and received no word that they were there, but in the morning the spoors showed they had crossed the river only some 200 yards from our camp. They had entered one of the lands, but left almost immediately, making off back across the river in great haste. We followed the spoor for a mile or two. It appeared as if they had run all the way. What had scared them we did not know. We could only assume that they had got wind of our camp. This was interesting as they took no alarm when they caught wind of Africans. Seemingly, the scent of Europeans scared them.

On the third night in camp the hordes of mice were worse. I am afraid we were guilty of encouraging them for, as we ate our evening meal, we would throw scraps of bread into the fringe of the firelight and watch the tidbits being snapped up. My wife is not one to be frightened by mice (in fact she has a soft spot for them), but Jim Till

86

decided he had had enough of being disturbed at night and next day he went to a kraal where he had seen some cats. He soon returned with one of them, a very friendly half-grown tabby. Before long this cat settled down to camp life like an old-timer.

As it became dark, the mice appeared in battalions but the tabby had one nailed in no time. Having made a kill she settled down to eat her catch, while several mice made the crossing of the bare sand between the river bank and our beds. The truce, however, did not last long. Tabby soon had them all cleared away from our beds and food boxes. This little cat was certainly a grand mouser, bless her!

For a couple of nights the elephant gave no trouble. Then suddenly their raids became frequent, but they remained as elusive as ever. Contacting the elephant in the lands at night was not proving successful, so we tried hunting them in daylight. After their next raid we picked up the spoor soon after sunrise, confident that we would find them within an hour or two but, to my surprise, we found that for a mile or two the three raiders had moved slowly, feeding as they went; they had then stopped feeding and had made off along an elephant path at a fast walk. This went on for close on five miles. It was nearly ten o'clock when we turned off the path and began the climb up the side of a steep flat-topped koppie. The top of this koppie was sandy and covered with dense bush. Here the spoor began to wander about and it was clear that the animals had decided they had done enough travelling for one day.

We had not been on top of the hill very long when they got wind of us and fled. We found they had gone over the side of the hill down a steep path. We followed on for about another three miles, but as they were running by this time we gave up the chase.

It was not my intention to shoot any of them, but merely to disturb them and see if they would leave the area. They did not raid again that night but the following night they were at the old game again.

In the morning we took up the spoor and this time they headed towards the game reserve. The boundary was about seven miles away and they seemed to be wasting no time. We did not intend to worry them once they were back on their way to their sanctuary. Just after midday, however, the spoor began to wander about and we found we were getting close. Half an hour later we spotted them standing together under a shady tree. I approached cautiously to within twenty yards and then both Jim Till and I fired two shots into the air. At the first volley they all spun round with their heads held high in alarm; when the second shot was fired, they were off towards the boundary.

We spent a full day searching for them but found no elephant. We had only disturbed three and knew that there were five about. As we had been in the district nearly a week, we decided to pack up. The tabby cat was returned to her kraal and we hoped the raiding would stop. Five days later an appeal came in for help again. I returned to the lands determined to shoot one of them if I caught elephant near the gardens. To shoot one, five or six miles away, would do little good.

On arrival at our old camp I was informed that two days after our departure, two elephants had raided the lands and now all five were causing damage to crops. My efforts to frighten them away without killing any had been of no avail. (In those days we could not afford to lose any of our elephant stock). That night there was no moon until the early hours of the morning, so when word came at midnight that the elephant were in the gardens, I did not turn out to try and frighten them. I just stayed in bed with the mice who, like the elephants, were as active as ever now that we had no tabby cat in camp.

My trackers and I were on the trail early next morning. There were only three elephants and I was sure they were the same ones we had tried to scare off during that last trip. Three miles from the cultivated land we came across a place where two of the animals had obviously been lying down on the bank of a dry river. From this point the spoor indicated that all three had stopped at frequent intervals. On approaching a patch of thick bush, we could hear breathing. The sound was just like a snore – which in fact it was. When I approached I found two elephant lying down flat on their sides, sound asleep.

I was able to walk up to within a few feet of one of them and, from a kneeling position, put a bullet into the back of its head into the brain. The other two immediately made off at top speed; they seemed to know this time that the shot had not been fired to frighten them and that one of their troop had been killed.

By the time we reached camp it was too late to remove the tusks and cut up the meat. The following morning, we returned to the carcass, which was terribly distended by stomach gases. Practically the whole population of the African kraals was there, dogs and all, but we missed our faithful tabby cat. Soon knives and choppers were busy hacking at the carcass while women and children stood by with baskets as the menfolk handed out chunks of red bloody meat.

Suddenly there was a deafening hiss, like escaping steam. Men, women and children fled in all directions and all the dogs barked. What had happened was that the stomach could no longer stand the pressure of gas generated within and, with the outer skin of the animal removed, the abdomen burst.

An examination of the stomach contents showed that the kaffir corn which the elephant had eaten was fermenting, thus generating an excessive amount of gas; this was also responsible, no doubt, for the drowsiness of the troop. The raiders were actually slightly drunk.

The shooting of this elephant stopped the raiding for that year at Lukosi, but in subsequent years raids by elephants caused great havoc. In the end it was the elephants who won. The Africans had to be moved farther from the boundary of the reserve.

This raiding at Lukosi took place right on our boundary but, in time, raiding by our elephant from the reserve went farther and farther afield. A herd of about fifteen found their way into the Gwaai Forest Reserve where their presence was not welcome and we were requested to get rid of them. By this time my assistant had changed and I had Bruce Austen, a fair, rugged Rhodesian of Finnish descent. Bruce and I set up camp near the forest station and, accompanied by the forest officer, we set about hunting down and destroying the offending troop. We soon picked up the spoor of six, which our Bushman tracker had no difficulty in following.

We had authority only to destroy these elephant on the Forest Reserve and not on neighbouring privately-owned land, so we were somewhat worried when the spoor headed towards the boundary. After some five miles the herd crossed the boundary which was marked by a cleared fireguard. This meant that we could not shoot them, but we decided to carry on and see where they had gone. When about two miles across the fireguard the herd turned and moved on a course parallel to it. We knew we were getting near the herd for the spoor was becoming very fresh; there were lots of flies on the droppings. The elephants were not moving fast but feeding as they went, despite the fact that it was nearly midday. To our surprise and relief the spoor suddenly turned towards the boundary again. Just as we came up with the

89

cleared fireguard we saw the elephant herd standing in a bunch, only some fifty yards inside the forest reserve.

There was not much difficulty in getting up to them. The wind was in our favour and, after a short engagement, we had all of them on the ground within a couple of acres. One had got away and may have been wounded as we could not account for all the shots that had been fired by the three of us. The follow-up was long and fast but we soon satisfied ourselves that the animal (a bull) was wounded. We just had to catch up with him. Eventually, after spooring for about two hours, we found him and had no difficulty in finishing him off.

This, however, was not the end of the hunt for, if our information was correct, there were about nine more elephant to be accounted for. On the way back to camp we crossed the spoor of another six which we did not think were the same ones we had hunted.

Next morning we were soon on the spoor of six bulls and it was not long before I realised that they were following a course nearly parallel to the spoor we had followed the day before. The spoor was converging slightly, and eventually the two spoors met. After that the tracks followed the same route but the ones we were following kept to the down-wind of the old spoor, anything from fifty to two hundred yards from it. At odd times the two spoors were on the same track for a short distance but not once did the one we were following cross the old spoor. It was quite obvious the six bulls were following their pals, doing so by scent even though that was twenty-four hours old.

We had a different tracker from the one we had the day before. He did not appreciate that the two spoors were following each other. Just as we were about to cross the firebreak for the second time that day the tracker stopped and peering ahead he said: "There they are lying down." At that point I had little hope of catching up with the herd as the spoor was somewhat old. I felt sure the elephant would get the scent of the dead animals and belt for cover. But no! The tracker pointed again and said: "There are others standing up" and, sure enough, they were. All the ones we were following were standing in a bunch close to the dead animals; as we watched they moved right in among the carcasses.

Again we had no difficulty in approaching them. We shot five and all fell where they stood. One which got away had been standing off to one side and no one had fired at him, so we let him go.

From the spoor we were able to conclude that this herd had followed the first one, but when they caught up with them and found them all dead they were nonplussed and did not know what to do. They had milled about for some hours, going off first in one direction for a few hundred yards, and then back to their dead comrades; then repeating the process in another direction. Why they had not taken alarm at the scent of blood and the scent of our spoor of the day before, I do not know, unless it was that the elephant scent held longer than ours did.

A thing like this could only have happened in the Gwaai Forest Reserve where the Africans do not eat elephant meat. The tribespeople were not at all interested in the carcasses. Had it happened anywhere else, the carcasses would have been swarming with Africans hacking up the meat. It was a dreadful sight. Ten elephant bulls lay dead within a few yards of each other, some of the bodies actually touching. The forest officer wanted to return to the spot and take some photographs, but I would not allow this as I felt sickened by this scene and did not wish to have to account to my friends for this slaughter.

Just why these elephant behaved in this strange way I do not know, unless it was because they were all strangers to the area, not knowing their way about. There had not been elephant in the Gwaai Forest Reserve in living memory.

It was common practice to rely on the "shot" carcass of a crop raider to scare off others; the scent of meat hanging up in the kraals being sufficient to make crop raiders quit an area.

I have had other instances of elephant following one another at a couple of days' interval. When herds are moving from one feeding ground to another they invariably do so in single file on one or another recognised route each time. This is how elephant paths come to be made, some of them having been used regularly for hundreds of years. There are well-defined elephant paths in country where there are no resident elephant today. These paths were made by the passage of elephant through the country at intervals over a very long time, a long time ago.

The Wankie Game Reserve is criss-crossed by hundreds of elephant paths. Nearly all pans are linked by well-worn paths. These are usually well marked near the water and tend to fade out on entering a feeding or resting place, re-developing again on the other side.

The game reserve country is mostly flat with no big ranges of hills to form obstacles to elephant passing from one side to the other. But where hills do occur, elephant have made paths across them and it is clear that they chose the easiest route. I do not think they achieve this by sight but rather by trial and error, until a line of march is decided upon, to which they stick for years.

Bruce Austin and I had another strange experience when on crop protection. At the request of the District Commissioner (then known as the Native Commissioner) we went to a group of tribal villages just south of the Zambezi about thirty miles down stream from the Victoria Falls. A small party of elephant had invaded the area and were creating havoc with crops.

We arrived late one afternoon at the kraal where the trouble was taking place and pitched our tent a few hundred yards from the village. It was a dull day, threatening rain and, when darkness came, it was exceptionally black with not a star in the sky. We had just finished our evening meal and were about to turn in; our four African servants were sitting around a big fire some forty yards from our tent happily chatting, when suddenly their conversation stopped. There was complete silence for a few seconds and then a wild stampede as the four of them rushed past our tent and off into the night. Bruce and I went out to see what had caused the panic and found a figure standing beside the fire. We walked up to discover it was a woman. She was stark naked with her hands clasped about her neck, and a huge mop of wild hair lagged in dust with little rings of mud around her eyes. There were large scars and scabs on her abdomen and thighs as if she had been burned by sleeping too close to a fire. The creature was not old, in her early twenties maybe, and she had a wild frightened look in her eyes.

We asked her what she wanted but she gave no sign of understanding us, merely sitting down near the fire, folding her legs beneath her, evidently intending to stay. Encouraged by our action, our four servants had come back and stood and stared. I despatched two of them to the kraal to bring some of the older women and it was some minutes before they arrived. In the meantime, our other servants had tried to get some sort of conversation going with this strange woman, but without any success. When the two old dames from the village arrived, they just beckoned to the girl to follow them – which she did without hesitation. From information obtained by my servants from the village women, it appeared that she belonged to another village, was a deaf-mute and mentally deranged. She would not wear clothes and spent most of her life in the bush, sometimes being away in the bush night and day for three weeks at a stretch. This was her first appearance for some time; no one knew where she had been; and this in country with herds of elephant and lions, too!

The next day we had some difficulty in picking up the spoor of the elephants who had not raided the gardens that night although they had done so each night for a week or more. Eventually we found the spoor of three young bulls only about half-a-mile from our camp and followed it. It was almost certain these were the raiders as there were no other elephant in the immediate vicinity. The spoor led off eastwards into the wind, keeping to thick bush where the sand was soft from the recent light rain. For long stretches all three elephants had been stepping into each other's footprints, making a hole anything up to four inches deep. They did very little feeding, keeping up a steady pace, for the spoor was getting older and older as we plodded on. Our local guide was of the opinion that the herd had decided to quit the area and were heading for a crossing place on the Zambezi, just above the Matetsi river mouth, and they were returning to Zambia from whence they had come. In the end we gave up the chase and headed back to camp.

When we got back an old man expressed the opinion that the elephant had quit because we had arrived and that somehow, he did not know how, the mad girl had contributed to this, making them aware of the fact. I was prepared to accept that the elephant passing our camp that night had got our scent and recognised a European's presence as being more dangerous than an African's, and had cleared out. I am not prepared, however, to accept that the woman had anything to do with it, although our trackers were convinced that it was so. The thought of this helpless creature being in contact with these huge beasts was frightening enough without the thought that she would actually approach them.

I had another experience of elephant discriminating between the scent of Africans and that of Europeans. Some elephant had been raiding repeatedly in tribal gardens in the Gwaai Native Reserve and I went there to try and attend to the matter. The locals reported that three young bulls were responsible. They were in one garden or the other every night. Despite a great din made with tins and drums they could not be driven out and they were inclined to charge if approached too closely.

I gave instructions that as soon as the raiders appeared I was to be called, but the customary beating of tins and drums was to continue as usual. It was quite early when the din started up in a garden about half-a-mile away. I went over to see if I could do anything, taking with me a 9·3 mm Mauser mounted with a telescopic sight, but unfortunately, I had forgotten to bring my binoculars.

I soon arrived at the lands and could hear all three elephant feeding rather noisily; but because of the height of the kaffir corn I could see nothing of them. There was a bright, nearly full moon which was behind me. This meant that I could not see any shadows. I tried to get around the elephant so that I could see the shady side and hoped this would make them show up better. I realised that by so doing I ran the risk of giving them my wind but, as they were so bold, I did not anticipate this would matter very much. As things turned out it did matter, for, on getting my wind all three bulls spun round and made off at full speed. They crashed a lane through the standing grain and dashed away the brushwood fence which enclosed the garden, not bothering to go through the opening they had made to come in. I could still hear them crashing through the bush when they were a quarter-of-a-mile away. They did not raid another garden that night nor the next but they did raid again about seven miles away on the third night.

CHAPTER TEN

NOT only are elephant extremely adept at picking up the scent of danger but they quickly follow scent of their own kind as well. All elephant have a gland on their temples between the eyes and the ears, which gives off a strong musty-smelling substance. At times this substance can be seen running down the animal's face when it is feeding quite happily while at other times it only starts discharging when the beast is angry or frightened. This is apparent in cows as well as bulls but has not been noted in calves or young animals. The discharge from this gland can only be for scent purposes and this scent can only be of value to other elephants. I am confident that by means of this odour elephant can convey to others of their kind their state of mind, such as anger, fright, sexual seasons, and so forth. When brushing its way through the forests a minute quantity of the discharge could leave a scent mark that could be picked up by other elephants, possibly weeks afterwards and is a means of marking out territory.

On one occasion when I was busy building a hide at Danga pan a single elephant came down a path towards the water but he heard the chopping going on and turned back. The animal walked a few yards along the path on which it had come and then turned off and went away. About an hour later, when all was quiet, a small herd of seven elephant came along the same path. On reaching the point at which the first elephant had turned off, their leader stopped and after some rumbling the whole party turned about and made off. I have no doubt in my

95

mind that scent left by the alarmed elephant had warned them of the presence of danger.

I once stalked up to a fine old bull with the intention of taking a photograph but he saw me when I got close to him and made off right away. As I followed I was very much aware of a strong smell, rather unlike an elephant, rather like fresh droppings of a guinea-fowl. I saw the old chap join up with the cows of the herd and all those on the down-wind side of him immediately stopped feeding and took on an alert attitude. Those on the other side of the bull took no notice until a cow screamed, when the whole herd took alarm and moved away. I have smelt this bird-like odour at other times when elephant have been alarmed. Elephant, of course, give off other scents and a recently vacated resting place can be smelt by human beings at a range of a couple of hundred yards, but this is mostly dung. The sweat from behind the ears also has a strong smell and I have no doubt plays its part in the day-to-day life of elephant.

This gland on the elephant's forehead is small in comparison with the size of the animal. The orifice is just large enough to admit a pencil, while the cavity behind the skin – which has the texture of tripe and is black or dark grey – is about the size of a pigeon's egg. This little pocket sometimes contains bits of wood or stones which may get in when the elephant is immersed while bathing or lying on its side. The Bushmen prize these oddments very much, claiming that they are very lucky charms.

The scent gland is not peculiar to elephant but is found in most herbivorous animals. In the impala it is situated under a tuft of black hair just above the hind foot. The duiker has it on the side of its face, between the eye and the nose. The stembuck has it in the groin on the back leg. Wildebeest, sable, roan, and hartebeest have glands on the face just below the tear ducts. Eland have the gland in a tuft of coarse hair on the forehead, while even crocodiles have one on either side of the lower jaw. Doubtless they all serve some purpose and must play an important part in the life of the animal.

I once had the unique task of finding an elephant's pituitary gland. A young university student had been asked for such a gland from an elephant by an eminent zoologist in Germany. He asked me if he might accompany me when next I had to shoot an elephant raiding crops, because he wanted to try and extract the gland. The day came and the young student joined me in the hunt. I am a keen exponent of the brain shot in preference to the body shot on elephant but there was a distinct danger that even though the pituitary was only about the size of a hen's egg I would put a bullet through it. We knew that the gland was situated somewhere in the brain cavity but neither of us was very sure just where. To be on the safe side, I placed my bullet a bit high, on the assumption that the gland would be at the base of the brain. The result was that I missed the brain with my first shot and was lucky to get in a second before the dazed animal was on top of us, as the first shot made it spin round and run straight towards us.

Then the task of hacking a way to the brain began. We only had two Africans with us so I had to lend a hand with some of the heavy work. We first cut off the head but, despite our combined efforts, were only able to turn it to one side and roll it over so that it rested on the forehead. Blood poured out of the severed neck and soon we were wallowing about in a pool of blood. Then it came on to rain. Neither of us had raincoats so we cut off the great ears and propped them up on sticks as improvised shelters. Though blood and mud soon started dripping on to us we decided to carry on with the job in spite of the rain.

After some time and much careful chopping we opened the brain cavity and were able to remove the brain more or less in one piece. It was about the size of a soccer ball and damaged slightly by the passage of one bullet. There was no sign of the pituitary gland. We examined the brain and the cavity very carefully and had almost given up when I happened to touch a part of the brain pan which I found to be soft. There in the lower part of the pan was a small piece of membrane which was just the same colour and texture as the bone structure. This thin membrane, which, was like the skin on an egg and no bigger than a hen's egg, was carefully dissected and beneath it lay the pituitary. It had taken us some four hours to reach it. The gland was not attached to anything and came out in one piece with ease. After it was carefully injected with preservative and placed in a bottle, we set off for home sopping wet, covered in blood and mud, our boots in particular being full of blood.

In due course my young student friend and I received a long learned paper from the German professor on his findings. The pituitary is evidently the master gland, just as the brain is the master nerve.

Elephant, or at least those at Wankie, are not badly infested with parasites, either internal or external, but we did once find a case of screw worm around the base of a tusk. The horde of maggots were eating their way into the gum, causing a very substantial sore which was bleeding but not septic. The tusk was not loose, but what may have happened had the infestation continued for much longer I can only surmise. Possibly the tusk would have fallen out.

Most bull elephants at Wankie have a type of big white worm or maggot in their mouth. These creatures live in saliva under the tongue and around the lips and a little way down the throat. They do not seem to do the elephant any harm or cause any irritation. I have collected these larvae and allowed them to burrow into a box of sand and pupate. The emerging fly was a bright blue creature with orange eyes and about twice the size of a bluebottle. These flies deposit their eggs on the tusks of their hosts.

Elephant seem to enjoy a very healthy existence and I very seldom saw a sick one, but they do die prematurely and the greatest mortality appears to be among the adolescents. By far the greatest number of tusks collected from elephant found dead are from young animals between five and fifteen years old. The number brought in each year amounts to about twenty-five or thirty animals, which is not a very high proportion, representing only something like one per cent. Of course, there are many more that are never found but I would not put the mortality of this age group at more than five per cent.

Just what happens to the remains of elephant that die of natural causes or old age is not difficult to explain. A common place for elephant to die is in the water, and when this happens the ivory and bones soon sink into the mud and disappear in a couple of years. Carcasses which are lying out in the open do remain visible for much longer but few of them exist for more than ten years. I have known big elephant carcasses to disappear in less than five years; all that would be seen after that time was a slight difference in the vegetation where grasses have changed due to the considerable amount of humus deposited. These, of course, are carcasses from which the ivory had been removed. The last of the skeleton on the site was the teeth. The tusks do outlast the bones but not for long. Those tales of untold wealth lying unfound in the form of elephant tusks is a myth. Very little of the "found" ivory handed in has any commercial value whatsoever.

I had occasion once to shoot two elephant bulls with tusks about the thirty pounds mark on a private farm. The farmer laid claim to the tusks in spite of the fact that the animals had been shot to protect his water installations. I left the tusks with him until his claim was settled when, after a lapse of three months, the government decided that the tusks were the property of the department and I was instructed to collect them. They had been lying all this time in the shade of a big evergreen tree but when they went on to the market they ranked as "stale" ivory and fetched less than half the price of a sound tusk. Ivory which has lain out in the open, exposed to the sun and rain for five years, has no market value.

I have said that I have seldom seen a sick elephant, in fact I can only recount one case. This was an elephant cow which hung about a pan for several days and spent so much time in the water that her trunk went quite pink. I kept a watch on her and never saw her feed or drink, but she would lie in the water for hours on end. Eventually she left the pan and I lost trace of her. Very old elephant, particularly cows, are relatively common. They become very thin and slow in their movements, usually bringing up the rear of the herds.

There is, naturally, some mortality among babies, that is animals who are dependent on their mothers' milk, but these are hard to trace as the little carcasses soon disappear after attack from vultures, hyenas and lions.

One can divide elephant into five age categories; babies, those solely dependent on their mothers for their food and drink, who do not eat solids or drink water; calves, those who still drink from the mother but also eat vegetation and drink water with their trunks. Babies, when they first begin to drink water, do so direct into their mouths, sucking it up just as they do when drinking milk from their mothers. Calves, on the other hand, drink just like their older relatives. The baby stage lasts for about a year but the calf stage lasts until the animal is about six or seven years old.

The third category, the adolescent, are those calves which have been weaned and, although they still stay with their mothers, no longer drink from her. They reach an age of about ten when they become young elephant and remain so until they in turn calve, in the case of females; or until sexually mature in the case of males, which is when they are about twelve and fifteen years old respectively. The fourth stage is maturity. They remain as mature elephant until they stop breeding at about fifty to fifty-five years of age, when they rank as old elephants – the fifth category. The gestation period of elephant has been determined by those kept in zoos and is about twenty-two months for a female calf and little more for a bull calf. The maximum age of elephant living in the wild state will possibly be in the region of seventy-five years, for an elephant can only live as long as the teeth last.

A common size for a herd at Wankie is about thirty-five individuals, and this is made up of one or two old cows, ten or twelve adults of whom one or two might be bulls, fifteen adolescents of which possibly six would be bulls with six or seven calves or babies. This might be termed a family group with all the individuals related. One frequently sees a herd of a hundred but this is made up of a number of family groups and will be subject to division from time to time into smaller parties. As the years have gone by at Wankie the herds have had a tendency to get larger and larger. In the early days I never saw a herd of more than sixty animals, not even when there was a temporary concentration at a watering place.

Just how fast or how slowly elephants breed is not easy to assess but one or two babies in a herd of thirty-five is not uncommon. The mortality rate is low; of all calves born perhaps eighty per cent reach maturity.

One of the causes of death in young elephant is the drinking pattern at the seepage springs, places such as Nehimba and Shakawanki. Here the water oozes slowly out of the fine sand into shallow wells dug by the elephant. At each place there will be only some six to ten wells, with great competition for the water in them, and the wells will be occupied all the time during times of stress. The adults and calves tended by their mothers can get a drink, while adolescents, who have no one to fight for a place for them, are unable to get a drink and spend so much time battling to get at the water that they sometimes die of starvation and thirst. This state of affairs was very prevalent during droughts before the advent of pumps, but today the pressure on these seepage springs has been much reduced.

Elephant meet death in some surprising ways. I have twice had to shoot an elephant because it had broken a leg and could hardly move; in both cases there was no sign of a bullet in the leg.

I came across the partly decomposed body of an elephant, a fully grown cow, who had met her death by walking or running into the top end of a fallen tree, where she had got a front leg wedged into a fork in the branches. The animal had fallen on her side and, unable to extricate her foot, was unable to get up. The marks on the ground indicated that she had evidently struggled for days before passing out. It must, indeed, have been a horrible death.

The carcass of an elephant was found in an abandoned well some twenty feet deep and quite dry. What induced the creature to fall into it I cannot imagine as normally they are very sure-footed animals.

On more than one occasion elephant have died of arsenical poisoning after drinking at cattle dip tanks. In one case we lost five elephants who drank from the dip tank on *Sunnyside* farm soon after the farm had been closed down and the usual water supply had dried up. In other cases there was other water available and there was no necessity for the animals to drink from the dip tank. One such dip tank had been disused for fifteen years and there was only a little rain water in it, but it contained sufficient poison to kill an elephant within a few hours. In all cases death seems to have occurred within a few hours and the stricken animals had not travelled far. In one case two elephants died within half-a-mile of the dip and one of them had died on its chest as if he had passed out without any struggle.

Since 1940 it has become quite a common occurrence for elephant to be killed by trains on the railway between Dett and Wankie. One would think that they would learn to keep clear of this hazard but they continue to cross the line and, I am afraid, will continue to get killed. After some of the injuries they sustain it is amazing how they still manage to wander away from the line and back into the reserve. One old chap got caught in a cutting and after the initial impact with the engine, got jammed between the cutting wall and the passenger coaches. At one minute his head was crashing through the windows of an African coach and the next his hind quarters crashed into the window of a second-class coach. When we found him the next day he had all of one side of his head crushed in as well as several broken ribs, but he was still on his feet.

One elephant, which met its death just outside the reserve, where it was shot for allegedly charging a car, was a particularly sad loss. We took over the carcass some hours after it had been killed. It looked just like any normal elephant cow and we noticed nothing unusual until the Africans cutting up the carcass (we were interested only in the recovery of the ivory) exclaimed that the animal was pregnant and that there were two calves. Sure enough, there were the two foetus. They were carefully removed and taken to headquarters, weighed and measured. Both were bull calves and must have been very near full term for they weighed 215 and 186 pounds respectively. I have since weighed live elephant calves which were estimated to be two or three weeks old and they weighed less than that.

The dimentions of these twins were:

	"A"	"B"
Weight	215 lb.	186 lb.
Height at shoulder	3′ 0″	2′ 9½″
Withers	2′ 9″	2′ 8″
Length, mouth to anus	3′ 8″	3′ 6″
Tip to tip	6′ 7″	6′ 6″
Length of trunk	1′ 6″	1′ 5½″
Front foot	5½″	5¼″

In common with many people I have never had any success rearing baby elephants. Calves which have taken to eating solid foods before their capture seem relatively easy to feed but as long as their natural food consists solely of the mothers' milk the feeding problem seems almost impossible to overcome.

The first baby elephant we had became separated from its mother by a passing train and as after two days the mother had not come back to collect her baby, I went out and caught it. Perhaps "caught" is the wrong word for all I did was to ride up to the poor little animal on horseback and as soon as it saw the horse it came towards me. My horse, however, would not allow it to approach very close so I dismounted and fondled the little elephant. It was very young with the umbilical cord dried but still attached. After some difficulty I managed to get it to take a drink of water from my water-bag. I walked the ten miles back to the house with the baby elephant follow-ing along behind. We fed it on things such as powdered milk and linseed meal gruel supplemented now and again with things like boiled rice and mealie meal gruel. It lived for some months but did not thrive. It suffered one tummy upset after another and eventually became very weak and died of pneumonia. We were extremely upset at its death, for at one time it looked as if we would rear it, and its friendly manner had endeared it to everyone.

Another baby we got was found walking around the pump house at Nyamandhlovu pan. The pumps were not working at the time, as it was during the wet season and the little fellow had evidently been there for some time, judging by the spoor, and had been sucking at the handle of the door. Evidently it had somehow lost its mother and seeing the pump house, mistook it for an elephant and adopted it. It was obviously pleased to have our company and sucked our fingers with vigour. I left one of my young sons with it and raced back to the house for a truck and a couple of Africans to assist in lifting it. This elephant was not so very young; we estimated its age at about six weeks. How long it had been without its mother there was no way of telling but it was very hungry and already had an upset stomach. By this time we had had an analysis of elephant milk done and mixed up from a dry milk basis a feed as near as possible to the elephant milk, but it was of no avail. The food we gave it and which it took readily enough just did not feed it, and after about a month it developed a peculiar smell which I have since learned to associate with baby elephants just before they die.

For some reason baby elephant are unable to assimilate anything but their mother's milk. They lack something in their digestion which they acquire later on, for once they are old enough for solid foods they are very easy to keep and rear. I know of a case where a baby elephant that was being reared by a friend of mine, John Posselt – who has a wonderful way with young animals – had the same trouble. Once he found his baby elephant eating the stomach contents of a goat which had been slaughtered by Africans in the compound. This was the first effort the creature had made to eat anything solid and one wonders if the little animal was in need of digestive bacteria which it would normally get from its mother.

I tried the same method using the stomach contents of a freshly killed wild pig. The little elephant ate it readily enough and showed some improvement for a week or so, but the end was just the same. Just why elephant abandon their calves is not known. Perhaps there is something wrong with them and they are unable to keep up with the herd. The mother may be forced to make the heart-breaking choice of either leaving her baby or leaving the herd. On more than one occasion I have found a cow elephant with her calf quite detached from any herd. These pathetic couples seldom wander far and can be found about the same spot for days on end.

An elephant calf about five feet high was reported at a pan about seven miles from headquarters. There seemed to be nothing wrong with it; although it was not in very good condition, but was feeding normally and its droppings were healthy. The calf spent days wandering about near the pan where there was very little to eat. Making no attempt to join up with elephant herds which came to drink, it would mingle with the herd as if searching for its mother, but when the herd moved off it remained behind.

Just for the heck of it we decided to try to catch the calf. But what we were going to do with the litle elephant if we were successful we did not know. It was rather a formidable undertaking but three of us set out with ten Africans armed with good ropes. The plan of attack was to stalk up as close as possible and then Bruce Austen was to rush in and place a rope around a hind leg. Tim Braybrooke and I were to try and get a hold of its ears and, if we could bring it to a halt, it was to be roped by the front legs as well as round its neck.

We found the little elephant easily enough and had no difficulty in getting up to within twenty yards of him without him becoming aware of our presence, but when he did detect us he was off. Bruce had no difficulty in overtaking him but, before the rope was attached, Jumbo turned round. Bruce held his ground and the little elephant concentrated on Tim and I, attempting to charge us, but by this time Bruce had the rope in place and had made some progress holding him back. Tim and I rushed in and grabbed an ear each and put our arms around his neck and held on for dear life. Only when we had got thus far did the Africans join in and take a hand on Bruce's rope.

We were all spun round a couple of times and dragged off our feet but with the added weight on the rope we brought our quarry to a halt. He did a lot of screaming and growling and tossing of the head from side to side in an effort to use his tusks, which were about six inches long. Fortunately, he did not attempt to use his trunk to ward us off, or we might have been in for a rough time. By the time there were people swarming all over the little fellow we managed to get a rope around the neck as well as one front leg. But it was some hours before we were able to get him on the move and to keep to any one direction as he kept turning around and getting all the ropes tangled up. There was no making friends with this calf as is so easy with most of the real baby elephants. He took a dislike to one of the Africans and would charge viciously at him whenever he came near, requiring all hands on the ropes. However, by getting him to charge this African to whom he had taken such a dislike and having him run in the direction of home, we were able to make some progress in short bursts of one hundred yards or so at a time.

After about two miles of this rush-and-stop travelling, Jumbo began to tire and would stop under a shady tree and refuse to budge. It was only after the elephant had urinated and the penis showed that we confirmed it was indeed a male. When the penis was retracted it was impossible to tell the sex. We decided to call our new orphan Joshua.

During the struggle we had evidently injured one of Joshua's ears for this began to hang in a rather limp unnatural way. Very much to our surprise the little chap began to put the tip of his trunk into his mouth and bring out about half a cupful of saliva at a time and dash this over the injured ear. Sometimes he missed the ear and anyone standing or walking behind him got the full benefit of it. This explains, possibly, a story told by Selous of elephant, after a long chase putting their trunks down their throats and extracting water from their stomachs and squirting it over themselves to cool off. The liquid that Joshua used to spray his ear and chest was not water in the true sense, but saliva, and it was taken from the tip of the mouth.

Eventually, after about four miles we arrived at a small pan with water in it. Joshua went straight into the water but did not drink. He merely sprayed water over his head and chest. By this time he was tired of chasing the African to whom he had taken such a dislike and progress was slowed up considerably. At this stage of the operation I left the scene and returned to the house to get a pen ready for the time when Joshua would arrive; which he did about 4 p.m., going like a lamb with no pulling or tugging. He was coaxed into his pen without much difficulty. Although he refused to eat or drink for a day he soon settled down and accepted the branches we gave him. He was very fond of fresh green couch grass which he would soon take from our hands. We used to have it tied in small bundles with bark and it was not long before he would manipulate the grass in his mouth and get rid of the bark. His next favourite was the saplings of the umTshibi (*Guibourtia coleosperma*) but he refused anything we gave him in the way of cooked mealie meal or bread.

Joshua became very tame and we were contemplating letting him out of his pen, when one morning we found him lying down unable to get on to his feet. We helped him up and until next morning he was all right, but the process had to be repeated. Each day it became more difficult to get him up until, eventually, he died. He had lived with us for about three weeks, but I fear that whatever the trouble was that made him leave his family herd eventually claimed him. We noticed that his ear did not regain its normal position and remained drooping down. I have seen other elephant in the wild with this injury, their great ears flopping about completely out of control; and usually carried sticking at right angles to the head. The first time I noticed this peculiarity I advised all staff of this "marked" elephant so that its movements could be recorded; but soon another one turned up with the opposite ear affected and since then we have recorded others. These elephants were, of course, called "floppy ears" and every one of the staff mentioned seeing them from time to time.

Another such marked elephant was a young bull with the left tusk turned down as if it had been twisted 180° in the socket. For a time its movements were recorded and it did not seem to wander very much, but there were periods of up to three months when there was no record of the animal. Then I shot one with exactly the same deformity, which was crop raiding about thirty miles from the reserve. I was satisfied that it was the same elephant, but no, our marker turned up again in the usual locality and we saw him many times after that.

Some of our naturally marked elephants ranged over an area of several hundred square miles. One old chap whom we called "Haemorrhoids," because he had a big swelling near the root of his tail, was seen at places as far apart as Guvalalla and Mandavu, a distance of fifty miles. Another, who had a hole in his right ear about the size of a cricket ball, wandered from Dom pan to Linkwasha, also a distance of some fifty miles. There were long periods when these marked animals were not recorded at all and it was not known where they had wandered to during that time. The marks, of course, could only be recognised by our own staff, in fact, many of the African rangers were not aware of them and thus failed to record them.

We tried daubing our animals with paint to see if it made a more recognisable mark, but it did not seem to last long enough. The method we used was to shoot an arrow topped with a rubber suction pad, the kind used on roof carriers of cars, filled with a quick drying paint. We tried red but this looked like blood and resulted in tourists reporting wounded animals, while white paint looked like bird droppings and was not recognised as a mark.

There is little doubt that elephant have definite extents of territory which they know well. From time to time they move to a new territory as circumstances dictate, such as the failure of water supplies or the shortage of food. The ripening of certain fruits such as the murula (*Selerocarya caffra*) can attract elephant while, for the rest of the year, they hardly visit the area. When they do visit these trees the herds move about calling at every tree in the area, shaking off the ripe fruit and picking it up from the ground.

The camel thorn (*Acacia giraffae*) is another favourite food of the elephant. They only feed off the tree itself to a limited degree – when the trees are young – but they are very fond of the seedpods which ripen and fall between July and September. As with the murula the seedpods are shaken from the tree and picked up off the ground. This is done by raising the trunk and placing the underside of the base of the trunk against the tree some eight to ten feet above the ground and giving it several quick jabs. This causes a sharp vibration of the tree but does not knock it over.

The same method is adopted when a tree is pushed over in order to get at the leaves. This happens in the case of combretum and the musasa (*Brachystegia speciformis*), but when elephant only want the bark off the tree it is left standing and the bark is ripped off with the point of a tusk. Once it has been loosened the elephant's trunk comes into play and the bark is pulled off either in big slabs or long straps running right up into the branches. This is particularly noticeable in the case of mufuti (*Brachystegia boehmii*).

Most of the acacia family provide food for elephant, the most important of which is the camel thorn which has already been mentioned. This tree grows only on the Kalahari sands, but in the hilly country to the north of the reserve and in the Zambezi valley another acacia (*A. heterancanthra*) produces a small curly seedpod which is much sought after.

Many trees such as *Pterocarpus rolundifolius*, a close relation of the mukwa and umtshibi (*Guibourtia coleosperma*), the mupani (*Colophospermum mopane*) and mangwe (*Terminalia sericea*) are eaten mainly as young saplings when the chief attraction is the bark. The sapling is pulled up by the roots and passed through the mouth where the great flat teeth grind off the bark; the wood with most of the leaves being discarded. The mukwa (*Pterocarpus angolensis*) is sometimes eaten in this way but the bark of mature trees is often ripped off and many fine trees are killed merely for the sake of a few square feet of bark.

Many fine camel thorn trees were also destroyed in a similar way, but in the case of these trees it was noted that the de-barking only occurred during the hot months of October and November and then only in certain localities. Samples of the bark taken at this time and from the areas where the damage was being done revealed that the bark contained a very high lime content. It was also recorded that only individual elephants were causing the damage and were small of stature, as the damage was in nearly all cases low down, some six feet from the ground. This suggests that cows were causing the trouble. A careful examination of the spoor showed that a single animal wandered from tree to tree, taking a piece of bark from each, and that in a herd of fifteen elephant only one was doing this. The inference drawn is that it was a pregnant cow on a special diet.

Elephant do, of course, eat a multitude of roots and bulbs, which they dig up. Some of the holes they dig with their great front feet to get a bulb or tuber only the size of an orange, are of considerable depth. The digging is done both by pushing the soil out with the toes and by scooping it out with the back of the foot. It was always a seasonal joke by people at Wankie that the elephant had started making their gardens. This occurred at the beginning of the rains, when acres of digging would be done on the open glades in search of a little bulb, a member of the garlic family. The patience of the great beasts is amazing, as a good deal of their food is small and hours of labour are required to obtain a feed.

Creepers and lianas and fruits such as grewias make up a great deal of the elephants' food supply. The fruit of the vegetable ivory palm (*Hyphaene crinita*) as well as the leaves are eaten to a large extent where they occur. Many fine palms are broken down to get at the fruit. The fruit has an extremely hard centre, about the size of a table tennis ball, like a small coconut. It is, as its name implies, as hard as ivory but, if anything, it is even tougher; for it takes considerable force to break one with a good heavy axe. Nevertheless elephant often break these hard kernels with their teeth while others, unbroken, pass right through. Just why they trouble to break them is not understood as there is nothing of food value inside; it is the pithy outer covering which provides the food.

These palms occur mainly on the poorly drained sandy soil between Kennedy and Ngamo as well as along the small streams in the north-west of the reserve, but the seeds can be found in almost all parts of the reserve, carried there, no doubt, by elephant. In the central-western area of the reserve just north of Domtchetchi there are hundreds of small palms, not one of which is big enough to have fruit.

Another fruit of which the elephant is very fond, and that has an extremely hard seed which passes right through them, is the fruit of the wild almond (*Ricinodendron rantanenii*). The seeds can be found all over the reserve while the trees grow only in a few localities.

Although principally browsers, elephant do eat a wide range of grasses. They seldom eat *Hyparrhenia*, which is the common thatching grass but they are very partial to the *Digitaria, Panicum,* and *Urochloa.* When they do eat *Hyparrhenia* they pull up whole tufts, roots and all. They beat it against their knees to shake off the soil, then eat the whole plant. *Digitaria* is mostly eaten towards the end of the wet season when the grass is in seed. When elephants eat this they pull up whole tufts and bite off the heads and upper half of the grass, discarding the roots.

Elephant will go to extraordinary lengths to get at *Loranthus,* a mistletoe-like parasite which is usually found growing on mupane trees. They will come right into settlements where these plants have escaped the ravages of other elephant and push down numerous trees just to get at this tasty morsel. At Robins Camp many fine trees were being destroyed in this way by elephant in their efforts to get *Loranthus.* Night after night one or more would come right in among the huts and send trees crashing to the ground, raising a cloud of dust and dry leaves. Some action had to be taken, not only to save the trees but for the safety of visitors. A gang of Africans was laid on to remove the growths, and this stopped the trouble.

Another titbit that elephant enjoy is the charred ends of young

Acacia giraffae saplings after they have been scorched by a grass fire. Just why these are sought after remains obscure, but the fact that the trees have been burnt has something to do with it. Elephant will wander about for hours on newly burned ground, often with logs still smouldering, eating off the charcoal tops of young shoots.

For many years there was no indication that elephant ate or damaged baobab trees, but in more recent years, since 1950, this has become more apparent. Reports of this sudden preference came to us from game authorities in countries to the north of Rhodesia as well as from the Zambezi valley. Not only the baobab (*Adansonia digitata*) but a similar tree, *Sterculia africana*, are suffering in the same way. The bark is ripped off and the pithy substance of the tree itself is eaten. Whole trees are destroyed. In Wankie Reserve there are not many baobab trees and it is feared they will, in time, be wiped out.

There are a few trees which the elephant does not seem to choose for food. These are: the ebony (*Diospyros mesiliformis*), pod mahogany (*Afzelia quanzensis*), the sausage tree (*Kigelia pinneta*), the mufumena (*Entandrophragma caudatum*), and the umgusa (*Baikiaea plurujuga*). It is perhaps significant that all of these trees are very valuable as shade trees. They seldom push these trees over, but they do damage them by doodling with their tusks while resting in their shade.

I once tried to gain some idea of how much an elephant ate in twenty-four hours. To do this I picked on a single elephant bull resting under some shady trees about two o'clock in the afternoon and waited until he moved off at about two-thirty. I then followed him until dusk, picking up and weighing every piece of dung he dropped. The next morning I picked up the spoor where I had left off and followed this through feeding grounds, drinking places, and salt licks to his next resting place. We came up with our bull again at about eleven o'clock but let him rest until two-thirty when we drove him off. The total weight of droppings, including those at one rest period, was 625 lb. Of this a fair amount was water, but the weight of vegetation must have been nearly 600 lb. We may have missed some droppings at the water as there had been several elephants there during the night, but we accepted that our elephant had evacuated once while at the water hole. The weight of a single evacuation varied from 6 lb. to 30 lb. and there were twenty-seven deposits spread along a route of about ten miles.

Elephants love their water and if they can get it will drink every day, but if food is scarce and they have to travel a long way to satisfy themselves, they will miss a drink and go for forty-eight hours without any hardship. We have been able to measure the amount of water an elephant drank from a trough. Three big bulls consumed 220 gallons in about twenty minutes, or about seventy gallons each. The average is about fifty gallons, not including calves which drink very little and babies who drink nothing at all.

Elephant suffer little from predators; man seems to be their only real enemy. Lions occasionally get a baby or a calf but this must happen very seldom. The old elephants treat lions with a great deal of suspicion and drive them away from a herd whenever they see or smell them. A young elephant, even up to about four feet high, will have very little chance if it should become separated from the mother and lose touch with the herd. Even hyena would kill an elephant under these circumstances. A small elephant (it was a bit big even to be called a calf) got separated from its family herd at Robins salt pan and hung around for three days, but eventually it was killed by a pride of lions. This kill, with the pride feeding on it, was much photographed by tourists.

Fights to the death between elephant bulls have occurred. One such fight took place near Nyamandhlovu pan. Unfortunately the carcass of the defeated animal was only found some days after the fight, but the signs of the struggle were plainly visible. The two monsters – they were both big matured bulls – had pushed each other about over a considerable distance. At times the spoor indicated that they had been chasing each other, while at other times there had been a pushing match going on for some time, as the grass and bushes and even quite big trees had been trampled and knocked over.

The defeated bull had only one tusk, and this had been broken a long time previously. When the carcass was examined a couple of months later after all the flesh had rotted off, I found that the roof of the poor brute's mouth had been smashed. Evidently the victor had got a tusk into its adversary's mouth and with a sharp thrust broken through to the brain. It was also discovered that the stump of the missing tusk was still in the socket and consisted of no less than seven small tusks each with a nerve cavity. They were all in the same tusk socket and came apart when removed.

CHAPTER ELEVEN

WE always experienced a feeling of relief when the reserve was closed to the public each year at the end of November. How long it would be before someone was killed by an elephant I did not know, but the danger increased year by year. As our animals became more tame and took less notice of tourists, so foolhardy people became a danger to themselves and other visitors as well.

My fears were justified when the report of the first casualty came in. An African had been killed by an elephant just outside the reserve near Lukosi and I was requested to go down and attend to the culprit. A guide led us to the spot where, in the middle of a recently ploughed land, he indicated a trampled area where an elephant had obviously been stamping about. The body was hardly discernable. It had been trampled into the ground and covered with sand and earth, almost completely hidden. We uncovered the body and found that not only had the unfortunate individual been trampled upon, but a big tusk had been driven right through his body into the soft ground beneath. Apparently the boy (he was only a lad of about fifteen or sixteen) had been missing from his kraal since midday two days before and his mutilated body had only been found at about midday on the day we arrived. There were no witnesses to the tragedy. Fortunately, some cattle had been over the ground and it was the unusual behaviour of the cattle which had attracted a herdboy's attention to the spot where the body lay, partly concealed. Up to that time no one had worried

Ted Davison with his first edition of Wankie - The Story of a Great Game
Reserve in 1967.

This gathering of National Parks stalwarts of different vintages, all at one time connected with Wankie, was taken at a Wankie symposium in August 1978, where they had gathered to celebrate the 50th anniversary of Wankie National Park. The picture includes Ron Thomson, Les Gregory, John Hatton, Les Stewart, Tim Braybrooke, Bruce Austin, Ted Davison, Sir Hugh Beadle, Cliff Freeman Graham Child, Jordie Jordaan, Boyd Reese.

(photo courtesy of Ministry of Information)

The Management Unit moved from Shapi Pan to Umtshibi in 1972, shortly after Len Harvey was killed by a lioness. Today the base covers a very much larger area.

(photo courtesy Tore Ballance)

Entrance to Umtshibi,
1998

(photo : Keith Meadows)

"Shapi Pan at midday, March almost over, with late season thundersheads building up ...."

(photo : Keith Meadows)

Culling ....

The last seconds of a cull. Clem Coetsee with tracker Mackson in close support holding reloaded rifle.

(photo courtesy Clem Coetsee)

All down ....

(photo : Keith Meadows)

The skulls of culled elephants, with the ivory destined for the security of storerooms at National Parks Headquarters.

(photos : Keith Meadows)

" ...the 'product' from the culled animals was not left to waste... harvested and used to feed hungry tribespeople ..."

And capture ....

Helicopter drive on wildebeest capture at Ngamo, 1972.

(photo courtesy Mike Fynn)

Black rhino calm down remarkably quickly after capture.

(photo courtesy Clem Coetsee)

An elephant bull, drug-darted for research and collaring, gets a helping
hand from National Parks staff.

Cliff Freeman (top) and Willie Koen (below) both headed the culling unit after Len Harvey.

(photos courtesy Mike Fynn)

Basil Williamson, ebullient ecologist, Wankie National Park 1977.

The unflappable pipe-smoking Boyd Reese.

Basil Williamson and senior ranger Mike Fynn with trackers, locating rhino

A random page of a flying log book. *"... alive or gone their names still crop up in campfire conversations on occasion."*

Clem Coetsee headed the Management Unit from 1979 until 1987.
Leasha Cull Camp 1980.

(photo courtesy E. Coetsee)

A white rhino (above) killed
by poachers for its horn.

(photo : Keith Meadows)

At left a warden cuts away
a snare that has worked
its way deeper and deeper
into a rhino's foot.

(photo courtesy Ron van Heerden)

" Sadly, Hwange... is decidedly ragged around the edges these days, in need of a lot of tender loving care."

Parts of the main link road between Main Camp and Shumba picnic site.

(photos : Keith Meadows)

Guvalala game viewing platform, burnt in March 1998, still unrepaired months later.

Direction signs long in need of facelifts.

(photos : Keith Meadows)

"There is too much being taken and not enough being given back." Mature teak trees logged **within** the park in the Wexcau region.

(photos courtesy Cam Spencer)

much about the missing lad for he was, according to reports, mentally deficient, often wandering from village to village without telling anyone where he was going. It was not unusual for him to spend a night away from home. Had it not been for the cattle pawing the ground and bellowing as they do when scenting blood, the body may not have been discovered for days or even longer.

When uncovered it was noticed that there was a dead bird tucked into the boy's belt and he held a small stick in his hand. We were told that he was in the habit of climbing down into a shallow well where the cattle were watered, and waiting for birds to come to drink and then striking at them with a stick. It seemed that he had been doing this when an elephant came upon him. We were able to reconstruct the incident from the spoor along the following lines:

One elephant, a big bull, had evidently come right up to the edge of the well in search of water and surprised the boy at his bird-killing activities. We could see where the boy had scrambled out of the hole and where the elephant had turned sharply away. The boy's tracks, as he ran away from the well, could be clearly seen, but he made a sharp turn where there was the spoor of a second elephant only some fifteen yards from the well, almost as if he ran right into it. The second elephant appeared to have given chase and pursued the lad for fifty yards or so, where it looked as if the boy fell or was struck down by the animal's trunk; for the elephant overshot the boy by several yards, whirled around in a circle and came back to the prostrate lad, proceeding to kneel on him and drive a tusk into the body.

We could see clearly the marks where both tusks had been driven into the ground and by careful excavation we were able to establish that the tusks were over two feet long and that the left one was slightly blunted.

Spoor indicated that there were, in fact, three elephant at the well at the time, all big bulls, and that they had not drunk any water. The spoor was much too old to follow so we scouted around all the other likely drinking places to see if we could pick up the spoor of the three. We found the spoor of the three bulls, but one of these was a much smaller animal than any of those we were looking for. There were other bulls about, but all were running singly. There seemed to be nothing we could do to bring the culprit to book, so we just stayed in the area for a couple of days to see if the killer would strike again, but nothing happened.

Only about a month or so later word came in that another African had been killed in the same area. I was on the spot within a few hours and learned that two Africans returning from a beer drink in the morning, much lit up with their night's indulgence, had come across two elephant on the path. One of the pair was all for making a wide detour around them saying that it might be the one which had killed the boy a few weeks before, but the other, full of Dutch courage, elected to run past the elephant, which were quietly feeding within about twenty-five yards of the path.

While one African watched, the other started to run along the path towards the two elephant, shouting as he went. One of the animals turned tail and made off at top speed but the other whirled towards the advancing African and just as he passed, it gave chase. In a very short distance the elephant overtook the fleeing man and, seizing him in its trunk, tossed him sideways into the bush, then followed him. This was the last the other African saw, for he immediately beat a hasty retreat along the path whence he had come, spreading the news that his companion had been killed by the elephant.

When I arrived on the scene, accompanied by my assistant warden, J. C. Tebbit, we found that none of the villagers had been near the spot. We found the corpse in a sitting position entwined with sticks and long grass. Again the elephant had seized the African in its trunk and swung him around and around, entangling him with grass and thorn bushes in so doing. The body and clothes were dreadfully torn but less damaged than had been the case with the boy killed earlier. There was a deep cut on the side of the neck which at first we could not understand until we discovered a very sharp table knife in the breast pocket of the deceased's coat. In the struggle this had inflicted the wound, although it was not the cause of death.

The spoor was fresh enough to examine closely and to follow. It tallied in size with the spoor of the elephant which had killed the boy; we were able to make a careful note of the formation of cracks and crevices in the footprint. We followed it until nearly dark, but the killer had not joined up with the other elephant, having gone off on its own in the opposite direction, at a fast walk.

We had to abandon the spoor when it got dark. Then we estimated that we were still some six hours behind the elephant. Again, early next morning we were able to take up the trail and followed it relentlessly all day. It wandered about a great deal, remaining more or less in the area where both Africans had been killed. Sometimes the spoor was easy to read and we felt we were gaining on the killer fast, but then the spoor would run into rough stony country with other elephant spoor about – where we obviously lost time. It was not until about four o'clock that afternoon that we came on a spot where our quarry had rested. The bull had evidently been there from about midday and perhaps had heard us approaching or may have got our wind, for he had gone off at quite a brisk pace, going up into a small koppie covered with very thick bush.

We made a detour and approached the hill from the right side of the wind and made our way into the thicket very cautiously. After a while we could hear the elephant moving about. Evidently he was quite alert. Suddenly he stopped and remained quiet, perhaps even listening for our approach or even watching us. Although we could not see him we were no more than fifty yards away. At one point it seemed as if he were coming towards us and we prepared ourselves for a charge, but it did not come. We followed him for about thirty minutes, our nerves tense, knowing that our presence was known to the elephant, but still he made no effort to bolt, showing that he was on the defensive.

At last I caught a glimpse of ivory, a long sharp tusk, but the body was hidden by thick bush. I managed to keep the tusk in view as the bull moved across our front, until I caught sight of his shoulder and then quickly put in what I hoped would be a heart shot. The animal swung half round and made off. We followed as fast as we could. We had not gone more than fifty yards when Tebbit, who was just behind me, shouted, "Look out!" I did – and looked up right into the face of the elephant who had stopped and turned around, waiting for us. We both fired into his face and, as he swung around again, we each put a bullet into his side. This time he went off slowly, evidently mortally wounded. In a very short time he stopped and began to totter on his feet and then went down.

The tusks were much as I expected them to be after measuring the impressions in the sand where the boy had been killed. We will never be quite certain that the same elephant had been responsible for both killings but at least we were sure he was responsible for one of the deaths.

These two incidents served to show just how easily a tragedy could occur, while it also showed that our elephant on the tourist routes were not as predictable as we could wish. Another example of unpredictable behaviour was noticed when a gang of African labourers, using a dam scoop and tractor, were busy cleaning the mud out of the bottom of Nyamandhlovu before it dried up completely. The only water available was a little in the drinking trough. During the morning one labourer had taken off his shirt and hung it over a small pointed ant-hill. During the lunch-break a herd of elephant cows came down to the pan and, when passing the ant-heap one of the cows suddenly charged at it and drove her tusk through the shirt. For her pains, she snapped off about eighteen inches of her tusk, leaving it embedded in the ant-heap. After that the herd went off without drinking. It served to show that even in a locality such as Nyamandhlovu where elephant were becoming used to the presence of humans, there was the danger of a determined charge with little or no warning if an elephant found itself too close to a human being.

Elephant repeatedly charge or chase cars but they never or very seldom catch them. There is no doubt that if they really made a determined effort they could catch many vehicles, and if they did so they would wreck a car completely. Only one accident has occurred to date; this happened near the Deteema dam when a cow elephant, separated from her calf, caught and overturned a Volkswagen but, fortunately, no one was hurt, and the two occupants of the car treated the whole incident as a rather frightening joke.

I have been chased by elephant many times when in a Land Rover and I have deliberately slackened speed to see what they would do. In most cases the elephant slowed up, too. There have been occasions when I was very glad to have a Land Rover under me with a good turn of speed if I needed it. I was once chased by two elephant cows on the Ngamo vleis in very open country but heavy sand. I was trying to stop the herd from drinking from a pan in the Gwaai Native Reserve when these two old girls took exception and gave chase. I had about fifty yards start on them and the two Africans in the back of the Land Rover were shouting, "They are coming," then a little louder, "They are still coming," and then louder still, "They have come!"

In the rear view mirror I could see little more than a cloud of dust but, on glancing around, I saw the two angry-looking old cows emerging from the dust no more than ten yards behind me. I have no doubt at all that they meant business and would have done some damage if they had caught up with the Land Rover.

Their speed for a short stretch must have been about thirty miles an hour, but I have seldom seen an elephant run as fast as that. I think the best speed I have ever seen an elephant make was on an occasion when two young bulls were chasing each other. The speed for such a big animal was amazing and rather frightening. On one or two occasions I have measured elephants' speed against a speedometer: they have been about twenty-three miles an hour both when chasing a car and when running away.

There is always the danger when pacing a running elephant that an African on the truck will panic and jump off, relying on his own legs rather than the vehicle. This did happen once to my knowledge and, as can be expected, the African whose legs were running before he reached ground lost his balance and fell right in the path of the oncoming elephant. Fortunately the driver had the presence of mind to stop, and the shouts of protest from the other dozen Africans on the lorry so demoralised the elephant that it stopped short and gave up the chase.

In the great majority of cases a charging elephant does not intend to press the charge home. Its wild trumpeting and outspread ears merely serve to intimidate its adversary. Should it be successful and its adversary take fright the elephant will, as often as not, stand its ground and let things be. To anyone who has been dealing with elephant for a long time it is not difficult to guess the animals' intentions but it is not the sort of thing I should advocate a tourist to try. A wounded elephant, or one being harassed or defending a very young calf, is a very different matter. In these cases the trained and experienced hunter can tell that the animal means business and, unless he is prepared to shoot, his best line of defence is to get out of sight as soon as possible and beat a retreat, screened by a big tree or bush.

Elephant who charge cars usually do so when the car has stopped too close to them. They then feel they have little chance of making an escape and go on to the offensive. Although elephant are big, powerful animals with a surprising turn of speed they are not really very dangerous. This applies particularly to the Parks elephant, but not to the same extent to animals outside the Park. The same elephant in an area where it knows it is safe can be a very different proposition in an area that it knows to be dangerous.

The weight of the African elephant has always been rather a matter of speculation. Big bulls weigh up to seven tons and cows up to about five tons. I have never accurately weighed a full-grown animal but Robertson-Bullock weighed four in Zambia in 1960. He gives some interesting figures: His biggest elephant, which he estimated was sixty years old, weighed six tons, 12,240 lb. of which the ivory was 161 lb. and the skin 1,104 lb. The quantity of flesh was two tons, 4,130 lb. This was possibly an average-sized good bull.

In Wankie Game Reserve elephant do not carry heavy ivory. A mature bull with tusks sixty pounds a side would be considered a good specimen and anything over eighty pounds a side exceptional. Cow ivory is, of course, much smaller and a thirty-five pounds cow tusk would be a good one. Tuskless elephant, particularly among the cows, are not uncommon and for some reason, possibly because they have an inferiority complex, they are more bad tempered than the tusked animals. This tuskless strain seems to run in females and I have seen a family group consisting of an old cow, two young cows and two big calves, with only one of them, a calf, having tusks. Probably this calf was a male.

Although elephant have learned that inside the reserve they are safe from persecution by humans, they have not lost their inherent fear of traps. At a pan called Mbobomchawa, a line of game pits can still be seen which had been used long before the reserve was proclaimed in 1928. These must have been big pits, for the depressions left today are still quite apparent. This method of killing elephant and other game may have been in general use towards the end of the nineteenth century but early writers such as Selous make no mention of them. Elephant, however, are very suspicious of any hole dug in the ground and give such things a wide berth. I have seen a cow elephant become very agitated when she came across an excavation of this nature. At one time I used pits about three feet deep as a hide for photography and I soon noticed that these holes caused consternation in elephant herds.

It sometimes happens that an elephant calf will get into a drinking trough and have difficulty in getting out. This invariably causes a bit of a panic and all the members of the herd, except the calf's mother, will stampede away from the trough. The mother, in most cases, gets the calf out by scooping it up with a backward swing of a front foot.

The pit method of killing elephant may still be in use in Botswana but I have not heard of it and I do not think that the elephant in Wankie have been subject to this hazard for a very long time. But they have not forgotten it.

A more recent type of trap into which elephant occasionally fall is a newly introduced steel wire snare. These are not set for elephant but they do get either the trunk or front foot caught in them and as a result suffer agony. However, they are learning. I had a good example of this when following a single crop raider along a game path. The spoor turned off the path and, after about fifty yards, rejoined it again. Later I discovered that a wire snare was in position on the path where the elephant made the detour, having been there for several weeks, perhaps even months. The elephant evidently knew of its existence and gave it a wide berth without going near it. There was no sign that this elephant had ever been caught in a snare; it must have gained its knowledge from other unfortunate members of its herd.

For some reason elephant which are suffering untold agonies as a result of having a wire snare embedded in their trunk or on a foreleg tend to seek protection near habitations. There was the case of an elephant bull which started frequenting a mining camp near Wankie Colliery at night and although it did no damage it did cause considerable alarm. When the unfortunate creature was destroyed it was found to have a wire snare tightly secured to its trunk about two feet from the end, and the portion of the trunk below the snare was gangrenous and paralysed. A similar thing occurred at Nantwich, near Robins Camp. A big bull elephant with a badly damaged front foot took up residence near the homestead and remained for several weeks, never wandering far from the houses. It disappeared and was later found dead in a ditch. The poor beast had fallen down when crossing this rather steep-sided watercourse and been unable to get up again.

Some of the examples of suffering inflicted by these dastardly trap contraptions are too terrible for words. There have been only a few at Wankie Game Reserve, but they are all too common in the Zambezi valley.

CHAPTER TWELVE

THE Wankie Game Reserve was only proclaimed a National Park on the 27th January 1950. Its official designation then became The Wankie Game Reserve National Park. It was only after this that the tourist development really got under way. But, of course, tourists had been visiting the game reserve long before that and by the end of 1949, the number of visitors had reached 2,771 in a year. At that time the roads and rest camps were open to the public only from 1st June to 30th November each year. By 1965 the number of visitors had increased to 25,351 in a year, while a part of the park and the rest camp at Main Camp were open throughout the year.

As far back as 1930 visitors began to arrive, but these were mostly friends of mine and the method used to locate and see game at that time was to go out with a tracker, pick up the spoor of some animal or herd and follow it. Naturally, most people wanted to see elephant and these were not always easy to find. In those days they did not seem to tarry about the water supplies to feed, but made tracks for good cover after drinking. It usually took a five-mile walk to come up with them. Even then it was by no means certain that they would be seen, for the slightest trace of human scent would send them scurrying off to seek shelter farther away.

Giraffe was another animal that visitors wished to see; these, too, were found by following spoor. One was lucky if one got a close look at them, for they invariably spotted the party before the visitors saw them and all one got was a view of these great animals lumbering away through the trees or crossing an open glade.

By far the most popular way of seeing game in those days was by the use of platforms overlooking water holes at night. I had a number of these platforms built in big trees at various water points. Access to the platform was by a rather rickety ladder made of cross pieces lashed to a long pole with bark. The procedure was to arrive at the pan just before sunset, complete with blankets, sundowners, evening meal and thermos flasks of tea or coffee. The party usually consisted of four or five people and all climbed up the tree just after sunset. I was always last up as, when everything was taken up the tree, I had to drive the car away and park it a good distance away from the pan; then I used to worry all night for fear some elephant would come along and damage the vehicle, which was not always my own.

The platforms were not very large and could only just accommodate five people lying down.

Once all the blankets had been laid in position and everyone had settled down, strict silence was the order, while anyone wishing to smoke had to do so without showing a light. The human voice carries a long way; an animal a mile away might be distracted from coming to drink if it caught the sound of humans at the water. Not only will a particular animal be discouraged but others coming in later on might be disturbed by the alarmed state of those frightened earlier.

After settling into the platforms no one could expect to come down until after sun-up, and the parallel poles and thick grass from which these places were made could become very hard before morning. But how tourists enjoyed these unique outings! There was nowhere else in Africa where they could do this. The famous "Tree Tops" in Kenya had not been thought of in those days. The game was very shy but nearly always something was seen, while elephant showed up more often than not.

Later on I built platforms in the frames of the windmills. These were much safer and easier to get into but were not large enough for more than four people to lie down. We had learned, too, that there was little activity at the pans after about 10 p.m., so we began to give up the all-night sittings, returning to camp about this time. The drive home in the moonlight was an additional thrill as we frequently saw lions on the road in the headlights of the car.

121

Of course, we only used the platforms during the moonlit periods each month. Even when the moon rose at about eight o'clock we discontinued the practice, for during the dark period before the moon rose and the light became strong enough to see by, the majority of the game had come and gone.

Using strong spotlights was not a success, particularly with elephant. They did not seem to be very much alarmed by the light itself but they were disturbed by other elephant or bushes which became illuminated in the beam of the light.

Once game became thoroughly accustomed to our use of these platforms at night and took little notice of either the sound of voices or scent of humans, we built proper platforms capable of seating thirty people, and these were used for game viewing in the daytime as well as on moonlight nights.

Towards the end of my service at Wankie these platforms became increasingly popular and the sights seen from them were truly amazing. It was no uncommon occurrence for 250 elephant to come to the pan at one time during daylight, often at the same time as 500 or more buffalo. Giraffe were fairly regular visitors to the water during the afternoon; it was not unusual to see as many as thirty-five of these tall creatures at the water at one time. Although these daylight scenes were an everyday occurrence, the moonlight sessions continued to be enormously popular. Somehow the nights were much quieter and any noise made by the animals seemed more audible. If two herds of elephant met at the pan, the trumpeting and growling which went on provided a never-to-be-forgotten thrill for visitors.

In a short time, relatively speaking, the animal population of Wankie had learned to trust humans to a degree which I never envisaged when I started my work of conservation and protection in 1928.

For photography we used hides built near the water on the downwind side of the pans. The hide consisted of a hole in the ground about four feet square and three feet deep, with a covering of leafy branches to provide shade and camouflage. We could build a hide in one day and get it ready for the following day when the human scent would have worn off. Frequently we found that during the night elephant had wrecked the shade part of it. This, however, was easily replaced and we only hoped that elephant would not wreck it again while the photographer was inside.

Scent played a big part in these operations, as animals in their cautious way would circle a pan before coming down to drink. They well knew that they were much more prone to attack from carnivora and poachers while at the water. To minimise the effect of scent we adopted the Bushman trick of burning dry elephant dung in the hide and this certainly did have the effect of reducing the amount of human scent. The very pungent smell of burning dung was not objectionable to animals.

Only the real enthusiast made a success of these photographic expeditions, as to sit cramped up in a hole like that was very trying. If in the course of an eight or nine hour session two herds of game came to drink, the photographer was considered lucky. Elephant did not come to the water in the daylight hours in those days. The most usual visitors to the pans were warthogs, kudu and sable. Occasionally a photographer would have the great thrill of seeing a giraffe drinking.

Gradually the tourist pattern changed. A large number of visitors used cars to see game, but the game was shy and suspicious of vehicles. Visitors would invariably stop when they saw groups of animals, which was the surest way of scaring them away. Lions would crouch down at the approach of a car, remaining only if the car drove slowly by. If the car stopped, the lions would be off in a few seconds. Not only did we try to get tourists to drive slowly past animals they saw, but we, ourselves, went out in cars specially to do this, to encourage our charges to accept that a car meant no harm. On occasions we would drive past a feeding herd and when out of sight, return and repeat the process. In some cases we found on our return run that the animals had gone, even although they had shown no sign of alarm when we drove past them in the first instance.

Speed, too, we found was a cause for alarm. A vehicle passing a herd at fifteen miles an hour gave little cause for panic, but the same vehicle travelling at twenty-five miles an hour would cause a stampede. It was not the vehicle itself which frightened the animals but the speed, which to an animal means alarm or danger. Game, particularly giraffe, would take fright at any fast moving object. Their attention was not directed at the vehicle but in the direction of the danger which they thought was chasing it. On occasions like this a general stampede would take place only after the vehicle had passed.

Later, when we had aircraft flying over the park, we noticed the same thing. Unless the aircraft was very low, game would stop feeding at the sound of the plane but they would not run off until after it had passed. If the plane was very low there was a general stampede as soon as it approached.

Pilots of light aircraft seem unable to resist the temptation to fly low over game to have a close look, especially if they have a paying passenger on board. Their chances of being seen are slight, more so in the remote parts of the park away from the road system. For this reason we soon introduced legislation to prohibit flying over the Wankie National Park and other game areas. It was quite noticeable that game would be seen more frequently drinking from pans during the day where they did not come into contact with tourists, while pans along the tourist route would be more or less deserted until late in the evening. It was usual to find that after the game had quenched its thirst it would move off quite quickly, moving a long way, possibly two miles or more, before starting to feed.

As early as 1937 we began giving visitors a list showing the game animals they were likely to see and requesting them to fill in the numbers they actually did see, together with the total distance travelled on their trip. These lists proved very useful as we were able to tell what results people were having. Some visitors would come back from a day's outing and hand in a list of what they had seen, being very pleased with their "bag." On the same day another party would come in disappointed with what they had seen but, on comparing lists, we found they had both had a view of about the same amount of game.

In 1937 the average amount of game seen by visitors varied from 0·3 to 1·09 head per mile travelled. These figures did not alter much until 1941 when they had risen to 3 head per mile, the peak months being August to October. By 1948 the figures had risen to 6·2 in October and in 1956 the figure was 8·6 in the same month.

From that point on, figures recorded by tourists began to be very unreliable as they were seeing so much game at one time that they were unable to count herds accurately, resorting to estimates. It was the task of someone in the office each month to wade through the hundreds of lists handed in and extract from them all those which were judged to be reliable. We had our own yard-stick by which we would judge. We knew, for instance, that there were very few reedbuck on the tourist route and if a visitor recorded hundreds of these we knew that he did not know the difference between a reedbuck and an impala; while it was unlikely that anyone would see a wild pig, although many were recorded. They were, in fact, warthog.

Estimates of the numbers of larger animals such as elephant and buffalo were nearly always too high but, on the other hand, the number of giraffe recorded were usually fairly accurate. We did not include on these lists animals smaller than warthog and impala, but nevertheless the list consisted of twenty-one animals, namely: buffalo, eland, elephant, gemsbuck, giraffe, impala, kudu, ostrich, reedbuck, roan, sable, tssessebe, warthog, waterbuck, wildebeest, zebra, cheetah, leopard, lion, hyena and wild dog. Rhino were so unlikely we did not include them, but one visitor reported seeing six. However, when we checked up with him they turned out to be warthog. Buffalo and small elephant were occasionally recorded as rhino.

We started the first rest camps in 1933, building pole-and-dagga huts with no windows and no furniture. These did not serve any very useful purpose as most visitors had their own tents and were prepared to camp out. Following these huts we got prefabricated wooden huts which had been used before. They were well made and quite comfortable but we found, after they were up, that they were infested with bed bugs; so we had to pull them down again without ever using them.

Our next effort was to build twelve huts of Kimberley brick, that is, large green bricks made from the soil of ant-heaps. Due to transport difficulties we had neither sand nor stone, so there were no foundations under the huts. The brickwork was laid on level ground. The roofs were thatched on indigenous timber. These huts served wonderfully well and were under their third roof when, in 1966, they were finally pulled down and replaced by modern brick huts, each with its own bathroom and flush sanitation. These were not the only huts we built. Another camp of twelve huts of concrete blocks with asbestos roofs was also opened to visitors, who, we found, preferred the thatched huts.

The first African tourist visited the park in June 1958. An African and his wife motored from Robins to Main Camp and were late in arriving at Main Camp. A search party found them about ten miles out, waiting for a herd of elephant to get clear of the road. They were both terrified and had been in that state for most of the day. It transpired that they had been held up several times on their trip, not only by elephant but by buffalo and lions as well. They did not enjoy their visit, but perhaps they enjoyed talking about it to their friends later on.

The African generally has far less knowledge of wild life than the average European. Many of the labourers who came to work for us had no conception of what a giraffe looked like, and believed that they were dangerous and would eat humans even more readily than lions. The inability of the primitive African to interpret a photograph leaves them with only a very hazy idea of what an animal strange to them really looks like. I once showed an African a photo of an elephant, and although he knew well enough what an elephant looked like, his comment was that there were no elephants as small as that. A surprising number of Africans have never seen a giraffe, elephant, lion or wildebeest – even those whose homes are near country where these animals occur.

European visitors to the park, too, have shown a remarkable dread of their first meeting with an elephant: "Do you think I will meet an elephant? – I hope not," they would say. But after their trip they emerge as heroes and heroines . . . "Yes, we met elephant, lots of them, and they were quite friendly," was the usual remark.

Just what they expected to find I have no idea. No doubt the exciting moments are the most talked of, and it is those odd occasions when elephant charge or chase a car that get the most publicity. During the hot months of October and November hardly a week goes by without a visitor, in a most excited state, reporting at the office that an elephant at such and such a place had charged them. Such types are somewhat taken aback when, after taking a note of what happened to them, we do not rush out immediately to hunt down the "rogue." Others again report the incident but insist that they do not want us to destroy the elephant as it had done no harm really. Most people who have experienced a charge and were terrified at the time, see it all as a big joke afterwards. The reactions of Ma who chastised Pa because he did not drive fast enough will bear telling for many years.

There was always the danger that one day something unfortunate would happen to a visitor, and that is why a system of checking cars in and out of the park was inaugurated. All visitors had to be out of the park or into a rest camp one hour after sunset. If anyone was not accounted for, a search party was sent out to look for them. Sometimes a breakdown caused their late arrival, while at other times a herd of elephant astride the road would have held up traffic for an hour and more. The heavy sand on parts of the road rather taxed the mobility of some old cars. I recall one motorist who, after labouring in a sandy road, had his radiator boil dry just after he had got clear of the sand. He was afraid to drive on for fear of wrecking the engine, so decided, after waiting for an hour or two for help (no one came), to push the car the ten or twelve miles to camp. When the search party found this driver and his party they were thoroughly exhausted but, as they said, nothing would induce them to leave the car and walk, for fear of meeting up with something dangerous – when they would have nowhere to hide. Our young rangers were very amused when they discovered that although there was no water in the car there were six quart bottles of beer. It never occurred to the stranded visitors to put the beer into the radiator and make camp – even at the risk of the car getting a bit tight and wandering all over the road.

As the tourist traffic grew, the pressure on the roads increased, the surface began to give way under the strain and, obviously, something drastic had to be done. Experts on road building had to be called in, but no one had much experience of building high class roads in the Kalahari sand country.

Following a good deal of exploratory work, a number of limestone deposits were located which provided good road material. Even the prospector searching for these deposits soon realised that lime existed at all the most popular game feeding and watering areas. It was an amusing sight to watch this chap and his staff of Africans taking samples of materials at various points, while elephants wandered around almost supervising their work. He was, luckily, a keen game watcher and only stopped his work when the elephant actually came up to his site, sometimes even smelling around the actual test holes.

Eventually, in 1962, a tarred road was built from Main Camp to Shumba (a distance of fifty miles) at a staggering cost, but the experts were satisfied that the money spent by tourists would repay the outlay.

As soon as the tarred road was completed, work began on a tarred airstrip, as today a high proportion of visitors arrive by air, landing right in among the animals. When the airstrip was being built a constant patrol had to be maintained day and night to keep animals, chiefly wildebeest and elephant, from damaging the surface. It is now standard practice for a Land Rover to go out on to the airstrip and drive the game off just prior to the landing of a plane. Hundreds of people now visit the park by this means and there is a fleet of small buses there to drive them around. How different from the days when it took a full day to reach the game reserve from Bulawayo and then one had to walk to see game!

The park soon began to attract another type of visitor. These were the scientists who were hankering for a field where they could work and study wild life in its natural state. One of the first to come was a Fulbright Scholar from the United States, who arrived in November 1958. He was very knowledgeable on the habits of deer, both in the U.S.A. and New Zealand, but knew little about the behaviour of African game and he arrived with preconceived ideas of what he would find. Although he may have been right in many of his conclusions, we were not prepared to accept them until he had proved them on the spot. He was anxious to study the local movements of animals and with this object in view he devised a bow and arrow with a rubber cup filled with different coloured paints, which was fired at animals. I have referred to this before, but it was not very successful as there were too few observers who knew what to look for. Red paint on an animal's rump looked like blood and white paint looked like bird droppings and could not be recognised as a distinguishing mark. This Fulbright Scholar stayed and worked in the park for over a year but did not produce much in the way of information which was of use to us.

Another scientist, Dr John Weir, came to us at intervals from the university in Salisbury. Ants were his chief interest. To catch them he put out a large number of test tubes filled with beer and soap flakes – the beer to attract the ants and the soap flakes to form a foam in which the ants were trapped. This research worker, however, had not reckoned with the ostriches, who proved almost as adept at finding the bait as were the ants. They swallowed the beer, soap flakes and the test tubes.

Later Dr Weir made a detailed study of dung beetles (*Scarabaeidae*), spending days and weeks following dung beetles as they rolled their balls of dung about the veld. He followed the road grader as it turned up the earth in the hope that it would uncover the buried balls of dung with larvae encased in them.

128

Yet another scientist studied biting-flies, and he engaged a couple of Africans to wander around a predetermined route with a coloured screen, catching all the flies which came to it and noting the degree of attraction of the different colours of the screen. What the Africans thought of this procedure is not recorded but their faces were a study as the exercise was explained to them. My rangers were, of course, always in demand by our scientific visitors to help with the interpreting for them.

Eminent veterinarians, such as Dr Zumpt, have been frequent visitors and their work on parasitic organisms have produced some startling results. To accommodate these research workers, sections of the rest camps were kept open during the wet season, when at times the camp presented a busy scene, bristling with microscopes, preserving jars and the like.

Most research seems to have centred on the entomological field and the unique pan system opened up a field of inquiry hitherto untouched. One of these highly qualified scientists pronounced the Kalahari pan system as the finest field for aquatic biological research in the world; not only for insect life but also for botanical investigation. Without doubt the number of research workers visiting the reserve will increase as time goes on, and when culling of elephant and buffalo starts (as it surely must some day) much valuable research will be done in conjunction with the work of thinning out the herds to balance them with their watering and feeding areas.

Two fields of scientific research which have not attracted many workers to Wankie are those of anthropology and archaeology. This is understandable, as the country which now comprises the park does not seem to have been inhabited in prehistoric times by man with the exception of wandering Bushmen in more recent times. It is obvious, though, that the Wankie area was renowned game country many hundreds of years ago, for rock carvings of game spoor made by early man are situated at Bumbusi and Deteema. These carvings seem to be associated in some way with fossilised trees which also occur in the same locality. Fragments of these trees – which are really not fossils at all, but silica replacements of wood which are much harder than the sandstone on which the carvings were made – have been found on the sites, and were more than likely used as tools to make the carvings. The eminent archaeologist, the late Neville Jones, formed the opinion that the carvings were the work of Wilton Age people when he carried out observations at Bumbusi in 1947.

At both sites the carvings are all of spoors, some of the best being of giraffe and kudu, but there are unmistakable spoors of zebra, impala, eland, rhino and lions. The fact that the lion spoors all show five toes rather suggests that the two sets of carvings were done by the same artist who specialised in animal spoors. There are some other carvings in the Bumbusi site which represent human hands and feet and "V"s, but these are so unlike the animal spoors in character that it suggests they are the work of another artist.

The Bumbusi set of carvings are on vertical rock sited in two caves or rock shelters and are well protected from the weather, but those near the Deteema dam are on flat exposed sandstone. They have weathered badly and are difficult to see when the sun is overhead. But in the slanting light of early morning or afternoon the lion and impala spoor show up quite well. There are no shelters near the Deteema carvings but, as in the case of Bumbusi, there are ruins built of stone. The Bumbusi ruins are much more extensive than those at Deteema.

Just what was the object of these carvings no one has yet been able to determine satisfactorily. The only other similar carvings are in a like situation in sandstone between Wankie and the Zambezi and these, too, are of animal spoors.

There are more ruins near Mtoa pan, in granite country where one would expect to find Bushmen paintings, but so far none have been discovered. The Mtoa ruins are better built than those at Bumbusi and have a little chevron pattern in the wall as well as monoliths on top of the wall, suggesting that they are associated with Zimbabwe.

CHAPTER THIRTEEN

ALTHOUGH tourism was beginning to play a big part in the development of the park, it had not yet emerged as the most important aspect. The National Parks Advisory Board had decided that where the interests of game and tourists clashed, the welfare of game should take preference. With this object in mind an ever-increasing number of watering points were created. From the visitors' point of view this was not a good thing as it tended to disperse the game, and where these water supplies were installed away from the tourist runs, the tendency was to draw game away from the areas where visitors could see it.

By 1960 the water supply was more or less assured as far as the requirements of the animals were concerned but a new problem was developing. A number of generations of our large animal family had now bred up in the park. These animals had been immune from persecution by humans and no longer treated the watering places with the caution which is natural to game.

In the ordinary course of events, it is near the water supplies where animals are subject to the greatest danger and it is natural for them – once their thirst is quenched – to get well away from the water to feed and rest in a secluded spot at midday. But with our parks-bred animals (such as buffalo and elephant) this was no longer happening and large numbers of them would spend a great deal of time feeding within a few miles radius of the water-holes, while they no longer sought out patches of dense bush to rest up in. In addition to this, animals have a sense of security from predators when they are in large numbers; while the grazing types, at least, like heavily grazed places on which to feed, as the grass is sweeter where the old dead grass has been trampled down. All these factors placed a great strain on the feeding areas around the waters and left a large part of the reserve untouched during the dry months. To counter this, the artificial watering points were spread farther afield, year by year, to bring an even larger amount of grazing and browsing into service.

Each year as the park dried out after the end of the rains (when small pans dried up) game densities increased on the bigger pans which lasted longer. Most pan areas consisted of a group of pans, some bigger than others, and in these game would concentrate, living in the vicinity of the drinking places, using first one and then another pan. When the water finally gave out, the herds would move to another supply. If the move was not too distant (that is about five miles or so), the game would return to the old feeding ground, making the journey to the water at fairly regular intervals. As the dry season advanced, with more pans and watercourses drying up, so game concentrated on the few remaining supplies. This movement each year had a definite eastward trend; as each group of pans dried out game moved to a fresh supply always in that direction; so that there was a steady convergence on the larger and more permanent waters along the watershed or east of it on the tributaries of the Gwaai river.

Over the years my observations revealed that game seemed most dependent on water during the months of July and August when the moisture content of the browse was at its lowest ebb. This was most noticeable among the semi-desert animals such as giraffe, eland, and gemsbuck. September saw many of the browse trees come into early leaf, such as the camelthorn (*Acaecia giraffe*), and the nyelenyele (*Ochna pulchra*). By the end of September the weather had begun to warm up, with concentrations of game increasing and large numbers of animals being seen at the water. This persisted until November when thunder clouds appeared and one could almost feel the tension as the animals waited for the rains, elephant standing in the shade fanning themselves with their great ears and other animals resting in every spot of shade available, panting in the heat. With the first storms these concentrations would break up and the herds would begin making their way back to their wet season feeding haunts, some using almost the same tracks each year. A herd of sable used the same path repeatedly about the middle of July when they moved across the railway into the Dett valley, where they remained until late in November, when they returned home to the reserve.

To determine what animals were present at these various concentration points and the frequency with which they visited the water, a number of observations lasting twenty-four hours were made simultaneously at a number of watering points during 1958, 1959 and 1960. The counts were made on the night of the full moon either in October or November, just before the rains. In all, some twenty-seven counts were made involving over 11,000 head of game. Most of the observations were carried out at pans supplied with water from a borehole. The number of watering places existing which were not under observation were known and, from the figures obtained, it was possible to arrive at a fairly accurate assessment of the total population of the park.

It became possible, from the data collected, to group animals into three distinct groups. Firstly, those that usually drink in the evening and at night, which included buffalo, elephant, zebra and, to a lesser extent, giraffe. Night and morning drinkers proved to be wildebeest and eland. The day-time drinkers were warthog, roan, sable, and kudu. Individuals of all species, except warthog, have been recorded from pans at most hours of the day and night, but the main trends show that various animals have a marked preference for set drinking periods. The greatest number of animals drink between 4 p.m. and 9 p.m., the peak period being at about 7 p.m.

Buffalo, elephant and eland favour the time just after dark between 6 p.m. and 9 p.m., while giraffe, sable, and zebra prefer the twilight just before dark, about 4 p.m. to 7 p.m. The main day-time drinkers, kudu, warthog and roan, drink in the afternoon between noon and sunset; while wildebeest and most of the carnivora seem to prefer the early morning hours – 5 a.m. to 8 a.m.; but a fair number of the latter drink between 1 a.m. and 4 a.m.

These twenty-four hour observation periods confirmed that many animals do not drink every day. In some cases a big herd of buffalo (300 or more), were known to be in the vicinity of a watering point but did not visit it at all during the observation time, and lions were heard repeatedly in the neighbourhood but did not show up at the pan while rangers were observing.

It is quite evident that there is a marked movement from one drinking place to another during the dry season, but some types of animals – mainly buffalo and elephant – move around in a circular orbit covering, in some cases, a hundred miles or more in a week or two.

In 1929 the only known buffalo in the reserve were confined to the dense bush along the southern fringe of the Deka basin, west of the Deteema river. These were by no means permanent in this area but wandered during the wet season over the border into Botswana, being back in their normal haunts by the end of March each year. It was not until 1935 that any buffalo were encountered in the open country during the middle of the day, and then only in small parties and usually all bulls. Steadily the herds grew, no doubt being augmented by migrants from across the border. They began to wander farther east and in 1937, the first big herd was seen at Shumba, and at Nehimba soon after.

It is possible that a small buffalo herd did exist in the south of the reserve near Labuti in 1929, although there is no record of this. A herd found there in 1935 numbered about fifty head. This herd did not move south to Sibaninni and the Nata area as one would have expected when water became scarce towards the end of the dry season, but moved north-west to Shakawanki where they spent a month or two.

During dam building operations on the Deteema river, the herd of working oxen, which had recently arrived, strayed away and could not be found. The herd-boys picked up the spoor travelling south; after reporting this they set out after the oxen. The next day the oxen – there were thirty of them – were found near the work, none the worse for the night out of their kraal. The herd-boys, however, did not reappear until I met them at Nehimba three days later. They had come to the end of the spoor at Skakawanki only to find that they had been following a herd of buffalo. These herd-boys were not Bushmen trackers, but knew their way about the park. The interesting thing about this movement of buffalo was that they had trekked straight away from Deteema without resting until they got to Skakawanki, a distance of about fifty miles. No doubt the disturbance caused by the dam building work at the Deteema water supply had induced them to move out.

The increase of the buffalo was much more rapid than any of the other animals, and it was recorded as early as 1950 that these would be among the first to present a problem of overstocking.

The grazing pressure first became noticeable in the north-west of the park for, as the herds moved steadily eastwards seeking out the best feeding, the problem spread right up to the railway; but for some unknown reason it was a long time before any herds crossed into the Gwaai valley. The size of the herds increased alarmingly. Where we once saw a hundred head, we were now seeing 1,000. In October 1963, while approaching Mandavu dam from the west, I came up with a particularly big herd. The first thing I noticed when about four miles from the dam was that the road and game tracks were just a mass of buffalo spoor, while ahead of me there was a cloud of dust in the air almost like the smoke of a veld fire. Then I came upon the stragglers of the herd. Old cows with calves at foot and those old bulls who seem to lag behind in the rear of a herd, taking no part in the day-to-day life or in guiding the herd from one feeding area to the next.

Soon I began to catch up with the main body of the buffalo herd and found myself driving along with a solid mass of animals on either side of the road; those in front stampeding off to the left and right to get out of my way. The road veered off to the left around the upper reaches of the dam where I arrived just in time to see the leaders of the herd reaching the water. I estimated the herd to be three miles long, and it took nearly an hour and a half for them all to get to the water.

As they came in, I was able to make a fairly accurate count of the numbers from a point of high ground on the opposite side of the water. There were a good 3,000 of them and they bunched up at the water's edge like a gigantic swarm of bees. Those in the forefront waded out into the water until they had quenched their thirst and then, turning round, forced their way back through the mob on to dry land. There was a continuous line of horns stretching for over 400 yards along the waterfront, backed by a huge mass of closely-packed bodies under a cloud of dust.

After drinking, the herd moved back a little from the water, where many of them lay down to rest. There was a steady trickle of animals drifting back to the water for another drink and returning to the main body of the resting herd. Some animals just stood and rested in the water. They were still there when I left just before sunset, some three hours after they had started to drink.

I had spent the afternoon with them and I felt that all my battles to obtain water and other help for my charges had been well worth while when I could look at this great herd contented and happy, as well as safe from the dangers which their ancestors had faced in the area, now their sanctuary.

The only predation to which buffalo in the park are subjected is from lions and this does not nearly keep pace with the natural increase. Occasional deaths have occurred, the cause of which could not be ascertained, but *Theilerosis* (a tick-borne disease) was suspected. Anthrax is always a danger, as in Botswana it is known to occur in both buffalo and elephant, but so far no cases have been recorded in the reserve. The phenomenal increase and the very large stock now carried in the park is largely due to the absence of any serious disease.

Grazing conditions have evidently been to the buffaloes' liking, for the east-west migration across the Botswana border is not nearly so marked as it used to be. Despite the heavily grazed areas the condition of the herds has also remained good. There is still a fairly marked migration into the south of the park in drought periods, to the waters of the Sibaninni, where there has been a number of deaths, but the main buffalo population of the park has not been seriously affected by drought.

Most of the buffalo calf crop seems to appear in July or August while there are a fair number in December and January. Bulls are seen to accompany the herds all the year round. A herd will usually contain about 5 per cent of mature bulls but there are many younger bulls, mature but not yet in their prime. It is these younger mature animals that seem to hold most sway in the herds. Some of the older bulls do little more than follow along in the wake of the moving herd, taking little part in the leading of the animals from place to place or in serving the cows. Small troops of bulls in their prime are a common sight and these mingle freely with the cows when they meet at the water without any opposition from the herd bulls. After slaking their thirst, however, they will wander off on their own, making no attempt to join up with the bigger herd.

Fights among buffalo do occur, but not very frequently. Bulls with broken horns are not uncommon, yet results of fatal encounters are not nearly so often seen as in the case of sable, for instance. Buffalo of both sexes will walk boldly forward to meet an intruder such as a lion, and even when in a pride, lions will give ground at the advance of several buffalo. It is not infrequent that a buffalo herd, when approaching the water, will encounter a slumbering pride of lions when, with obvious enjoyment, several buffalo will pursue the lions well out of the vicinity before returning to join up with the drinking herd. The lumbering great beasts chasing the streamlined lions is a sight that provides great amusement to tourists, and happens quite often.

Yet lions do kill a good number of buffalo; in fact, some prides seem to specialise in this type of sport. Some big bulls have been killed in their prime. In one case I recorded at the Deteema, two such bulls were killed by the same pride of five lions within a week of each other. In both cases the buffalo had not had its neck broken but, judging by the badly mutilated nose and face, it seemed to have been rendered helpless by lions getting a grip of its nose and by others either throttling it or tearing open the flanks.

I witnessed one such encounter between five lions and a lone buffalo bull. When we came upon the scene the buffalo was standing in the water at Deteema dam. It was only some ten feet from the water's edge, with the lions sitting or lying down within a radius of fifty feet. Neither seemed to be taking much notice of the other but it was obvious that the buffalo was at bay. After about ten minutes the animal tried to make its escape by running along parallel to the water's edge and, when clear of the water, made off into the bush. The lions just watched this until their quarry was well clear of the water, when they gave chase. The buffalo did not have the speed to maintain his lead, being soon overtaken. When the poor beast realised escape was impossible it whirled round and made a dash back to the water with the lions in hot pursuit. This happened a number of times. On the second occasion one of the lions sprang on to the buffalo's hind quarters, being dragged along until it reached the water's edge when it let go as if afraid of getting its feet wet. This happened a number of times without the buffalo suffering much damage. At times the harassed beast dashed out of the water right at the lions but it was much too slow and clumsy to get near the more agile lions.

A small troop of elephant came down to drink and proved a diversion but the buffalo did not take advantage of this, making no attempt to escape by mingling with the elephant. A large troop of impala also came down to water – some of them within fifty yards of the recumbent lions, who made no attempt to catch one.

Things seemed to be stalemated until, after these dashes out of the water and back again at intervals of about fifteen minutes had gone on for some three hours, one lion eventually fastened on to the hind quarters as the buffalo was on its way back into the water. The buffalo lost its balance and fell. Immediately the lions closed in, one seized the nose, another the throat while two others were on the flanks. Then the buffalo seemed to give up the fight and made little effort to regain its feet.

On another occasion I saw a buffalo give up when attacked by lions. It was a single three-quarter grown animal. Perhaps it was not very well or it would have been with a herd. As it approached the water two lions, who had been lying in the shade of a tree, got up and made a stealthy approach. For the last one hundred yards they were following only about fifty or sixty yards behind the bull. At the time, one of my young sons and I were in a boat fishing on Mandavu dam. When we saw what was happening we rowed over towards the buffalo to have a closer look. On seeing us approaching, the animal stopped drinking and turned to move off when it was confronted by the two lions. It made a half-hearted rush at one lion which was sitting up in a most unconcerned manner. The lion merely side stepped and grabbed the buffalo by the back of the neck with both front paws and its teeth. The buffalo stood for a moment with its head down then rolled on its side. The lion released its hold and leisurely walked around to the other side, taking a grip of the animal's throat. Only then did the buffalo try and regain its feet, but the lion held it down with a paw on the shoulder.

In the meantime the second lion was walking slowly up to the struggling animals, but showed no inclination to participate in the struggle. The fight, such as it was, soon subsided. We could hear the buffalo bellowing every now and then. Twenty minutes later it was still bellowing while the second lion had begun to feed on its rump. In fact, a large hole was eaten out of the leg while the animal was still alive.

But not all kills are so one-sided. The pump attendants at Guvalalla pan reported that they had been charged by a sick buffalo and, on investigation, we examined the spoor of what proved to be a buffalo

138

bull. We followed it for about a quarter of a mile and found it dead. It was a big bull in its prime. It had been lacerated about the shoulder and flank but this had not accounted for the copious amount of blood we had seen on the spoor. On closer examination we found that the scrotum had been badly torn and one testicle was missing. Evidently the buffalo had been attacked by lions but had beaten them off and suffered a wound from which it bled to death.

What must have been a great battle between buffalo and lions took place at Shapi in 1955. A tourist reported that he had seen four dead elephant at one spot. He was sure they were elephant; they were all lying together with their feet up in the air. This sounded serious, calling for immediate investigation, because four elephant do not just lie down together and die without some good cause.

We found the place easily enough, as the carcasses were visible from the road and there were thousands of vultures about. But the dead beasts were not elephant, they were buffalo bulls. There were five of them all dead within a radius of some fifty yards. Lying in the shade of a big diospyros tree near by were seven lions, all fine males. I drove round each carcass in turn and satisfied myself that all had been killed by lions. There were no signs that they had been shot – which was what I had feared. The spoor indicated that a fierce fight had gone on for some time. All the carcasses were near the edge of the pan. It seemed that some of the fighting had taken place in or near the water.

The animals had been dead for about twelve hours and a little had been eaten from each beast, but some of this had been consumed by hyenas. Even with this vast supply of meat at their disposal the lions were keeping watch over the carcasses, driving vultures away. The lions could not possibly eat all the meat, so abandoned the scene after two days of gorging.

This wasteful killing by lions is not at all common. They usually make full use of any kill they make. Just why the pride of seven chose to kill five animals at one time is difficult to understand, but it may have been that all seven of them attacked at once and the kills were made simultaneously.

CHAPTER FOURTEEN

THE carnivora have not increased at the same rate as the herbivorous animals with the protection they have enjoyed. It will be remembered that when the reserve was first proclaimed it was considered that there were too many lions, which I think there were. If they had increased as their breeding potential suggested, they would soon have presented a problem. However, lions were only shot up to 1935, when it was considered that the population had been sufficiently reduced.

Carnivora as a whole (including wild dogs and hyena) have not exceeded 0·1 per square mile. In 1950 the figure was 0·07 and in 1935, only about 0·01. This is a ratio of about one carnivora to one hundred other animals, excluding elephant. There are some losses in the elephant population due to predation but this is very slight. The buffalo and giraffe herds suffer fairly heavily from lions, but very little from other carnivora. It is the smaller animals such as kudu, sable, eland, impala, reedbuck and warthog which are preyed upon by all the carnivora, particularly wild dogs.

There is a certain amount of predation among carnivora themselves. Hyenas undoubtedly cause some losses among lion litters. We have a record of three young cubs being killed by two hyenas in one night. The lioness was evidently away at the time, for the hyenas were heard howling and laughing at 10 p.m. one night. On investigating the following morning, the lioness was found at the spot. When she was driven off it was seen that she was at her lair and one partly eaten cub together with three front paws were found. The spoor about the spot indicated that two hyenas were responsible. Whether they had chased the lioness away is not known, but she made no sound when the hyena concert was going on.

Two hyenas have been seen pursuing a half-grown lion in daylight. The end of the chase was not recorded but, unless the lion was able to join a pride of adults, it is thought that the predators would have killed and no doubt eaten the youngster.

I have recorded, too, a case of a leopard springing on a full-grown cheetah as it was walking along a game path. After despatching the cheetah with very little difficulty, the leopard proceeded to eat half of the unfortunate animal. This particular leopard was trapped on the carcass and its stomach contents were found to contain parts of the cheetah.

One of my rangers, Harry Cantle, witnessed two fully-grown lions killing and eating a half-grown male lion cub. The incident happened near Main Camp late one evening when the ranger was observing a lioness with three half-grown cubs lying under a tree near the road. Suddenly they all looked up and bolted as two lions appeared. The lions gave chase, overtook one of the cubs and pulled it down. The scene was visited next morning when all that remained of the kill was a few bones, the skull and a little skin.

It is possible that wild dogs account for some of the carnivora losses. Once a pack of these animals was seen leaping at a tree in which they had a fully grown female leopard at bay. Attempts were made to dislodge the leopard in order to make a photographic record of the wild dogs in pursuit of the animal, but without success. It was not until the wild dogs were well out of the way that the leopard came down from her refuge.

It is doubtful if a leopard could defend her young cubs successfully against a pack of wild dogs. I have no doubt that when these animals come across undefended lion or leopard cubs they make short work of them. Wild dogs and hyenas do not seem to be subject to attack by other carnivora, and their litters remain safe in burrows until well able to look after themselves.

It might be expected that the meat eaters in the Reserve would increase rapidly as the game became more plentiful and easier to find, with less necessity for parents to leave their cubs undefended while they hunt for food. This has not happened yet, despite the fact that the park is fast becoming overstocked with elephant and buffalo. These two species do not affect the carnivora other than lions and hyenas. There is a danger that the present balance might be upset if extreme culling measures among elephant and buffalo were carried out, with the resulting large quantities of meat and offal becoming available for a number of years.

Observations made on a pride of seven lions showed that they killed about four head a week of animals ranging from warthog to zebra. This is an average of only thirty head per lion per year. They will possibly kill less when their main prey is buffalo. There is no doubt that at times lions go for six or more days without a feed while, when they kill a big animal such as a giraffe, it will serve them for about ten days, that is, provided they are able to keep the vultures away.

A big kill like this, when cleared up, may be followed by ten days when the pride will do little or no hunting. This works out at one kill in twenty days for seven lions; but it often happens when a pride of this size are feeding on warthog and impala, they will kill more than once a day, so that I think thirty head per fully grown lion each year is a fair estimate. The estimated lion population of Wankie in 1960 was about 300, which means that they kill an estimated 9,000 head of game a year. This represents about the number of natural increase from 50,000 head of game a year, with the exception of elephant.

Leopards do not often kill animals bigger than impala but do occasionally take toll of young kudu, eland, waterbuck, sable, and roan. The leopard population at Wankie is not as high as the lions, but they do, possibly, account for about 3,000 head of game in a year. They are not wasteful killers and make full use of their kills, sharing them with neither hyena nor vultures.

Wild dogs are seldom wasteful killers. They rarely, if ever, kill except for food, while they do not, as a rule, pull down animals bigger than they can eat at one sitting. But they do devour enormous quantities of meat and seem to be hungry again in no time. A pack of seven will kill every day. One such pack numbering nine, hunting near headquarters, killed three kudu and two duiker in one week. These were the kills which were actually found. The amount they kill in one year must, I feel sure, be equal to that of the lion, in spite of the difference in size of the two animals.

The estimated number of wild dogs in Wankie is 300, so that the amount of game killed by them is in the region of 9,000 head per year. Unfortunately, they prey on the smaller animals and do not harass the more common types such as buffalo. Reedbuck and young tssessabi are among their common prey and it is the wild dog that has kept these two species at such a low ebb in Wankie. In fact, reedbuck are in danger of becoming extinct within the park.

There are two varieties of hyena in Wankie. The spotted (*Crocuta crocuta*) and the brown (*Hyaena brunnea*). Neither of them is very common, so that they do not kill a great deal.

There is one record of a pack of spotted hyenas killing near headquarters. They killed animals as large as zebra and were exacting a very heavy toll in the days when we could not afford to have losses. Some action was considered necessary. They would not return to a kill but made a fresh one almost every night. By a stroke of luck I heard them killing one night and was able to drive them off and lay down poison. The next morning there were five dead animals around the carcass.

Unlike the wild dog, the hyena is not a very fast breeder. Hyenas have their pups in ant-bear holes or rocky crevices, usually one, or at most two, to a litter. The pups live a long time in the burrows and do not accompany the parents on hunting and foraging trips until they are well grown. They spend their young lives near the burrow where they are in company with the parents during the day, lying and playing about near the lair, to which they retreat if there is any hint of danger. The parents, on the other hand, run off into the bush when disturbed. I have dug out the burrows of both the spotted and the brown hyena and have found pups, never more than two, and I have never found an adult underground.

The breeding capacity of the wild dog is far greater than any other carnivorous animal. A bitch will litter each year for five or six years, possibly more. Litters consisting of five and even six pups have been removed from bitches which have been shot. As many as nine pups have been removed from a breeding burrow, thought to be the progeny of only two bitches. All the breeding females of a pack will litter about the same time, which is usually between the beginning of May and the end of July. They litter in old antbear holes, from where the pups will come out and play in the sun when only two or three weeks old. They do not leave the burrow finally until they are about two months old, but will move from one burrow to another and sometimes back again when about a month old. If disturbed, a bitch will carry her pups several miles to a new home, but sometimes not all the pups survive the journey.

Given immunity from persecution and an adequate game supply to feed on, the wild dog population soon builds up but, thank goodness, they suffer from dog diseases such as distemper and rabies.

The wild dog method of killing, or rather of eating its food on the hoof, is perhaps unique, in that all other carnivora do at least kill their prey before eating it. Not so the wild dog. It makes no attempt to kill, it simply tries to tire out and then to eat the unfortunate animal it selects as its victim. It is usually the more defenceless types such as kudu, impala, reedbuck and duiker which are its prey, but occasionally a big pack of twenty-five or more wild dogs will tackle a sable or roan antelope. Fully-grown eland are seldom killed, but eland calves fall an easy prey, as do young wildebeest and tssessebi.

Cheetah are not an important factor in the herbivora-carnivora set-up. They are by no means common in the park and are not local in their habits, seldom being seen more than once in any one locality. They do not concentrate at water supplies, seeming to be largely independent of water, and often being found in very dry areas many miles from surface water, where they live on small game such as steen-bok, duiker, and hares – which are also independent of water.

Their method of killing is invariably to seize their quarry by the throat after knocking it over on the run. Having lacerated the throat they will then lap up all the blood which may escape from the punc-tured jugular vein. Cheetah are very slow breeders and the young are not concealed in burrows but in a sort of nest in long grass or bushes. The parents offer no resistance to any intruder such as a human being or a hyena, wild dog or leopard. They are usually seen in pairs, but there have been occasions when five have been seen together, for example, two females with three cubs; possibly the cubs were all of one litter.

The crocodile must be included in the predators, but, apart from two in pans near the Main Camp, they occur only in the Mandavu dam (where there is one) and the Deka river and its tributaries. Just how much game they kill is not known but it is, possibly, quite an appreci-able amount. There are some big crocodiles in pools on the Deka –

twelve-footers and over. On one occasion two big buffalo were killed one night at a pool where there were known to be three big crocodiles and a number of small ones. When examined, some ten or twelve hours after the killing, the only injuries found were facial. One buffalo had a slight cut under the tail. The carcasses were not removed but they disappeared in ten days, with vultures and hyenas playing their part in the disposal.

Hyena are very careful of crocodiles. A donkey which was taken by crocodiles in the dam at Robins was dragged on to an island, and although hyena were very interested in the carcass they did not cross a narrow strip of water only a foot deep to reach it. In the pan country it is a common practice for hyena to hide their food in the water in order to protect it from vultures, but this has not been noted where crocodiles are present in the water.

I was once attracted by the repeated screams of an elephant which sounded as if it was really annoyed. My approach to the scene was very cautious as I did not know what to expect and did not want to get mixed up with a charge. I arrived at a small pan, only about fifteen yards across, in which a young elephant bull was having a mud bath. All seemed peaceful enough until a hyena hove in sight and approached the water and waded in beside the elephant. The elephant turned on the hyena and with loud trumpeting chased it for one hundred yards or more away from the water before it came back and resumed its bath. After a lapse of about five minutes, the hyena came back, but this time he was spotted before he reached the water and the elephant, thoroughly annoyed by this time, gave chase in a most determined manner. (I was very glad that it was in a direction away from me). Having chased the hyena away this time, the elephant did not return to the water, but the hyena did; and he began wandering about in the water with his head down and nose and mouth under water. This went on for some time but, unfortunately, in my eagerness to see what was going on, the hyena spotted me and made off. With the help of two Africans, I searched the pool and found a big bone with a fair amount of meat on it in the water. I am confident that the hyena had hidden it there and was trying to retrieve it when the elephant took exception to him sharing his bath.

CHAPTER FIFTEEN

AT the inception of the reserve there were no rhino present in the area. However, there were a number, possibly five, on the Mabali river, a tributary of the Gwaai not far east of the railway. Reports indicated that black rhinoceroses had existed in the area now comprising the Wankie National Park up to about 1925, but there was no trace of any being alive when the reserve was declared. A farmer at *Sinamatela* ranch had a horn, found in 1926 just south of the ranch. Selous records rhino in fair numbers prior to 1896, while the late Mr Kelly Edwards saw one at Old Ngamo in 1912.

It was not until 1942 that the first signs of rhinoceroses were recorded, when two appeared on the Deka, thought to have come into the reserve from the west. These animals did not settle down but continued to wander from place to place, often two months or more elapsing without any spoor being recorded. They spent some time in the Sinamatela and Deteema areas and were also seen at Shumba and Shapi pans.

These rhino continued to roam in this fashion until 1946, when they wandered on to *Sunnyside* farm, a small-holding owned and run by a widow and her daughters, which jutted into the reserve near Mukwa siding. One of the daughters, a girl of about seventeen, out hunting for a buck for the labourers' meat, fired at what she thought was an eland but turned out to be a rhino. Unfortunately, she hit it in a vital spot and it died. The rifle she used was an old sporting ·303 in such a worn state that it is amazing it could kill anything at all.

This was the bull of the pair wandering about the reserve. The other animal, a cow, remained about for a few months and was seen at Ngwashla – where it successfully drove six elephant bulls away from the drinking trough – and again at Nyamandhlovu where it was equally aggressive towards other game. My wife and I saw it at the pan one evening when it took over an hour to get a drink – so intent was it on investigating every other animal that came down, making short rushes at them, snorting wildly. The animals merely got out of its way and took little further notice.

The next morning Bruce Austin and I followed up the rhinoceros to have a better look at it. It had evidently hung about the pan for some hours and then wandered off along an elephant path. It kept to the path for about four miles, and then we suddenly came upon it asleep in the middle of the track, right out in the open, about ten o'clock in the morning. We all got safely into the branches of trees before waking it, but the rhino made no aggressive moves. It ran off snorting, after giving us just sufficient time to satisfy ourselves that it was a cow.

Soon after that, it disappeared from the Nyamandhlovu-Ngwashla area although spoor was reported at Ngamo, and later well down the Sihumi vlei near the junction with the Linkwasha. There was no trace of the animal after that for a couple of years, when a piece of rhinoceros hide was found in an old Bushman camp near the Nata river. Since then there has been no trace and we conclude that that was the end of our rhino.

In 1961 displaced rhinoceroses from the newly formed Kariba lake became available. These were rhino which were trapped on recently formed islands which, in many cases, would be submerged when the dam filled to capacity. Most of these rhino were captured by darting them with an immobilising drug and transporting them to the mainland in an unconscious state, where they were given an antidote and re-leased. We decided to try and re-establish black rhino at Wankie and, with this object in view, a crate was built at Kariba, big and strong enough to hold a fully-grown rhino when it recovered from the effects of the drug. The habitat, we knew, was suitable, as there had been – according to old records – black rhinoceroses· in fair numbers in the early days.

Rupert Fothergill, his assistant, Tink Haslem, John Condy, a veterinary surgeon, and myself found ourselves on a small island some fifty miles from the dam wall where a single rhino had been trapped by the rising waters of the lake. Rupert Fothergill was in charge of the catching. By the time I arrived he had cut a number of lanes through the thick bush which covered the island, in such a way that the island was divided up into ten or twelve blocks of about three acres each. By placing an observer in a high tree in each block it was possible to keep a check on where the rhino was. This was of great assistance in finding the animal when the darting was to take place and, more important, it enabled a watch to be kept on the rhino after the dart struck home and during the twenty minutes or so before the animal became unconscious. The weapon used to project the dart with the drug was a "Cap Chur" gun, a new tool somewhat like a child's popgun. The accuracy of this weapon left much to be desired, even at ranges of as little as twenty yards.

After two misses due to the dart falling short, the rhino became very worried and, instead of standing still, he kept running from one block of thick cover to another. Shouts of "It's here" went up from one observer after another, and the route taken by the animal could be traced round and round the island. The temperature in the meantime was about 100 degrees in the shade and the rhino began to perspire profusely, becoming very black. Eventually it went to bay, not far from the tree in which I was parked, and refused to move. Rupert stalked up very close behind it but, just as he was preparing to fire the dart, the animal turned round and faced him. He had to retreat and stalk up again from another direction. This time the dart went home but still the rhino did not vacate its stand. The drug did not take effect and after an hour another one was fired. It was found later that the needle of the first dart had gone right through the tail and the drug had been discharged harmlessly on to the skin between the legs.

Just after the second dart had been fired, I stood up on my perch to see better how things were going. The branch under me snapped without warning and I fell a couple of feet before the calf of my right leg became impaled on a jagged dry piece of wood, breaking my fall – which would otherwise have been about fifty feet. I was unable to dislodge my leg and called John Condy to come to my assistance. He had to climb down from his safe perch to reach my tree. He pulled my leg up some six or seven inches before the piece of wood which was holding me like a meat hook came free. I was able to climb down and walk to the boat. John came with me and, after dressing the wound, he sewed it up with six stitches of fishing line.

When this was all over, the rhino was down and unconscious. It was dragged to the water's edge where it was loaded on to a raft and placed in the crate. When it was pulled away from the shore the raft with the crated rhino barely floated. Fortunately, there was little loss of blood from my torn leg and we decided to take the rhino to Kariba before I was taken to hospital.

We set sail from the island just about sunset, with the big raft in tow, but the whole contraption was so unsteady that it was in danger of capsizing each time the rhino shifted its weight. We had a small boat with about ten Africans ranged on either side to pull on ropes to keep the raft upright but, as our captive came out of the effects of the drug, he lunged about more and more until about eleven o'clock – when we had done about ten miles – it was decided to put the rhino ashore on the mainland. The first attempt proved to be another small island, not the mainland at all. Eventually, the animal was released and I was safely deposited in Kariba hospital, where the doctor, after examining my leg, decided that the veterinary treatment I had received was satisfactory and he did not undo the stitches. I spent a week in bed before going home.

This, our first attempt at rhino destined for Wankie, did not come off; but Rupert got a system going and eventually delivered nine animals safely to pens which had been built for them just below the Mandavu dam, where there was a nice stream of water running as seepage from the dam. After being kept in the pens for a fortnight or more the rhino were released to fend for themselves. One of the released rhino, a young bull, took up residence close to the dam and later, when a cow was released, they fought so desperately that they both died of their injuries.

The next rhino introduction was from the shores of the lake near the point where the Sengwa river now runs into the lake. Rupert Fothergill was again in charge and he successfully caught and moved to Wankie no less than forty adult rhino.

It was amazing how quickly these great big aggressive beasts became tame. Before they were released, after being in pens for only about three weeks, they would come up to the bars of the enclosures and have their noses rubbed, behaving like great soft pets. This tameness was achieved by feeding them lucerne hay which, when they had learned to eat it, they loved, associating their human captors with this titbit. The danger was that they would become so attached to humans that they would lose all fear of people and become a source of danger to tourists. One of our rangers spent an uncomfortable night on the roof of his Land Rover, his African servants up trees, while a friendly rhino wandered about his camp turning over pots and pans and generally making itself at home.

One of these "introduced" rhino has calved and now, after a lapse of several years, Wankie again supports a population of black rhino. Forty-nine were released and while some of them have wandered out of the park (two, in fact, being reported to have reached the Nata river) the majority have remained near Sinamatela.

There is ample proof that white or square-lipped rhino existed in this country until after the turn of the century. Selous recorded them on the Dett vlei just before the rinderpest of 1896, and there is little doubt that they were present at one time in what is now the Wankie National Park. There were reports of the existence of white rhino in the Chizarira hills in the Sebungwe district. Very few people had visited this area; in fact, there had been no official reports on the locality since Messrs Jack and Henkel visited it in 1912. I was particularly interested in visiting the hills to see if I could find any trace of rhino other than the black variety. With this object in mind, Bruce Austen and I went there in August 1956. As a preliminary, we flew over the area in a Dakota because we anticipated difficulty in finding guides. All we learned from the flight was that once up on the plateau, the country was uninhabited, but very well watered. We saw little game beyond a few sable, tssessebi and impala. Game tracks, such as there were, did not seem very marked.

We began our walk from a drift on the Lubu river and by nightfall were at a kraal near the foot of the escarpment. We had seen this kraal from the aircraft. Here we were fortunate enough to find a Batonka who was willing to act as guide. With him we set off next morning, much easier in our minds about finding a way up the escarpment. For about ten miles we followed a dry watercourse. By midday we were hemmed in by high hills but we had made no ascent. Our guide assured us there was water ahead so we pushed on, and about 2 p.m. he stopped and, pointing to a damp patch of sand covered with brightly coloured butterflies, said: "That is the last water; beyond this the country is black and I do not know it."

We soon had a hole scooped in the damp sand, into which some water percolated, sufficient for our needs. We had not brought many containers as we were confident of finding water. By the time we were ready to leave, a swarm of birds (waxbills) was drinking from the pool we had made, and we interpreted this as an indication that our guide was right and that there was no water farther on.

We moved on, still hemmed in by steep cliffs on each side, even higher than before. Only one hundred yards or so from the river bed, but ahead of us, we could see big green trees which indicated water. Sure enough, we came upon a stream of clear water which developed in the river bed and increased until, in a few hundred yards, there was a strong flow. There was little sign of game, merely a game track, but it was not much used and we were doubtful if it would lead us out on to the plateau. The cliffs closed in even more until we found ourselves marching in a narrow defile among big trees, being forced to cross and re-cross the stream many times and climb up small waterfalls. After some time the ravine on either side began to recede and the ground opened out. What was more encouraging, the game track seemed to be more used, chiefly by rhino; but all the dung was from black rhino, being browse and not grass – as would have been the case if there had been white rhino about.

The spruit divided here and we took the one to the left as the game tracks on this seemed more hopeful and it was going in the direction we wanted to go. Gradually we got higher and higher, with no very formidable climbs, until eventually the stream failed and we topped a rise from which we could see we were crossing a watershed with the streams on the other side running north and not west as was the case of the one we had followed.

That night we camped in a very pleasant spot in a grove of big musasa trees (*Brachystegia speciformis*) which seldom occur in the Zambezi valley, these being the first we had seen. We were now at an altitude of about four thousand feet, or some two thousand feet above our starting point. Our guide, who was still with us, maintained that he had never been on the plateau nor had any other member of his village. He said no one ever went there because it was too dangerous. We indicated the beautiful water and asked why his people did not live there. His reply was that it was too cold.

We spent several pleasant days wandering about the plateau, coming on some lovely places with abundant water. One of these spots was a large pool covered with huge water lilies. It was almost big enough to be called a lake. It is called *Mansituba* (white water). We examined hundreds of deposits of rhino dung, some in big middens, but we found no trace of white rhino, although black rhino were present in large numbers.

For two nights we camped on a stream which plunged over the northern edge of the escarpment on its way to the Zambezi. We fished in the big clear pools and had some wonderful catches of silver fish, a type of barbus, which our carriers were only too pleased to eat. We spent that day exploring the gorge of this stream with its thickly-wooded hillsides and big clear pools, full of fish. As we got lower down, the wooded hillsides gave way to steep precipices, several hundred feet high, with only a narrow ravine at the bottom. Like the one we had recently ascended, game only frequented the upper reaches of the gorge and seemed to be restricted by the numerous waterfalls.

At the end of our trip we had seen nothing which would suggest the presence of white rhino, but there were some big black rhino in parties of five and six, spending their rest periods out in the open grassland, a characteristic of white rhinoceroses.

Another area from which we frequently get reports of the presence of white rhino is the Chewore, an area in the Zambezi valley, east of the river of that name. A game ranger from the Game Department, "Lofty" Middleton Stokes, collected a specimen of dung from that area and sent it to me. It is the nearest approach to white rhino droppings I have seen, but it was not from this animal. It contained about 75 per cent grass and the rest twigs and leaves – which is definitely a black rhino sign.

The Africans of the Zambezi valley distinguish two types of rhino. The *Fura Uswa* (grass eater) and the *Eja Mtowha* (eats Mtowha) or *Diplorhynchus condylocarpon*. This is more than likely left over from the days when the white rhino did occur in the valley. Now the name is applied to any bigger-than-usual black rhino which spends its time in the open country. I was told of the presence of a *Fura Uswa* near a village in the Doma area. So confident was my informant that it was not the common black rhino that I cycled twenty miles to try and find it. This animal actually was easy enough to find. All the villagers seemed to know from day to day where it could be found and had no difficulty in approaching it, but what they showed me was a big black rhino bull. I thought at one time that the black rhinoceroses never ate grass, but this one did to some extent and I am now sure that many of them do. The bigger and older black rhinoceroses seem to have a tendency to spend less time in the thickets than their younger progeny and seem less aggressive, so there is small wonder that the Africans have different names for the two types.

One rhinoceros I saw in the Chizarira, a young bull, was wandering along a small dry watercourse in a most purposeful manner, as if looking for its companions. At intervals he would stop, turn his hind quarters towards a small bush or patch of grass and emit a blast of urine spray in a backwards direction. It would move on for a hundred yards or so and repeat the process. It was evidently laying a scent trail by which it hoped its companions would be able to find it.

The black rhino is well known for its habit of scattering its dung. The Africans have a story that long ago a rhino became involved in a fight and got its skin so badly torn that it had to have it sewn up. In the process the needle slipped inside and was lost. Now the rhinos of today are still looking for the needle. This story is based on the assumption that rhinoceroses scatter their droppings with their noses and horns, when in fact they do not; they do it with their hind feet, much the same as a dog scratching. Even baby rhinos do this.

Just why rhinoceroses use middens is not clear. These middens (some of them contain large quantities of droppings) are not used by one rhino only, but by any passing rhino. Middens may be a form of territory demarcation.

The Africans have a story to the effect that long ago the elephant and the rhinoceros had a competition to see who deposited the greatest pile of dung. The rhinos got together and hit on the idea that if they all deposited their droppings in one place they could beat the elephants, which they did. The elephants later heard of this trick and became very angry and beat up every rhinoceros they met. The rhinos, thoroughly beaten, decided to hide their droppings from then on, so that the elephant would not be reminded of the deceitful trick; and that is why today rhino scatter their droppings.

When it was decided to re-introduce the white rhino into Rhodesia in 1962, the preference was for young three-quarter grown animals and, as these would stand little chance against the lion population in the Wankie National Park, it was decided not to release them there. I was in charge of a party sent to Natal to bring up eight white rhino captured in the Umfolozi Game Reserve. We had no part in the capture but did witness one animal being caught by means of an immobilising drug. This was the same as that used by Rupert Fothergill at Kariba. It all seemed so simple, as the rangers at Umfolozi had got the technique taped to a fine art. To capture a rhino was to them just a morning's outing. I had seen white rhino before, having visited the Natal game reserves several times, but never in the herds such as are found at Umfolozi. I was struck by the hippo-like characteristics they displayed. They lived in small troops like the hippopotami, up to about twelve head, and when feeding behaved just like hippo. When resting, they often stand in a bunch with all their rear ends together, with their heads facing outwards from the circle that they form. I have often seen hippo asleep on the sand adopt just the same position. White rhino droppings, too, are much more like that of a hippo than that of their cousin, the black rhino.

Of the eight white rhino introduced, four were taken to Kyle Dam Game Reserve near Fort Victoria, and four to the Matopos National Park near Bulawayo. After being unloaded from their trucks, they were kept in pens for three weeks to accustom them to their new surroundings and adapt themselves to the new types of grass they would have to eat before they were completely weaned from the lucerne and teff grass "hay diet" on which we had been feeding them. During this time they were treated for worms and some of the stomach parasites they passed were truly amazing things, nearly four inches long and half an inch thick.

Two black rhino were also placed in the Matopos Park. One was a young cow called Sal who was originally sent to Wankie from Kariba. As she was much too young to defend herself against lions, she was sent to Matopos, by which time she had become very tame. Here she was joined by Rupert, a bull who was captured as a very young baby at Kariba and hand-reared by John Condy in Salisbury until he was about two years old. Unfortunately, Rupert died about a year after his introduction to Matopos.

CHAPTER SIXTEEN

ONE noticeable absentee at Wankie was the hippopotamus. This is not surprising as, until the Mandavu dam was built, there were no stretches of water big enough or permanent enough to accommodate such a large aquatic animal. The Mandavu dam had not been completed long when we recorded, with great surprise, the presence of a hippo in it. Just where it came from or how it found its way to the dam remains a mystery.

The filling of Lake Kariba jeopardised the hippo population of that part of the Zambezi and it is more than likely that, with all their feeding grounds submerged, some of the hippo wandered off up the tributaries in search of better areas. It is presumed that the hippo which appeared at Mandavu came from this migration of its kind and worked its way up the Lukosi river to the dam. Once into the water of the dam it only showed itself at night, and was not in the dam during the day. It would be found lying under the shade of trees a long way from the water. Gradually it changed its habits and settled down. After about six months a calf appeared, which must have been born there, but just when is uncertain. Since then these two hippos have been joined by a third, a young animal about three parts grown which, we hope, is a bull. Exactly what our hippos feed on is difficult to say as there is very little grass about the dam. This piece of country supports a large buffalo population and is subject to much over-grazing. Hippo on the Sabi river, who live under similar circumstances, are known to eat dry mupani leaves and it is more than likely that the Mandavu family do likewise.

The giraffe, being an animal of semi-desert country, has done well in Wankie, and giraffe are more plentiful on the Kalahari sand veld than in the more stony country north of the watershed. Although they have flourished under protection afforded them in the park the increase has not been spectacular.

Giraffe live in small troops, usually about seven head together, while sometimes herds of twenty-five or thirty animals are seen; but this is about their limit in Wankie. Giraffe do tend to concentrate to some extent in the open glades where they feed on a short type of grass (*Eragrostis viscosa. Trin*) which grows there. When feeding on it they have to straddle their legs just as they do when drinking. On one occasion I recorded an old bull lying down to feed on this grass. They are, of course, browsers. Acacia leaves from all types of this species and many combretums are, perhaps, their main source of food. There must be, in fact, very few leaves that giraffe do not eat. On the other hand, they eat very few fruits or seed pods. *Acacia giraffae* seed pods are one of the very few they do eat and then usually only when these are half formed. On one occasion I examined the stomach contents of a giraffe which had been killed by lions and was surprised to find fragments of wild oranges (*Strychnos spinosa*). How the animal contrived to break the hard shell of this fruit and chew it up I cannot imagine. They are fond of the leaves of this tree but I did not know that they would take the fruit.

Although they can do without water for long periods, giraffe will come to a pan regularly as long as it lasts. Once the water has gone, they do not move to another supply and suffer no hardship by doing without.

Most of the calves are born during the rains from January to April, but there are others which appear at odd times throughout the year. There does not seem to be a definite mating season and bulls have been noted fighting in September and April. These fights are ludicrous affairs and neither party seems to suffer much damage. Only the head and neck are used, while the hooves, which are such formidable weapons, are not brought into play at all. The head is swung round with considerable force in a backward sweep striking the adversary on the flank, the neck or head. The blows struck at the neck seem to have most effect. These fights will continue for half an hour or more and are usually concluded when both animals are so exhausted that they are hardly capable of striking any more blows.

Giraffe defend themselves against attack from lions by a downward and forward chop with the front hoof, sometimes one and sometimes with both feet together. They also kick out sideways with one back hoof at a time. These blows have great force and would put paid to any lion with which they made contact. One frequently sees giraffe with a small bare patch on the flank (or even both flanks) as if it sustained some injury, but this is caused evidently by a nasal parasite. When this worm causes irritation in the animal's nose and there is some discharge, the giraffe wipes its nose on its flanks, which makes the hair fall out.

The yellow-billed ox-pecker (*Buphagus africanus*) seem particularly partial to giraffe and several of these birds can be seen with nearly every troop. Frequently, when a giraffe bends down to drink, the ox-peckers will run along the animal's neck and enter its ears. Each of seven giraffe, all drinking in a row, have been seen with a bird in each ear. The first action when they stop drinking is to shake the head vigorously to dislodge the birds, which make no attempt to re-enter the ear until the giraffe resumes its drink again. Just what the birds are after has not been ascertained, but it is most likely to be wax and scurf.

Giraffe seldom lie down, but when they do it is invariably in the shade of a tree during the heat of the day in October and November. In areas where they are not subject to attack by lions (such as at Mcllwaine National Park) they lie down much more often. Frequently the whole herd will be seen lying down together. They lie on their chests and not on their sides, with the neck folded back along the flank. They rise (like all bovines) hind feet first. When in the process of getting up from a lying down position they must be very vulnerable.

Great strides have been made in the domestication of eland. John Posselt has, perhaps, done more to promote this in Rhodesia than anyone else. He started his herd near Lupani when, after some initial success, he moved it nearer to Gwanda and then sold the entire herd to the

Rhodesian government. There is a very good chance that this herd will form the nucleus of a big eland breeding project.

Eland introduced to Lake McIlwaine National Park have done exceptionally well. The first batch consigned consisted of nine heifers and one bull in 1960. Unfortunately, the bull escaped almost immediately and it was not until a year later that three young bulls and a further eight heifers from Wankie were added to the herd, bringing the total in 1961 to three bulls and seventeen cows. There was no mature bull with them, but a wild bull broke into the paddock from outside the park and stayed with the herd for a couple of weeks before it had to be destroyed for killing giraffe. After taking service from this wild bull, nine months later no less than eleven calves were born in the herd in one day. The herd at the end of 1966 number fifty, having increased from the original stock of twenty in five years.

Steps have already been taken to cull this herd and there is every indication that of the several animals suitable for game ranching, the eland is the best.

In their natural state eland are gregarious animals, showing a marked preference for heavily timbered country, but they avoid the bush. They sometimes come out into the more open savanna country, particularly during the mating season in September and October. At this time the herds have formed up into their maximum seasonal strength, and the cows are joined by the bulls for about six weeks or two months. At the end of this period the bulls again leave the herds and live either singly or in small troops of up to about a dozen. The herds then consist exclusively of cows, calves, and immature animals of both sexes. About April or May the young animals which were born about July or August in the previous year, form up into small herds accompanied by one or two mature cows; the main herds are then accompanied by only a few calves. This has sometimes led to the mistaken impression that the calving rate is very low.

Even newly weaned calves, when they are about four months old, will form up into troops of their own, but these usually remain not far from the main herd. They remain in these juvenile troops until they mature, gradually drifting away from the parent herd. The big herds of mature animals tend to break up into small groups, remain in these throughout the rains and begin to form big herds again about April when they join up with, not only other cows, but the mature young animals as well. The calves are born while the cows are in these big herds, some of them being well over 300 strong.

This breaking up and re-forming of the herds is no doubt a safe-guard against inbreeding, for, during the period when the herds have dispersed, the small troops wander great distances and it is doubtful whether the herds which bunch up during the dry season are made up of the same animals each year. Individual animals with outstanding characteristics have been noted with herds, but although herds have been seen in the same locality the following years the marked beasts have been missing. A fine bull with no horns at all was seen in a herd of 150 animals at Nyamandhlovu pan in October 1934, and seen again in 1936 at Shumba with a herd of fifty. In June 1937 it was again recorded at Nyamandhlovu, but this time it was alone. A cow, with the left horn curved back and without any spiral, was a member of a herd near headquarters from August to the end of October in 1942. She was not seen again in a herd in this locality, but a cow, thought to be the same animal, was seen in a troop of seven in January, near Ngwashla in 1946.

A common deformity among cow eland horns is the absence of the spiral with a backward curve, like those of a roan. In some cases both horns are thus formed and are rather long, being as much as thirty-five inches in length; whereas in others one horn is normal while the other is curved and smooth.

In sandveld country eland develop rather long hooves. When they walk the two halves click together as the foot is lifted and this sound can be heard a surprisingly long distance away, particularly at night. It is possible at night to hear an old eland bull approaching the water as much as half a mile away. The first time I heard this I was watching over a pan when I heard what I thought must be a pack donkey approaching carrying two or three empty tins, striking against each other as he walked. The noise would stop and start again, each time growing closer. I was all set to arrest some poachers when two eland bulls hove in sight. I was then able to determine what made the noise.

Eland do not remain in any one locality for long. A herd may be seen coming to water at regular intervals for several days. Then it will disappear from the area and live for days or sometimes weeks well away from water, to return to it again for a spell. These antelopes are essentially browsers but they do eat grass on occasions, particularly in the early summer when the new shoots of *Hyperinia* come through after a fire. The chief food supply consists of leaves and fruit or seed pods, the main ones being: *Ochnapulchra,* ebony shrubs, *Euclea spp. Protea, Bauhinia,* wild rubber,. *Diplorynchus, Condylocarpon,* as well as many other trees and shrubs.

The scent gland in eland is situated on the brow of the bulls, covered by a heavy growth of black hair. During the mating season, when the bulls are running with the cows, they are very prone to rubbing this brush of hair in the mud at pans, even dipping it into the water.

Eland are not normally aggressive and seldom fight among themselves. But once, when we were attempting to capture young eland with a Land Rover, a big eland bull made a determined charge and drove a horn through the door of the vehicle. This was obviously an attack in defence of itself. But attacks of another nature were recorded at McIlwaine National Park. A wild eland bull broke into the park and joined up with the cow herd there which, unfortunately, had lost its bull. After it had been there for a couple of weeks a giraffe was found dead with a gaping hole in its abdomen. A second giraffe was found in a similar state a few days later and the eland bull was suspected. It was proved when a third giraffe was lost. The bull had then to be destroyed.

The few gemsbuck present in the Wankie Game Reserve when it was proclaimed are, possibly, the only ones in Rhodesia. They are rather local in their habits. The main herds occur along the Kennedy and Linkwasha vleis. The combined population of these two areas was possibly 150, and I doubt if there are any more today. They are one of the disappointments of the park. These beautiful animals do not seem to have responded to protection in the same way as other species have done.

They occasionally frequent the glades along the watershed during the rains in small parties of six to ten and there is one localised herd near Labuti in the south, while a nice herd of about thirty wander about in the north-west of the park, being seen occasionally at Robins Reserve.

Gemsbuck come to drink at intervals at small pans but do not seem particularly interested in water. Ngwashla pan lies between Kennedy and Linkwasha valleys and, at one time, was the only water anywhere near the area for at least six months of the year. Pump attendants, tending the pump all day and every day from August to November at this pan, report gemsbuck visiting the water in small numbers only on rare occasions. They are, nevertheless, quite frequent visitors to the salt licks near Ngwashla. They seem to be rather unsociable animals, and are seldom seen in company of, or even in close proximity to, other game. I have seen a gemsbuck lower its horn and charge the legs of a giraffe, while on another occasion I saw one charge a warthog.

Gemsbuck are sometimes taken by lions and wild dogs, while leopards kill a fair number of calves. These appear in August and September and have not been noted at other times of the year.

In habit they are essentially browsers but do eat a fair amount of grass, especially new grass which springs up on burned areas. They are, in fact, very partial to burned patches. They dig for the large moist tubers of a creeper *Merremia spp.* which grows on the open glades in the cotton soil in the north-west of the park. These tubers grow to about the size of a football and contain a great deal of moisture and, presumably, food.

Sable and roan are the animals which have suffered most as a result of overgrazing by buffalo. They are substantially grazers and favour the best grass areas which are, of course, also favoured by buffalo. Their numbers increased fairly rapidly during the early days but there has been no marked increase since about 1952. They are among the most noticeable migrants. Usually they start to move in May or June, appearing about this time on the upper reaches of the Deka and on Robins Reserve. They usually reach the vicinity of headquarters, Kennedy and Ngamo, about June, when many of the sable – but not the roan – continue east into the Gwaai valley. The return migration westwards is not so marked, being spread over the wet months during the early part of the rains. By no means all of them migrate in this manner; a few herds can be found localised in odd parts all the year round.

A feature of the Robins and Nantwich area is the number of fine sable bulls which are to be seen; one herd, usually numbering about thirty head, is a regular visitor to Little Toms vlei on Robins reserve and consists entirely of bulls. Single bulls, many of them very fine animals, are quite a common sight.

For some reason, which is difficult to understand, sable are disposed to worm infestation which seems to affect the nerve system and cause paralysis of the hind quarters. It is not apparent in roan; in fact, I have only recorded one case in roan.

Sable are great fighters. Fights to the death are perhaps more common among sable bulls than any other animal. But there is a sable display or dance – which is a sparring up of two bulls, usually well matched, which goes on for hours without a blow being struck. The two bulls will arch their necks and present their horns to each other, sidling around each other in a most dignified manner. Occasionally they will stop, facing in opposite directions, standing like statues for a few seconds and then proceed with the circular movement again. This performance does not end in fighting, and seems to be some sort of display for the edification of the cows, who are sometimes present, but not always.

Warthog (*Phacochoerus aethiopicus*) are common in Wankie Game Reserve wherever the water supplies are reasonably good. They are for the most part very local in habit, but occasionally records come to hand of a family of warthog travelling along a game path or road for over twenty miles, not necessarily when water was giving out but when supplies were good. At other times during drought the spoor of warthog on the move has been noted twenty miles from the nearest water. They have also been recorded twenty miles from water, but have been permanent there and in quite good condition, having been without water for over six weeks. One such family of one old sow and four young were at Tchompani when the pan dried up in early October and were still there, having been seen regularly up to the first rains in mid-November, when they moved.

Warthog are among the few strictly diurnal animals. I have spent many nights watching game come to drink at pans, and have travelled many miles by car and on horseback on moonlight nights but have never seen a warthog abroad after dark. Warthog families can often be seen going to ground before sunset and in the cold weather they are sometimes still abed an hour after sunrise. If surprised in a burrow, a warthog will throw up a shower of dust with its nose before bolting. A family of six have been seen to leave an earth in this way, each one in turn preceded by a shower of dirt and lumps of soil – most disconcerting to the predator trying to get them out of their retreat in hope of a meal.

The reason for going to ground is possibly twofold : first, for warmth during the cold winter months, and secondly, for protection. I doubt very much whether a warthog can see very well in the dark. It does not show any reflection of the eye to a light at night, as nearly all nocturnal animals do, including even the elephant. Warthogs I have kept as pets appear to be rather helpless and at a disadvantage in the dark.

At Wankie the warthog seem to be suffering from a severe housing shortage, due to the small number of antbears. Many of their homes have been used for years and years; where, during the cold weather they make them more cosy by carting large quantities of dried grass down the burrow. Those who were our pets were given to taking all sorts of household oddments in place of grass, including my small son's hats, shirts, and other articles. Although not able to dig the initial hole themselves, warthog are capable of enlarging existing holes and construct a large cavern in which the whole family sleep. With this housing shortage more than one family will occupy a burrow. As many as fifteen warthog have been recorded coming out of one home. Protection seems to be the main reason for the use of these often deep burrows, as they are used just as much in the hot weather as in the winter. They will even still be in use when flooded during the wet weather. Unfortunately, this method does not afford complete protection as lions seem to have little difficulty in digging them out and many of their burrows are destroyed in this way.

Litters of up to five piglets are quite usual and in most years these appear in November. Occasionally the season is late and none appear until December. It is a rare occurrence to see a new litter earlier than the end of September.

During normal seasons the wildebeest population is confined to the mupani country in the south of the reserve, where the numbers fluctuate greatly due to the migration into the reserve from the west during the dry months. This migration does not extend far, covering only the mupani areas. Other rather isolated herds occur in the open glades at Ngamo, Kennedy, and near headquarters, with a few on Robins reserve. There is a little movement of the herds between headquarters and Ngamo but, on the whole, these animals are very local. Yet, in drought years (that is when rainfall is below normal), over the whole of the Kalahari sand area and including Botswana, large herds of wildebeest migrate north and north-east, appearing at all the water supplies, particularly Shakawanki, Nehimba, Shumba, as well as in the Sibaninni area. These herds do not remain once rain has fallen and have usually gone by the end of November.

Up to 1935 there were no wildebeest at all, either at Ngamo, Kennedy, or headquarters; the last of these animals having been shot near Kennedy in 1926. During the drought of 1934, large numbers concentrated at Sibaninni, and when the water there gave out many of them moved up the Sihumi and Kennedy valleys and a few were able to reach Ngamo and Kennedy, where they survived. Following this drought, when we were on patrol to Sibaninni, we found the pathetic heaps of bones of those who did not make it to the waters at Ngamo and Kennedy. (For this reason I made my first and foremost task the creation of more water supplies). Of those who survived the trek, about twenty-five with some young calves remained and have not left the area since. These have increased now to well over 3,000.

Each year these wildebeest, which have settled on the glades along the watershed, disappear from their usual haunts in October and, after moving about a good deal, appear again at the ordinary places in November or early December, bringing with them the new calf crops. Very few calves are born at other times of the year. The annual calf crop is usually well over 50 per cent; that is, one calf to every two mature animals. These little creatures are preyed upon largely by wild dogs and cheetah, but not by leopards or lions to any great extent, although lions get a fair number of adult wildebeest. Their habit of keeping well out in the open puts the large cats at a disadvantage and prevents any surprise attacks.

The breeding rate in the Sibaninni area is not thought to be as good. Reports from this part of the reserve are not very accurate, because only African rangers patrol there in November, as water supplies are very low and foul by then – if any water exists at all.

Wildebeest are exclusively grazers, cropping the grass very close and are to blame for the big expanses of bare ground at Ngamo, Kennedy and Main Camp. They love open country with short grass and concentrate on land which offers either of these attractions. Coupled with this preference for open country is an awareness of the danger from predators. For their midday rest period they invariably choose an open piece of vlei with good visibility all round with, if they can find it, a clump of trees.

Even at night wildebeest have a rest period and at Main Camp it is quite remarkable how whole herds of 200 to 300 of them will come right up to the houses and spend from five to six hours quietly lying down, some of them within thirty to fifty yards of occupied houses. They take little notice of barking dogs. And even the dogs become accustomed to this nightly arrival of the wildebeest and take no more notice of them than of the cattle and horses being brought home for the night. The arrival of the wildebeest was very interesting to watch on moonlight nights. The herd would assemble in the open vlei in front of the houses and stand there for an hour or so until all had become quiet, except for the throbbing of the electric lighting engine. They would then begin to file off towards the open spaces between the dwellings. They were usually all settled in their chosen spots by about 10.30 p.m. in the evening and, beyond an occasional snort, nothing would be heard of them until they began to move off about 4 a.m. When resting in this place it was noticeable that a far greater proportion of the herd lay down than is the case when they rest out in the vlei.

The migration into the Sibaninni area when there has been a drought in Botswana is most impressive. Some seasons the whole population from the west seems to arrive at once. Once when I was camped there, the migrating herds arrived. Up to this time there had been a few herds of about a hundred or so and the water in the pools was reasonably clean. About two o'clock in the afternoon we became aware of a distant noise of wildebeest calling to each other with that peculiar nasal grunt, together with a cloud of dust which was visible about a mile away to the west. Soon a solid line of animals appeared moving through the trees and, as they neared the water, they broke into a gallop. The thirsty creatures came on like a swarm of ants, striking terror into our horse and mules who had been turned out to graze. By the time we realised the danger it was too late and my pack animals and horse had bolted. Soon the whole place was alive with wildebeest and the pools were full of them. I estimated that in my immediate neighbourhood there were 2,000 animals.

The horse and mules had gone off in the direction from which we had come, along the river. In following them, we found the same huge concentration of wildebeest at all the pools. By next morning there must have been 12,000 of the creatures on the Sibaninni and they completely ruined all the water in twenty-four hours. In later years these vast migrations included buffalo and elephant as well, but in 1936 it was wildebeest alone. The waters did not last long and soon the herds moved on to other supplies on the Nata river.

For some reason wildebeest do not occur in the Zambezi valley in Rhodesia, east of the Victoria Falls. This is due, possibly, to the absence of open grasslands in this part of the country. They are present right up to the main watershed, not only in Wankie National Park, but in other districts as well; but very few herds have established themselves north of it.

There is one small herd in the Robins area just within the Deka basin and another at Sinamatela, with one very small herd between the Gwaai and Shangani rivers, about twenty-five miles from the junction; but all these herds seem to lead a very precarious existence with no increase. The only other wildebeest that I know of are near the Ngesi National Park, just east of the Umnyati river; but these, too, only just exist and their numbers remain static.

Zebra were rather rare animals when the reserve was first proclaimed, being purely dry-season visitors to the eastern and northern parts of the reserve. Only in the north-west were any found during the rains. The trek into the reserve to the east began each year about June when small parties came in from the west. Zebra are really what game wardens of East Africa refer to as "plains animals," and Wankie Game Reserve is not this type of country. They were not known at Ngamo, Kennedy, and were rarely seen around Main Camp before 1950. Even today they are not very common and one seldom sees more than ten or twelve together. They are still absent from the southern end of the reserve. Any migration which takes place seems to be from Botswana into the Deka basin, with none at all in the Nata area. Although the spread eastwards is fairly well established, zebra have not crossed the railway in any numbers.

In spite of the fact that we have always had horses and donkeys at headquarters, we have not recorded any zebra fraternizing with them, although this is a common occurrence on ranches in parts of Matabeleland where hybrids are a common sight. We did on one occasion, many years ago, have a zebra mare who attempted to join up with our donkeys. The horses and mules were terrified of her and came galloping home as if lions were after them. When the donkeys were kraaled for the night the zebra remained outside the kraal, but she had

166

disappeared by next morning. I am sure that the same animal appeared at a farm on the Gwaai river about a week later, where she actually went into the kraal with the donkeys and cattle and was made welcome. She was still alive on a Gwaai farm twenty years later, having produced a number of donkey hybrid foals.

The impala is another animal which occurred only in the Deka and Lukosi basins; the Kalahari sands being totally unsuited to them. However, one or two pockets on the main watershed were recorded, one of which was seen between Shapi and Mtoa, where impala are still present today – yet with no increase above normal, considering the protection now afforded these small antelopes. Small troops have now appeared at Tchebema and Nyamandhlovu but these are out of their natural habitat. Impala do not occur in the mupani country in the Sibaninni area, but one small troop of ten was seen on the Nata river in Botswana about twenty miles west of the border.

Impala seem to be dependent on water as long as it is available, coming to drink regularly every day at the same time in the same spot, often using the same path to the water; but when the supply gives out they are able to do without for upwards of two months and without undue loss of condition, provided the browse is good.

The mating season is in May and June, while the lambs are dropped in November and December. During the early part of the mating season the rams indulge in a good deal of fighting, surprising in these gentle little animals which most visitors call "Bambis." It is not uncommon to find a ram killed as a result of these fights. The noise during the rutting season made by the duelling rams is one of the common night sounds in the Deteema and Dorililo river valleys, where the main impala population is situated.

Kudu are present all over the reserve, there being few parts where they are not found. They are as common in the hilly country as on the Kalahari sands, with a few resident at all the water holes. Kudu drink daily as long as water lasts and will move a few miles to find other supplies, but do not migrate long distances. They suffer badly when water supplies give out, and lose condition; but many of them get over this and can remain in one locality for as much as two months without water. Stomach contents of animals shot under these conditions were found to be as moist as in animals with access to water daily.

167

The bulls run apart from the cows for most of the year, joining up for the mating season in April to June and again, to a lesser extent, in September. The young are born in August and March.

The kudu of Rhodesia is, of course, the greater kudu (*Strepsiceros capensis*) and is rated as one of the best-looking antelopes in Africa. There is another race known as the lesser kudu from East Africa, which has the same characteristics but is a much smaller bush animal. Visitors knowing this animal are always much impressed by the fine kudu bulls at Wankie, who are tame and stand well for photographers.

The Cape hartebeest is, perhaps, the rarest animal in the park. When I did my first patrols I found a small troop of twelve near Sibaninni and a skull in one of the Bushmen camps. At that time they had not been recorded in Rhodesia and did not appear on the game list. Since those early days one or two small herds in the Sibaninni area are all that we have recorded, with the exception of two animals which appeared near Kennedy. Of these, one was killed by lions, while another hartebeest which appeared at Ngamo was thought to be the other animal seen previously at Kennedy. There have been reports of a single animal at Robins on one occasion only.

It is disappointing that hartebeest have not responded to protection and increased, as they are relatively common in the Makarkari area over the border in Botswana.

Tssessebi, too, have not increased. They occur in small troops in the Robins area and there is a troop near Shumba but, apart from these small numbers, they are not present elsewhere in the reserve. They calve regularly in September each year but the young seem to be mopped up by wild dogs. Like the hartebeest, they are one of the failures under protection as far as Wankie is concerned.

Waterbuck are relatively common in the Deka river basin, as well as at Mandavu dam, but scarce in all other parts of the reserve. Despite the fact that these handsome animals are very dependent on water, a small herd have persisted near Danga pan. They disappear when the pan dries up and return again when the rains come; but where they go to is not known. Waterbuck were entirely absent from the Sibaninni section for many years but a few put in an appearance about 1945 and have remained in this part of the park, yet without increasing to any extent.

CHAPTER SEVENTEEN

Closely linked with the grazing and watering problems is, of course, the fire hazard. The park has few natural fire breaks within its boundaries. The railway formed an excellent fire guard along one border, but in the early part of the dry season, before the fire breaks are cleared, the locomotives are a continual source of fire. Even after the breaks have been cleared and the intervening strip burned off, there is always a danger of fire from the human element, in the form of working parties along the line leaving their fires unattended after they have cooked a meal, or when they have been robbing beehives, and a hundred other causes.

Once a fire started there was nothing in the form of rivers or other natural breaks to stop it. The roads in the park were quite useless for delaying a fire, which would rage for weeks, dying down at night, only to erupt again next day, sending up great billows of black smoke topped by a white cloud.

It was imperative that something be done to arrest this annual destruction of valuable grazing and browsing. The game itself did not suffer to any great extent. More often than not, animals would walk calmly ahead of the flames about a mile away. When the flames died down at night (as they usually did) the game would find gaps in the chain of fire and get back onto the burnt-out areas.

During the early part of the dry season – that is May and June

169

when the grass still contains some moisture with a suggestion of dew at night – fires will only burn during the day. So to form fire breaks, long strips of country are burned early in the year and as much as possible is done before the fires start to burn right round the clock and the next day.

Parts of the reserve, which had not been burned the previous year, containing old dry grass, would burn before areas which had no old grass and, by burning these patches first, it was possible to create a huge patch-work of burned areas all over the park, thus preventing the sweeping fires which resulted if an attempt was made to keep the whole reserve fire free. A large area like Wankie could not be kept free of fire for long.

Game of all types show a marked preference for burned-off country, when the new grass grows. Localities which have not been burnt for two or three years are not nearly so popular as feeding grounds as those which have been burnt and cleared of old grass. Quite apart from the grazing aspect, an area which had not been burned or heavily grazed for a number of years takes on an unhealthy appearance. Dead grass, leaves, and other types of litter accumulate, and in many cases this layer of dead material suffocates the growing grasses.

A fire late in the season, when all vegetation is dry and the air is hot and dry, can be a fearsome sight, with the excessive amount of litter generating great heat and destroying shrubs, and even large trees which had been able to withstand the early annual burns perhaps for even one hundred years. There are many parts of the park with hardly a tree to be seen, the whole area being covered with scrub growth, the result of repeated large hot burns. These low-lying scrub areas are, to a certain extent, linked with the severe frosts which kill off the young growth, forming a profuse amount of litter.

Fires, which occur late in the season, after some rain has fallen, do little damage to trees and bushes but do have a very bad effect on the grasses. Annual grasses which have germinated by this time are all killed off, while the perennial grasses will have sent up their early shoots and these, too, will be killed. The presence of moisture in the tufts of grass seems to act as a conducting agent, driving heat right down into the grass roots, which does not happen if the grass is dry.

Heavily-grazed areas which are becoming larger each year do not burn, or are at worst subject merely to slow-moving light fires which do little harm. Just how to control the fires in the vast acreage of Wankie National Park, other than by the early burning method of selected parts, has not yet been solved. To divide the whole area up into blocks by effective fire breaks is not practical, except at terrific expense. To exclude fire altogether might have a very detrimental effect on many animals, particularly those such as gemsbuck and tssessebi who prefer the sparse but succulent early grasses after a fire; as well as buffalo, who show a marked preference for grazing veld which was burnt the year before.

The outbreak of disease among the game at Wankie was always a source of anxiety. Right from the early days a careful watch has been kept for unexplained deaths, while any carcasses found were treated with the utmost concern. Any animal which was obviously sick or in very poor condition was subject to examination by blood smears, or in some cases examination of organs such as lungs or kidneys. This meant destroying the animal in those days, as there were no tranquillisers by which we could immobilise a beast and examine it and then let it come round again, as is done these days.

From 1932 onwards there has been maintained at Wankie a herd of what we called "indicator" cattle. These animals were isolated from any other domestic stock but mingled freely with game, using the same drinking points as wild animals. When any of the progeny of this herd were disposed of they were sent to the Cold Storage Commission for slaughter and the carcasses examined by the Veterinary Department.

The first disease in our indicator herd was *Trypanosoniasis* from tsetse fly which doubtless invaded the reserve from the north-east, but we had only two deaths among the cattle and lost one horse. The disease did not recur. The anti-tsetse operations east of the railway were possibly successful.

All went well; there were no more deaths from disease and our game kept free of dangerous epidemics such as anthrax (although we heard the occasional rumour of deaths among elephant from this disease in Botswana). For many years we enjoyed a clean bill of health and there was no trouble until foot-and-mouth began to rear its ugly head. There were a number of outbreaks in cattle both in Rhodesia and Botswana, and game were blamed as the source of the infection. Accompanied by a veterinary officer we shot and examined a fairly large number of animals which looked suspicious, but no positive trace of foot-and-mouth

171

could be located. The wildebeest showed a number of cases of foot rot but all specimens examined by the vets were proclaimed free of foot-and-mouth. There were quarantine restrictions imposed on the movement of cattle in the farming areas. Expensive cordons were also established and maintained – through which no cattle were permitted to move; but game in the area had no restrictions put on their movements beyond a few head shot on the cordon line. These precautions seemed to answer well enough, for in a few months the disease died out.

Then there was another outbreak in native cattle at Gwaai Native Reserve in the Ngamo area, right on the boundary of the reserve, where grazing and water were shared between cattle and game, mostly wildebeest. After this outbreak had been active for a month, two cases were found in game at Ngamo. The signs were unmistakable, particularly in the case of sable and kudu. The loss of condition was rapid and the stricken beasts were reluctant to move off when approached. Animals seen to be affected by the disease were kudu, sable, roan, impala, reedbuck, giraffe and, last of all, buffalo.

After foot-and-mouth had run its course, which seemed to be only a couple of weeks, signs of the disease soon appeared in the form of a ridge, not only around the hoof of the stricken creature, but also around the horns where the horn growth had been arrested during the time the disease had been active. There was also a scar on the tongue of some animals but, more often than not, this was missing while the ridge on the hooves was quite plain. Of course, we had few occasions when the tongue was available for inspection, as the majority of the carcasses we examined had been dead some time, quite often being the kills of wild dogs and lions.

Foot-and-mouth spread from Ngamo and soon became noticeable at Ngwashla and near headquarters, but it eventually died out. All quarantine restrictions were lifted, but still both the indicator herd at Main Camp and Robins remained unaffected. In the meantime foot-and-mouth was widespread in Botswana, with the annual migration of wildebeest from that country up the Nata river across the southern tip of the game reserve into the Gwaai Native Reserve, giving the Veterinary Department many sleepless nights.

Then, a year after the outbreak in game had subsided, in 1960, the indicator herd at Main Camp contracted foot-and-mouth. This was a definite "go ahead" for the Veterinary Department to take restrictive measures against game. It was resolved that the game must be isolated from the cattle, so steps were taken to erect a fence running from the Gwaai river along the boundaries of the farming area and then south to the Botswana border. This meant that the fence would run along the boundary of the park from Ngamo to the Nata, a distance of about 110 miles. The fence, however, was so frail and inadequate that most varieties of game could get through it or smash it down; so the Veterinary Department decided to shoot all game which could break a fence – that is game within a mile of the fence – and my staff had to hunt down elephant who habitually broke the fence but who could not be located within this area during the day. This caused a very heavy drain on the game population, which might have been avoided if the fence had been worthy of the name and strong enough to withstand the pressure put upon it by game.

Fences are things quite foreign to game. The animals just cannot understand the obstacle and will spend days trying to find a way through or around it if the barrier happens to be across their chosen path. They will walk along the fence for miles, then turn round and walk back again, repeating this over and over again. Some of the animals, such as kudu and eland, could easily jump the fence and did so regularly if disturbed; but left to their own devices the poor beasts would remain against the fence until they managed to break through, or were shot by the fence patrols. It was usually when disturbed by the fence patrol that the break-through occurred.

On one occasion when patrolling the fence, I came across a herd of ten eland cows with four young calves against the wire trying to get into the park. On being disturbed, all the old cows leapt the seven-foot fence, only damaging the top strand, but all four youngsters remained behind against the fence. The country was fairly open and we were able to catch them by driving them up to the wire and then we pushed them through on their sides, letting them go, and hoping that they would be able to rejoin their mothers who, by this time of course, were a long way out of sight; but they would be likely to return later in the day to look for their calves.

A herd of kudu trying to get to a pan outside the park near Ngamo, spent days trying to find a way through the fence. There was water at the pump inside the Reserve, only about two miles away. The herd was driven away from the fence in the hope that it would abandon its efforts to reach the pan and go to another water supply. But no; the animals came back to the wire at the same spot time and time again. The fence line was worn into numerous narrow dusty paths where these creatures had trodden a weary path in their efforts to get to water. In a couple of weeks, they became so thin and weak that they could hardly run away. It was then decided that it would be more humane to destroy them.

One of my rangers on patrol came upon a herd of sable in much the same state, trying to get at the water in the Sihumi. On his approach one of the sable charged the Land Rover and collapsed after striking it a heavy blow with its horns. So maddened by thirst was it that it would have inflicted severe injuries on anyone patrolling the fence on foot.

Buffalo, elephant and wildebeest seemed to have little difficulty in breaking through the fence, but giraffe encounters with the wire were nearly all fatal. The animals would walk up to the barrier and try to step through it, getting first one front foot entangled and then another entangled beween the strands. This invariably resulted in the creature falling down and being unable to rise again. Whole herds of giraffe perished in this way. One party of officials inspecting the fence counted thirty-five giraffe carcasses up against the wire in one section.

Elephant breaking through the fence on their way from the park into the Gwaai Reserve would nearly always break through again before the next day or, at the most, a day or so later; in many cases using the same path for their return, breaking the fence again within a few yards of the gap they had made on their way out. Generally, elephant treated the fence with utter contempt. The only ones who had any difficulty in getting over the wire were calves and babies which, in many cases, were abandoned by the herd.

What the fence patrol men thought and said about these things could not be told in this book. We, of course, mourned the loss of our animals, and the suffering they endured distressed everyone on my staff. But the conflict between game and domestic stock goes on all the time and one can only hope that science will find cures for all the ailments which game animals are supposed to carry with them and unfortunately transmit to the farm animals near the reserves.

When the big migrations of wildebeest and elephant came up the Nata river across the southern end of the park the fence became a huge problem. The animals bunched up against it and then when panic broke out among the herds – as it does under such circumstances for no apparent reason – the animals just swept the fence away in a mad stampede. At one stage towards the end of the dry season of 1964, fence patrols reported fifteen miles of wire flattened and in many cases carried away by elephant and wildebeest moving up the Nata river.

One wonders if the fence (and there are two of them now, the other being to the north of the park) is really justified. The Wankie district has not remained free of outbreaks and quarantine restrictions despite the colossal expense and wastage of wild life.

When the threat of a game fence along the south-eastern boundary of the park became a reality, the danger to game living near the boundary was realised. If the shooting in order to protect the fence was rigorously enforced the results would be devastating. Fortunately, none of our artificial water supplies were situated near the proposed fence line. There were few big natural pans near the boundary, but there were one or two – or rather a group of pans – near the boundary, but these were just outside the park at Ngamo, which was a very popular spot. The glade surrounding these pans carried a very good permanent herd of wildebeest as well as a few giraffe, zebra, and sable. Some elephant and buffalo, as well as eland, were frequent visitors to the area during the dry season. It was clear that the proposed fence line right across the Ngamo flats, would cut off much of this game from the park and enclose it in the African reserve, where it would have little hope of survival.

In an effort to save some, at least, of this game it was decided to catch as many animals as possible and transfer them to McIlwaine National Park near Salisbury and the Matopos National Park near Bulawayo. It was hoped that the general disturbance caused by the catching would induce some of the animals to move into the park where they would be safe. An area of about 2,000 acres was fenced in both at McIlwaine and Matopos, and when this was ready we set out from Main Camp to start our catching operations. We equipped ourselves with a short wheelbase Land Rover with the cab and windscreen removed. Bruce Austen, who by this time was my second in command, had put in a little practice by catching some wildebeest on the glade, just to try out the possibility of the scheme, and then releasing them again. He found that the scheme worked well. The plan was to have two or three Africans who were skilled at catching cattle by means of a

Rhodesian lasso, a loop of rope attached to a long light stick and used in the manner of a landing net when fishing. The animal could be caught by the neck or, preferably, by a hind leg which was the usual method with truculent cattle. We established a camp at a convenient borehole in the African Reserve near the boundary and constructed some pens in which to hold the captives before starting them on the 450-mile journey to McIlwaine.

Bruce had gained a little experience with the capture of the wildebeest. My experience was limited to the capture of young giraffe on horseback. Neither of us knew exactly what was in store for us when all was ready and we set off to make our first captures. Bruce drove the capture vehicle and I the bigger Land Rover which was to be used to transport the animals back to the camp.

We approached a herd of about fifty wildebeest and set them on the run. We followed close on their heels and when the herd made a wheel to the left or right we would whirl in and attempt to cut out one or two weaners that were less than a year old but no longer dependent on their mothers' milk. After one or two attempts we succeeded in cutting off a small party of five which included three young animals. Then the pace quickened; in about five minutes Bruce was able to range alongside one of the young animals, and the African with the lasso succeeded in getting the rope around its neck. As soon as it was brought to a standstill the Africans on my truck leapt off and secured it by the horns, ears and tail. In a surprisingly short time it gave up struggling.

Within ten minutes of starting the chase the first wildebeest was in the pens. By the time I had returned to the capture area Bruce already had the second roped up, and we soon had this one loaded and on its way to the pens. This seemed too easy, we thought; there must be a catch in it somewhere. After four animals had been caught in this way we swopped vehicles, and I drove the capture Land Rover and caught another three. By this time the herd had got wise to what we were up to and got into full gallop as soon as they saw the vehicles coming. But still they kept to the open glade and we had little difficulty in singling out young animals and running them down.

We knew that over-exertion must be avoided, so we were careful not to chase our quarry too far. If they got into difficult country where the catching vehicle could not travel fast enough, the chase was abandoned rather than carry on too long.

"... nevertheless... Hwange still offers a fine wildlife viewing experience.

(photo courtesy Lynn Taylor)

Young visitor and young warthog in mutual contemplation (above).
A herd of buffalo move across the road near Msuma, (below).

(photos : Keith Meadows)

Three old soaks.

(photo courtesy G. Groshart Wildlife Explorations client)

A small family unit (above). It is about now that one should have the gear lever in reverse. Watering elephant cows (below) keep a weather eye on a passing lion, on the Lukosi river.

(photos : Keith Meadows)

Lions are not always efficient killing machines. This kill took over two hours to complete.

(photo courtesy G. Claeys, Wildlife Explorations client)

A fine buffalo bull (below). Buffalo form the favoured prey of lion in most of Zimbabwe's wild areas.

(photo : Keith Meadows)

One of the wildlife enthusiasts 'mega-ticks'. A fine rare night picture of a leopard in relaxed mode.

(photo courtesy Paul Greenway)

The cheetah population in Hwange seems to be decreasing.

(photo courtesy G. Claeys)

Gathering of the clans. This group of giraffe provides seldom seen
symmetry in the bush.

(photo courtesy Mark M^{C}Adam)

Zebra always seem to look better in groups.

(photo : Keith Meadows)

The kill ratio of the painted hunting dog is more successful than that of
lion. The animal is the subject of considerable research in Hwange, and
is an endangered species.

(photos courtesy Sean Lues)

The spotted hyena is a successful predator in its own right, as well as being a scavenger. Essentially nocturnal, it is well represented in Hwange, and a campfire without its night music is not quite complete. A black backed jackal (below) has just seen off some rivals, white-backed vultures.

(photos courtesy Mark McAdam)

Sable antelope (above), with its cousin, Roan antelope (below).

(photos courtesy G. Groshart)

Kudu bulls, senior and junior (above). A pair of kudu bulls and impala
rams warily watching lions on the move (below).

(photos courtesy G. Groshart)

An eland bull (above)
watering at Ngweshla.
(photo courtesy G. Groshart)

Trains running along the
one boundary of the Park
take an annual toll of
wildlife.
(photo courtesy Paul Greenway)

A fine waterbuck male, the symbol of the Department of National Parks
and Wild Life Management.
Impala and baboon are often to be found in each other's company

(photos courtesy G. Groshart)

Small game ....

Bat eared fox (above) are not as often encountered as the gregarious banded mongoose (right).

(photos courtesy Paul Greenway)

The rock hyrax is credited, by virtue of anatomical similarities, as being the closest relative to the elephant.

(photo : Keith Meadows)

Hippos, resident at Mandavu Dam, will travel long distances between pans
and waterholes when their 'home' water dries up.
A cock ostrich with his three hens. These large flightless birds are often
seen in the more open Main Camp and Ngweshla areas.

(photos : Keith Meadows)

Hope for the future? A helicopter hovers over a drug-darted elephant
family unit. In recent times entire herds have been moved, alive, to new
areas. Revolutionary, but costly, this capture method may one day provide
an alternative option to culling.

(photo courtesy Clem Coetsee)

By the end of the first catching day our pens were nearly full and we hurriedly set about building more. When we resumed catching, we turned our attention to zebra and we hunted out small herds which were not accompanied by wildebeest. The same technique worked, but we had much more trouble with the capture after the initial roping. The zebra fought far more than the wildebeest and we had to be careful to avoid being bitten. To avoid being bitten we took the precaution of having a soft rope muzzle made. This was used on the first two or three, but then we gave it up as we found that the zebra were, in struggling, inclined to get a hind foot caught in the thongs holding the muzzle in place. They either succeeded in getting the muzzle off or in getting their legs caught up, so we decided against its use and risked their biting us.

Soon our pens were full again and we had to stop catching. We then began the training of our captives, that is, induce them to eat grass which was cut and given to them; we also had to get them accustomed to humans around them. At all times of the day and night we had someone near the pens. We slept within a few yards of the enclosures and tried to keep our presence known at all times. It soon became evident that attempts to escape were only made when no one was in sight. One zebra did manage to get out by clambering up the eight-foot sides of the pen and falling heavily on the outside when it got over. We did not attempt to catch it again as, in any case, it was a little too big for our purpose and was reluctant to be tamed.

At last we were ready to begin the move and the first batch of animals were carefully inspected by an official of the Veterinary Department, who went over them thoroughly for signs of foot-and-mouth. Fortunately, he found nothing; if he had, the whole scheme would have fallen flat. The necessary permits were issued and the convoy of lorries with crates built into them started off at 7 o'clock in the evening and arrived at the Matopos Park early the following day.

On arrival at the park the animals were again penned up for a few days to allow them to recover from the strain of the journey and to be in a fit state when released. There were leopards in the Matopos and any animal released in an exhausted state or in a run-down condition would stand little chance of survival. Strangers to an area or exhausted animals always attract the attention of carnivora.

Our activities at Ngamo had induced some of the animals – but by no means all – to move back into the park. When we were ready to begin the next move the fence was up. We had requested that a mile-wide gap be left in the wire where we could attempt a drive and get some of the game through it and close it afterwards, and before any of them had time to recross the line. The Veterinary Department thought otherwise and the gap was not left.

During our second catching operations we concentrated not only on wildebeest and zebra, but on giraffe, buffalo, eland, and sable as well. Much of the game was trying to get through the fence, some animals succeeding, so it was only a matter of time before most of them would perish. We operated on both sides of the wire, trying to drive the game away from the area. This time we established a camp and holding pens near one of our own windmills, which was situated in a convenient spot in the centre of a group of small pans, most of which contained water. Only the wildebeest spent the whole day in the open; the other animals would come out into the glade only, either to drink or feed towards evening. From the vantage point up the windmill a watch would be kept on the whole glade and on those animals seen coming out into the open when they were a mile and a half or more away. This made selection easy. First we caught our quota of wildebeest without difficulty and then turned to the other species.

When a herd, which included suitably sized animals (we were still only interested in yearlings), was sighted coming into the open, we would allow it to get well out on the glade and then we would leave the camp in the opposite direction, entering the bush on the fringe of the glade. We then circled round the vlei and got between the herd and the bush before coming into the open; thus cutting off the animals' retreat. The two Land Rovers would then give chase, keeping the herd out on the flat country until one or two suitably sized youngsters were cut out of the herd. The hunt was then concentrated on them. This technique worked well, taking usually only from two to five minutes from the start of the chase to the time of capture, when the captive was brought to a standstill.

When young giraffe were captured, the technique was altered somewhat. The actual capture was much the same but then a special harness was strapped on to the captive and, by using guy ropes to the front and either side, it was walked to the pens. This harness was designed when I captured the first giraffe way back in 1929. It was made of leather thongs or riems consisting of a collar around the lower neck attached by straps to a second collar around the girth just behind the shoulder. Long ropes were attached, which extended forward and to either side. For the present operations these harnesses were made of webbing.

When the giraffe was first caught, either by the neck or by a hind leg, it was brought gradually to a standstill. It was then blindfolded by placing a light blanket over its head, lifted up on one of the catching sticks. Once blindfolded, all struggling stopped and the animal would stand quietly while the harness was being strapped on. Then the blanket was removed and, by putting the strain on one or other of the guy ropes, the animal was guided with no difficulty towards the camp and into the pens.

None of the animals were fed on artificial foods such as lucerne or grain, but were given their natural food which was collected near by. In the case of giraffe, long branches of green browse trees were cut and propped up against the ten foot by ten foot pen and they were taught to drink from a drum set on a stand about six feet above ground. Considering that none of them had ever had a drink without having to bend down to get it, it was amazing how quickly they adapted themselves to this new procedure.

Giraffe, above all other game animals, had to be handled with great care and humoured while in the pens. If they were left alone for a few minutes during their first week in captivity, they would take fright at the approach of a human being; but with someone in attendance and close to them all the time, they soon lost their fear of man and accepted his presence. It was significant that they would take no notice of humans moving about the camp at night but would take fright if a hyena should put in an appearance. All-night watches were kept and we put up our stretchers close to the pens and kept lights burning all night. This was a two-fold precaution, partly to keep the animals docile and partly to guard against a raid by lions, which were quite capable of upsetting the whole show and terrorising some of the captives into injuring themselves or even breaking out.

It was really remarkable how tame some animals became in such a very short time. One giraffe, which was not in very good condition when captured, was released only thirty-six hours after capture. It spent the first hour of its new freedom wandering about among the vehicles, tents and pens before making off. An eland cow which was a little big for our purpose would keep horning the other in her pen and we decided to release her. She had to be roped and led out of the pen, but when the rope was removed she immediately broke back into the pen. We roped her again and released her a second time. This eland then spent the next twenty-four hours wandering about the camp, feeding on the leaves which were cut and brought to the pens for the giraffe.

We had very few escapes from the pens, but one giraffe did succeed in crawling under the bottom rung of the pen which was only three feet from the ground. Once out of the pen, it only ran off for about 200 yards and then stopped. It was still about when morning came and it was easily recaptured.

When the time came for the second batch to move (it had been decided to send this lot to McIlwaine) the problem of getting the giraffe into a lorry had to be overcome. On previous occasions when we had sent giraffe away – once to Pretoria and once to Livingstone – we had loaded them on to railway trucks using an earth ramp at truck level. But this time instead of building a ramp upwards we dug a wide trench downwards and reversed the lorry into it, bringing the floor of the crate on the lorry down to ground level. The giraffe were walked in, using the guide ropes as before. The front ends of the tall crates were covered with sails to keep the wind and dust off the animals. The journey to McIlwaine for giraffe was much more trying than for any of the other animals but, like the Mapopos consignment, the journey was done non-stop, travelling through the night.

In all our catching experiences we had very few instances when animals showed any inclination to attack us or the Land Rovers. Even buffalo would show no aggressive behaviour when they were being chased or their calves were being caught.

We did have a wildebeest swing off its course beside the Land Rover and, with a sideways sweep of its horns, break a headlamp. An eland bull once made a determined charge with lowered head and drove a horn through the door of the vehicle. The Land Rover had been stripped of cab and windscreen but, fortunately, the doors had been left on. This was to prevent the driver or his passenger falling out on the sharp corners.

As with all activities connected with the running of a game reserve, the game-catching exercise at Ngamo yielded some very useful information on the speed of the various game animals. A game warden is, in the ordinary course of his duties, always doing research of one kind or another and the translocation of game was no exception.

When catching game by Land Rover on the Ngamo flats I found it difficult to take an accurate speedometer reading, as it was impossible to gauge the wheel-spin in the sandy soil and the frequent bumps when the wheels were off the ground. But there were some smooth hard patches where I was able to note that sable could put on bursts of speed up to thirty-five miles an hour, but they could not maintain this for long. When allowed to make their own pace, it was about thirty miles an hour. Wildebeest were about the same and so were eland. Giraffe, however, were much slower, seldom exceeding twenty-five miles an hour. Ostrich, on the other hand, were faster than any of the antelopes and could top forty-five miles an hour when hard pressed.

Travelling by car on one occasion near Robins Camp, I came on a small herd of tssessebi and they, as usual, tried to cross the road ahead of the car. The last member of the herd just failed to make it, running parallel with the road. By keeping abreast of the animal I was able to gauge its speed fairly accurately. It seemed to have no difficulty in keeping up thirty-five miles an hour, while every now and again it would put on a spurt of speed, trying to get ahead of me sufficiently to cross the road, when I would have to accelerate to forty miles an hour to keep abreast of it. This race went on for over a mile without the tssessebi showing any signs of distress. Finally, it doubled back and got across the road behind me to rejoin the herd which was still visible about a quarter of a mile back, running almost as hard as the animal I had been pacing, which was still in fine spirit.

A roan which acted in much the same way, seemed to have difficulty in maintaining thirty-five miles an hour and soon showed signs of exhaustion and distress, running with its mouth open and frothing. This might seem understandable when one considers the thick-set build of this animal. Its appearance does not give the impression of speed as is the case with other antelopes.

Just why so many animals try to cross the road when running away from motor cars is interesting. It would seem that they try to keep one eye on the vehicle and this causes them to circle round as they pull ahead and eventually they cross the road. I have seen zebra acting in this way make 180 degree turns and end up running in the opposite direction from which they had started.

CHAPTER EIGHTEEN

Naturally, over the years as game warden of Wankie, I visited a number of other places where matters of common interest to all game wardens could be studied. Some of these trips were at the request of authorities other than my own head office, and others I arranged personally to further my knowledge of game habits.

One of the adjacent areas, which was of immense interest to me, was the lake Makarikari area where most of our migrant wildebeest population came from. This lake is just over the border in Botswana.

In November 1951, I made a quick trip to the lake. There had been exceptionally heavy rains in the Nata river catchment and the river had been in flood for several days. This meant that there would be some water in the lake. The rain was followed by two weeks of dry hot weather and there seemed little prospect of more rain for some time.

I was anxious to see the lake with some water in it and to see the bird life as well as the game there, particularly elephant, buffalo, and wildebeest; and to find out what numbers of these had made the move into Botswana now that the rains had broken.

The trip began at Nantwich in the north-west corner of the park, in a Land Rover with one African game scout. Neither of us had ever been to Makarikari before but we knew the route leading to it was well populated with Bushmen families and some Tswana tribespeople. Our direction took us south along the Mpande Mutenga road, which was little more than a track at that time but much more distinct than when I first used it in 1929.

The going was easy and pleasant, the sand firm and damp. New grass had shot up after the rains and everything was beginning to take on a springlike look. Some of the pans even contained a little water and almost all of them had a few pairs of knob-bill ducks on the surface.

We travelled south along the road to the Sibaninni pan and all went well until we turned west down the river into Botswana. Then we began to encounter some mud and were bogged a couple of times. We had no difficulty in picking up a guide, an old Bushman who had been to the lake several times to collect salt. He knew where a relative of his lived on a small stream running into the lake from the south. On the whole the surface was good and the Land Rover covered the ground with no trouble. We crossed the Nata river at a bridge at Sure and then travelled west along the south bank of the river. To my surprise our guide stopped us and said that the place where he collected salt was on the other side of the river and we would have to walk. This obviously could not be the lake, but I was interested in seeing what there was, and at the risk of having our belongings stolen by Bushmen or Tswana herdsmen (there were a number of cattle about), we left the Land Rover and walked across the river.

At our guide's suggestion we took with us, in addition to our rifle and all the ammunition, an axe, and a tyre lever to dig up the salt. The walk was not long, half an hour or so, but I saw many birds which were new to me including the handsome black korhaan, a much more noisy bird than the red-crested variety which is the common korhaan in Wankie. Our guide told us that there used to be some of these birds at Sibaninni on the border but they had all been snared. Apparently these birds are very fond of the gum of a certain acacia bush not very common at Sibaninni and, by setting snares around the few bushes there, the birds were easily cleaned up. I certainly had never seen the black kind at the pan or in that area.

Arriving at the salt deposit we were confronted by a fairly large pool of dark brown water rather like strong tea with, to my joy, half a dozen greater flamingoes standing in it. They took off at our approach and did not return. There was no sign of salt but the water was extremely salty. However, our old guide waded into the pool, feeling his way with his feet until he came to the edge of a hole in the bottom.

Here he said there were rocks of salt. He and my game scout worked away with the tyre lever for a few minutes and succeeded in breaking off a piece of rock salt about the size of a clenched fist. It was pure salt, like a block of ice.

In another half an hour he produced a piece about ten pounds in weight, which he gleefully informed us he would take back to his kraal, for it would keep his people in salt for about a year. They would be the envy of many. I questioned him about the flamingoes and he told me that he had only once before seen them and then they were in greater numbers.

When we got back to the Land Rover about three o'clock in the afternoon a big grey cloud had developed in the direction of the lake. It looked more like a veld fire than a rain cloud. This, our guide informed us, was smoke off the lake and it was a very bad sign as it would make sleeping near the lake uncomfortable. He was all for camping where we were until morning when the cloud would have gone. Furthermore, the water in the Nata river was drinkable, whereas the water in the lake, apart from being muddy, was salty. But I pushed on, knowing that we had eight gallons of fresh water with us, and I was interested to see what this mysterious cloud was.

Soon the track, which had been recently used by a donkey-drawn cart, led out of the bush into open country covered with coarse spiky grass. The cloud by this time was quite menacing and not far off. Soon we came within sight of the water. There in front of me were thousands, perhaps tens of thousands of flamingoes. To a keen bird man the sight was out of this world. The beauty of these birds as seen in even good illustrations was nothing to this, the real thing, and I stood entranced.

The grass ended abruptly on the edge of the lake and there was a pebbly beach of about fifty yards between the grass and the water. The beach proved to be hard and it was possible to drive along the shore. I climbed on to the roof of my vehicle and with the glasses had a good look round. This bird life was wonderful. Not only were there flamingoes, some in big masses and others in long lines evenly spaced off, but there were big concentrations of red-billed teal and numerous waders and plovers, all busily feeding in the shallows. Just how shallow the water was, surprised me. It looked deep but ducks and waders were standing on the bottom well over 300 yards from the shore. Flamingoes half a mile out were standing in water only about six inches deep. I could not see further than this as the haze was too thick. There were countless thousands of birds in the air, including many pelicans. Birds flying at only a few hundred feet above were hardly visible due to the thick haze.

The bird concentrations seemed thickest to the north, so it was in that direction that I turned. I soon found that the beach narrowed and there were treacherous soft patches. To get stuck in one of these would really present a problem as there were neither stones nor sticks with which to help ourselves out. I parked the Land Rover and walked, soon arriving at a sandy delta where the Nata river ran into the lake. Here there were hundreds of pelicans and some saddle-bill storks together with some terns. Evidently there were fish here, possibly coming down the river into the lake which, I gathered, had been very dry a month before. I returned to the transport as it was getting dark and found a level bare patch of ground on which we could camp for the night. Our guide had thoughtfully picked up a few pieces of dry wood with which to make a fire, or we would have been hard put to find enough to cook our meal.

Soon after dark a slight breeze sprang up and blew from the lake, bringing with it a thick fog which soon enveloped us, making everything damp and clammy. I was soon in bed and lay listening to the strange noises coming from the water. At intervals there would be great splashings and squawkings with the flapping of wings as flamingoes either took off or landed; but towards midnight all was quiet, as if the birds had either departed or gone to sleep.

It was an uncomfortable, hot, dark night and I was awake early when the birds seemed to come to life, too, as the noises from the lake increased in intensity. The morning was bright and clear. We could see for miles over the water where the flamingoes and ducks were still in sight, but the pelicans had gone.

I questioned our old guide about flamingo nests. He said he had seen dozens of eggs laid on the sand at the mouth of the river but, when asked if they were on any sort of mound, he was emphatic that the eggs were laid on flat ground. The eggs were pure white and each one laid singly, not in clutches. He had never seen a chick but his "broer," who lived not far away, knew the lake well and he would be able to tell us more about the nesting of these wonderful birds.

We set off south along the shore of the lake and came on the tracks of

185

the donkey cart again and followed it. This soon led us away from the water and into wooded country where we found a typical Bushmen settlement: little temporary grass shelters with no doors. We were greeted by three half-starved dogs, the only sign of life. Our guide called out a greeting and soon an elderly woman appeared from the surrounding grass. She recognised our old guide and, after greetings were called out, in no time two men appeared armed with spears. There was much talking and laughing with our guide and then they gathered round the Land Rover and we got down to business. Yes, they had seen flamingo nests. The eggs were laid on the top of a stone surrounded by water, a little grass on the top holding two eggs. They had seen young ones and had to chase them with dogs to catch them. They offered to take me to the place farther along the lake, but they were not sure if the recent water had reached to that place. They thought not, but the "stones" would still be there.

We started back to the lake with two Bushmen as guides and drove along the shore in a south-westerly direction. There were plenty of flamingo about, not only on the main lake but on the smaller pans near the shore line. The guides told us that the good rains had brought the birds and they had been there for about two weeks only. If the rains continued and the lake did not become too salty they expected the flamingoes to stay for two or three months, but one never knew, maybe they would soon depart, leaving only the ducks and the pelicans.

We saw little game, only an occasional wildebeest and one small herd of Cape hartebeest and some springbok. The guides assured us that to the north of the Nata there was plenty of game and they would find us some herds of wildebeest. Their disappointment was apparent when I said I only wanted to look at birds.

We had not gone many miles along the lake shore when the water receded from the grass and the beach increased in width. We had some difficulty in getting across a small stream which ran into the lake (the same one on which the Bushmen were camped) but we managed and went on. I kept as close to the water as I dared and spotted two humps far out in the lake. Through the glasses they looked like big water-tortoises, but they did not move. There were a few flamingoes near these odd-looking things and I waded out hopefully. Perhaps they were flamingo nests in the early stages of construction? About 300 yards out I came up to them and found, to my disappointment, that the humps were two big bubbles. The water was about two inches deep and the bottom of the lake was covered with a thick green scum about a quarter-of-an-inch thick. Gas had collected under this to form bubbles which stood about three inches high and about eighteen inches in diameter. When I pricked them with my finger they quickly subsided and sank.

The water was farther away from the grass verge now and I was soon motoring over the dry bottom of the lake, well away from both the grass and the water's edge. Our guides indicated a course leading away from the water. After a few miles a white object came into view, well out in the middle of the dry lake. It looked like a building or at least a tent about a mile away. We drove on and on and the object became smaller and smaller until at last it developed into a white lump of limestone about half the size of the Land Rover. This was desert mirage indeed. This rock, our guides assured us, was the site of flamingo nests. The birds nested on the top of it. Sure enough, there were some remnants of bird nests on the rock, about a dozen of them, but they were not flamingo nests, looking more like those of darters or cormorants. There was a water mark about half way up the stone showing the level to which the lake does rise on occasions.

Disappointed, I set course back from the rock towards the water's edge. I could see nothing but haze all around. There was no horizon and no sign of the water. When we eventually reached the water we were cut off by a wide stretch of slippery mud and slime, the same substance which had caused the bubbles. There were surprisingly few birds about.

When we arrived back where the water and the grass again formed the verge, we saw what looked like two huge dark objects a long way off out in the water and almost hidden in the haze. They were definitely moving, as they seemed to come together and then part again. Even through the glasses, I could not make out what they were. As we went on we came nearer the moving objects and I saw that they were ostriches. I don't think my game scout believes it even now, for they looked bigger than elephants, and what on earth ostriches would be doing out there in the middle of the lake in water about a foot deep, we just could not understand. But ostriches they were definitely, our guides agreed on that.

Desert mirage was indeed responsible for our confusion and odd discoveries in this part of the world; it was something I had never encountered before and of course my game scout was even more bewildered than I was. He, naturally, thought the area was full of ghosts and wanted to get out of it as soon as he could.

From under the canopy of the haze over the lake it was impossible to see what the weather was like. The sun was just a big copper disc, sometimes completely invisible. Once we though we heard thunder. As I most certainly did not want to get caught in rain in this treacherous country, I decided to make tracks for home. We dropped our guides on the lake shore where their stream joined it, and their joy when I presented them with a tin of bully beef each and half a crown was quite embarrassing.

On our way back up the north bank of the Nata, near Sibaninni, we saw a troop of impala, the only ones I have ever seen in the Nata area, and indeed the only ones I have ever heard of in those parts. There are, still today, none in the park at this point, although there is suitable country for them.

CHAPTER NINETEEN

ANOTHER one of my jaunts away from my own work in the park took me to the Linyanti (a part of the Chobi swamps) with a museum collecting team sponsored by the late Bernard Carp of Cape Town. The object of the trip was to try and collect a specimen of the red sitatunga, about which very little is known.

The party in two vehicles consisted of Bernard Carp, a genial Hollander of middle age, Reay Smithers, the Director of the National Museums, a taxidermist named White from Pretoria, and myself. For part of the time we were joined by a friend of Mr Smithers, who came specially for some fishing on the Chobi. Our first stop was at the Kasani rapids on the Chobi, just inside the Botswana border. We transported our camp kit and collecting gear across the Chobi just above the rapids by boat, camping on Impalila island in a delightful spot right on the river bank, with big shady trees and short green grass beside the rushing waters of the rapids.

My first task was to hunt for a Chobi bushbuck, which I did in the thick bush in the centre of the island where there are patches of wild sisal (*Sansieveria*). It was in these patches that the bushbuck were in the habit of lying up. I only discovered this after some hours of hunting near the water's edge of both the Chobi and the Zambezi, as I was working near the confluence of the two rivers. Failing to find anything other than a half-grown doe, which I did not want, we picked up the spoor of a pair and followed it along an elephant path right into the centre of the island. The spoor was not difficult to follow as the buck kept to the elephant paths, while when they did turn off into thick bush they soon came out on to another path. At intervals the bushbuck would lie down, but on each occasion they walked off at their leisure and did not appear to be disturbed. At last I spotted the ram standing watching me, just the head and back showing above a particularly high patch of sisal. I had no difficulty in putting a charge of buckshot into the animal's neck and he fell in his tracks. The doe gave me a chance of a shot but we had all we could manage, so I left her alone. I had two Africans with me, one a local guide and the other a Bushman tracker whom I had brought with me. We carried our quarry back to camp slung on a pole, well satisfied with my first day's hunting. While White busied himself with the preparation of the bushbuck for the museum, I turned my attention to a bit of fishing. With Reay Smithers and his friend I had some good sport fishing in the fast water just above the rapids where the water starts to break.

Tiger fish were on the bite and we soon had several each. The yellow bream (*Serranochromis robustus*) were not taking readily but we did land a few good ones. I had fished the Chobi before away back in 1933 when my wife and I and a friend of hers hired a barge paddled by fifteen Lozi paddlers under the command of a boss boy named Ukaleli, also a Lozi. There were few motor boats in those days on the Zambezi and travel was slow but very enjoyable. There was also plenty of time to study the birds, and my wife's friend, Molly Bromley, amused herself modelling a head of our *Capita Ukaleli* in the clay she collected from the river bank. The likeness was so good that even the Lozi paddlers could recognise it. The beauty of that early trip cannot be repeated to-day. The river was then a highway for trade of all the goods that come out of the swamps, and the people of the river were unsophisticated and friendly. We saw much of interest gone for ever now; store goods and fast river launches having brought civilization to the area.

It was on the first day out that I caught the biggest yellow bream I have ever recorded. We were nearing the Chobi rapids and the paddlers were tiring. The pace of the barge had slowed down to a speed at which I could comfortably troll with a big spoon. I had caught several nice tiger fish when I got a bite which was rather different. It should be pointed out that in those days I was a novice at Zambezi fishing and I thought I had hooked into a tiger which had gone into a bunch of weed. There was a heavy drag on the line. Occasionally the fish would give a bit of a pull. I had to give a little line but the fight was, as I thought, hampered by weed. The girls were hanging over the side, all excitement, and to my surprise when I got the fish up to the boat at last there were cries of *Membwe* from the paddlers, and a great yellow bream came to the surface. It had put up a very poor fight but everyone in the boat was delighted. This bream weighed just on eleven pounds. When hung up its great belly sagged as if it were either full of spawn or had just consumed a big feed. When opened up it proved to be a male fish with nothing in its stomach. The bulge was caused by two big layers of fat. The paddlers seized this with glee as, added to tiger fish, bream evidently improves the flavour. The "tigers" were so truculent that in a few days we had lost all our big spoons and found that on small ones we only caught small tigers. If we got a big one the hook would not hold it. We improvised big spoons, using a big hook and a piece of jam tin which seemed just as effective as the real thing. All the tigers were interested in were the glittering objects in the water.

But to return to my second visit to the Chobi. By then I had much better tackle and had gained a lot of experience with tigers. In spite of this we did not catch as many fish; in fact, the fishing was not nearly so good. Over the years there had been a development in the commercial fishing by Africans using gill nets and fish traps in the rapids. Added to this the Chobi rapids were by now easily accessible and much patronised by anglers. This may have accounted for the falling off in the fishing. I shall always look back to fishing in the Chobi–Zambezi in those good old days.

After a couple of very enjoyable days at the Kasani rapids we moved on to Linyanti, taking our trucks across the Chobi at Gomo by means of a very rickety pontoon. We called in on the District Administrator, the late Major French Trollope at Katimamolilo on the Zambezi. After completing the necessary formalities there – for we were now on the Zambezi and in South West Africa – we again crossed the sandy strip of country between the Zambezi and the Chobi. Linyanti proved to be an enchanting place, very flat with big ant-heaps covered with bush and tall trees. The swamp, which we could see from our camp, appeared to be just one huge extent of reeds about ten feet high, extending for miles without a break. I thought of some of those "early-day-men" who had reached this spot, Livingstone and his fellow travellers, unprotected from malaria, savages, and all the rest; and here we were safe from all these things travelling in their wake – men who had opened up Africa to the world.

We were told that sitatunga were plentiful and that every now and again a red one turned up. The local Africans hunted them fairly consistently with muzzle loaders and we had no difficulty in finding skins in the kraals. At our request an old man produced the skin of a red one. It was no use as a museum specimen but was, nevertheless, a valuable acquisition and a good start to our collection.

The local inhabitants assured us that the sitatunga lived in the swamp among the reeds in water about knee deep, but at night they came out on to the grassy plains and could sometimes be found in the open in the early morning.

The first night, Bernard Carp and I went out with a spotlight to try and pick up a sitatunga near the edge of the reeds. We found that in most parts there was a stretch of water up to 200 yards wide separating the reeds from the dry land and we soon picked up eyes of some animals out in the water. We went towards them but before we got near they disappeared into the reeds. From the numbers, we concluded they were lechwe and not sitatunga. We saw a few single animals but these too retreated before we got near enough to identify them. We had not learned to walk quietly enough in shallow water.

The next day I set off with a local guide and my own Bushman into the swamp. The guide lead us up to a deep channel about fifty yards wide where it was clear of reeds. The water, to my surprise, was flowing west when I had expected it to be running to the east, towards the Zambezi, if it were moving at all. Once over this river by a dugout, we were really in the swamp, surrounded by a dense curtain of reeds with visibility limited to about ten yards. Our guide explained that this was the time of day when the sitatunga would be lying up on ant-heaps and that everything depended upon absolute quiet. If the water was up to our waists it was easy to keep quiet, but with water only up to our knees care had to be taken to withdraw the foot carefully and put it back into the water equally silently.

We tried to walk quietly but our guide shook his head and indicated that we were making too much noise. He demonstrated, and with his toes pointed down, he slowly took his foot out of the water and moved it forward so that the drips of water made no sound. It was easier to place the foot back into the water quietly than to take it out. Another snag which we had to learn to avoid was dead reeds which were rotten and noisily snapped off at a touch. These were mostly lying horizontally, some floating on the water. They were best avoided, for any attempt to move them invariably resulted in a slight splash.

We were unfortunate in that there was no wind blowing, for without any noise created by the wind in the reeds the sitatunga could hear us approaching long before we could hope to see them. Our only hope of a sight was a very quiet approach. After about half an hour of "quiet approach" practice, our guide led us off along a small game trail in water about six inches deep. The going was painfully slow and our chances of getting a shot seemed slim indeed. Up to then I had not found a spot where I could see a buck at more than ten to fifteen yards, and for three of us to approach quietly enough to be undetected at that range seemed out of the question. Of course, we had to hunt up-wind as well. I soon realised, too, that my gun had to be kept pointing forward. Any attempt to lower it from the shoulder invariably resulted in it getting tangled with a reed, usually a dried one which snapped off with a noise like a bursting balloon.

Everything in the swamp was extremely quiet. There were a few reed warblers calling, and now and again I heard the drumming of an Ethopian snipe. Our guide stopped at frequent intervals and listened intently, but at first I had no idea what he was listening for. I found out later that he was listening for the noises we ourselves were trying not to make. He evidently expected to be able to hear a buck moving through the water by an occasional pop of a breaking reed or a slight splash. For a long time we neither heard nor saw anything – then our guide indicated that we must be even more quiet and I saw a gap in the otherwise complete coverage of white plumes on reed tops. It was this gap which we were approaching. Slowly the gap in the reeds developed into an ant-heap rising above the water, devoid of reeds. In fact, there was little vegetation on it, as when we walked on to it we found it a mass of sitatunga spoor. There was little fresh spoor, but there were several marks where an animal had been lying down in the damp earth.

Not a word was spoken, even in a whisper, but our guide indicated that there would be other ant-heaps about. After a brief rest, we set off along a game trail again and within a hundred yards were able to make out the gap in the reeds indicating another patch of dry land. This, too, was approached at less than a snail's pace but we saw nothing on it. There was, however, fresh spoor, while some bubbles in the water pointed to the hasty departure of a buck at our approach.

When this procedure had gone on for several hours, our guide indicated that he could hear an animal moving about, pointing in the direction of the sound. I could hear nothing. Little sounds like this are beyond me, due possibly to the use of heavy calibre rifles or from taking too much quinine over long periods to guard against malaria.

We did not approach the source of the sound, but tried to determine the direction in which it was moving and to intercept or get ahead of the creature making it. Had I been able to hear the sounds, I would have gone on alone but, as it was, I had to keep with the guide. After about twenty minutes of this the guide stopped for a long spell and then indicated that the animal had gone.

About four o'clock we were approaching an ant-heap, when the guide held out his hand and indicated that an animal was moving about to our left. He listened and then whispered that it was a herd of lechwe. Just to break the monotony I indicated that we should go for them and our guide abandoned much of his caution, retraced his steps, and after going back for one hundred yards or so, turned, took up a position off our track and waited. Sure enough, I soon heard the snapping of reeds and saw the plume on top of a reed move. We were standing in water up to our waists. Then I saw a long low creature moving silently through the water towards us. It came up to within a few yards and then stopped. Once it stopped it was quite invisible but, as it turned round, I saw that it was a lechwe doe. It had evidently seen us, for it swung quickly away and we could then hear several others also making off.

That ended the day's hunt. We made tracks back to the dugout we had used to cross the river in the morning. By the time we reached it I was extremely weary, for I had been on my feet for nine hours – bar one short rest of about ten minutes on an ant-heap. I was not thirsty, but how I wanted a cup of tea!

The next day we tried another locality. This did not necessitate the crossing of the river and we found the ant-heaps were bigger and sometimes in groups connected to each other by strips of exposed land. There was a great deal of spoor but most of it was of lechwe. The sitatunga is noted for its long hooves which are sometimes as much as six inches in length. This is a development caused by living in marshy ground. The long splayed-out hoof enables the animal to walk on soft mud and even on floating vegetation like the jacana. Lechwe, too, in this locality, had grown long hooves, not quite as long as those of the sitatunga, but much longer than those of the same species which live on firm ground.

During the day's hunt we came upon so many lechwe and they created such a disturbance when they ran off, that it was not surprising that we saw no sitatunga. I was back in camp in the early afternoon.

Our next hunt was in the same area as we had hunted the first day. When we crossed the river in the dugout I was surprised to notice that the water was running strongly in the opposite direction to that in which I had first seen it. The water lilies with six-foot stems were extended well off to one side and in some cases the leaves were submerged and vibrating like fishing spoons.

We had not gone far when we came across the spoor of a lion on one of the ant-heaps. The guide assured me that it must have swum across a wide stretch of water, as the area was surrounded completely by deep water. Soon we came on more lion spoor; there seemed to be several lions, some of them big cubs. This disturbed our guide. He obviously did not relish stalking quietly up to an island only to find that it was occupied by lions. His eyes were continually scanning the little patch of sky we could see through the tops of the reeds in search of vultures which could indicate a kill and an area to be avoided. He implored me not to shoot if we did come across the lions, as it was a particularly dangerous place in which to hunt a wounded lion. I agreed, as I had no intention of shooting a lion, partly because I did not need a specimen and partly because the shot would disturb the sitatunga for miles around, sending them off the ant-heaps into the reeds.

We were stalking quietly towards an ant-heap when my foot touched a piece of wood. A sunken log about four inches thick and eight feet long moved slightly. The guide instantly leapt off to one side and dashed away for several yards. He thought that the moving object was a crocodile. I had seen very little sign of these and I was somewhat surprised at his reaction to the movement and his obvious fear of crocs. This piece of wood was the first sign of timber I had seen in the swamp and when asked how it got there the guide said that it had been used to set snares. This, too, surprised me as we had seen no sign of snaring until then, although it seemed an ideal place in which to snare both lechwe and sitatunga.

Not long after this we came upon a hippo run. This was in water about eighteen inches deep, like a narrow canal, when the water was deeper and the reeds had been pushed aside. With a reed we tested the depth and found it to be about five feet. We wandered along the hippo track until eventually we found a shallow part and were able to cross. The next ant-heap we approached had fresh lion spoor on it and our guide expressed the opinion that the area had been so disturbed that we were unlikely to find any sitatunga out of the reeds that day. We, therefore, made tracks towards camp. We had gone about a mile when we passed two ant-heaps with no lion spoor on them. Some sitatunga had just recently left them. We could see the trail of bubbles in the shallow water which they left behind. Resuming our quiet approach, when about fifteen yards from the next ant-heap, I could just see through the dense cover, a small brown patch. It could have been part of the ant-heap. When I moved a yard or two to one side I could see a distinct red patch. This certainly was not part of the ant-heap. I decided to fire at it, even though I could not see what part of the animal it was.

I was using a 12-bore pump shot gun with 3A shot, being ready to fire a second shot instantly if the animal bounded away. At the shot, however, there was no movement, but the patch had disappeared. I advanced cautiously and, on reaching the ant-heap, I was delighted to find a young red sitatunga lying dead and right beside it another young one about the same size, but of the usual dark brown colour. It was disappointing that I had not got a fully-grown animal or that I had not seen a sign of the parents. But at least I had established that there were red sitatunga and that they consorted with the ordinary brown variety.

Next day Bernard Carp was lucky enough to surprise a young sitatunga ram near the edge of the swamp. This he bagged, so we had brought our collection of specimens to three. During his hunt Carp had walked on to an eight-foot crocodile and shot it at very close range.

We now had all the sitatunga specimens we wanted so I turned my attention to birds and other small mammals for a few days. Although my legs were raw and sore with the long immersion in the brackish water and the continual rubbing against the reeds, it had been an enjoyable trip and so different from the type of hunting I had become used to.

Before we packed I collected, in addition to numerous birds, some otters and two buffalo bulls.

On the way back we were delayed for a short time at the pontoon over the Chobi, as it was in use bringing a rickety old truck across and, when it arrived on our side, I was surprised to find on it the parson who had christened my second son, Gerald. He was travelling complete with wife, church (organ and all), going to give services to some of the most outlandish places in Africa. While we were waiting to cross we watched a wonderful succession of the biggest whirlwinds I have ever seen. The open flats had been recently burned off and these huge whirling turmoils carried a very dense cloud of dust thousands of feet up into the sky. At times there were five or six of them going at once. As they disappeared into the distance, new ones would form at intervals of about five minutes.

CHAPTER TWENTY

THERE are some strange animals in Wankie National Park, not seen by visitors and in some cases only recorded once or twice in all my years of service there.

One of the most interesting of these is, perhaps, about the smallest mammal in the world. The pygmy mouse (*Mus minutoides*). This little mouse is only about three inches long including the tail. It is claimed that the smallest mammal is a mouse which occurs in Russia, but *Mus minutoides* must be a very close second.

Another is the Angola hedgehog which has not yet been recognised as a Rhodesian species. We found ours living near the house. The fox terriers were barking at something under a dead log. I suspected a snake, but when we moved the log we found a ball of black and white spines. When the hedgehog was curled up all the spikes pointed in different directions and were just a mixture of black and white. But when it was uncurled and walking about, the white spines formed into stripes longitudinally along the otherwise black body, and it had a fringe of black and white spines along the forehead. At the slightest indication of alarm this frontal flap was quickly flicked down and covered the face.

We kept Reggie (as we called him) for several months and he became quite tame. He would sleep under the settee during the day and come out at night for a feed of grasshoppers or white ants. When we felt we had learned all about him we gave him his freedom. The museum has no specimen, but we could not bring ourselves to kill him merely to make a permanent record of the occurrence of *Angola frontalis* at Wankie.

Over the years, I have recorded odd incidents and fragments of information which are still not explained conclusively. No doubt my successors at Wankie will have the opportunity to give some explanations of these matters, when, as time goes on, they have better facilities for dispatching specimens for examination. I had no means of sending anything except by post, and this was no use for getting information on mammals, and so on. Preserving in spirit was possible but not acceptable to the postal people. Botanical specimens were easy and we sent in some interesting ones over the years. One such unsolved mystery comes to mind.

I had often noticed that the oxen at Robins would have a streak of blood on the lower neck or shoulder and wondered what could have caused it. I examined several animals but could find no puncture in the skin or any other cause for the blood. The herd-boy maintained that it was an engorged tick that had been killed in some way that produced the blood streaks.

One night I was camped on Jambili pan and was lying awake as the horse and mules were very restless. Then a bat hovered above my bed and actually settled on my blankets. It stayed there for several seconds, and may have stayed longer had I not moved to try and get a better look at it in the bright moonlight.

The next morning the horse had just the same streak of blood on his neck as I had seen on the oxen at Robins. Could it have been caused by the bat? According to the books there are no vampire bats in Africa.

Perhaps one of the most remarkable birds in Wankie National Park, and the bird most closely associated with animals, is the oxpecker. There are two varieties, the red-billed oxpecker (*Buphagus erythrorhynchus*) and the yellow-billed oxpecker (*B. africanus*), both of which occur in Wankie, the latter being the more common. They are so common that the average visitor soon loses interest in them, accepting them as just part of the life of the park.

Unlike most other birds, their life is spent on animals. They seem to feed exclusively on their hosts, as I have never seen an oxpecker feed on anything other than what they find on the hide of the animal they choose to ride about on; although if kept in captivity they will eat grasshoppers and white ants. One which we kept as a pet for some months, after we found it injured and unable to fly, came to an untimely end by eating flies which had been sprayed with D.D.T.

This bird was particularly adept at catching flies but did not show any great interest in ticks, although it would eat them. It loved to perch on the back of one's neck and run its beak through the hair at the back of the head with a scraping movement – which could be quite painful. It reserved this treatment for the men and did not indulge in it with the women members of the household. Its normal feeding place was a donkey which we used to tether in the garden and put our oxpecker pet on it for the day.

In the wild state these birds seem to favour giraffe and buffalo but they are a common sight on other animals including eland, sable, roan, kudu, warthog, impala, wildebeest and sometimes on steenbok and duiker. Occasionally I have seen them on lions and once on an elephant. The bird was sitting well back on the hind quarters and seemed to be resting and not feeding. I should imagine that feeding on an elephant would be rather precarious, as if within reach of the trunk it would be likely to come to harm. Even the frequent applications of dust and sand would make life for an oxpecker rather trying. These birds are well known for their habit of feeding on rhino and they frequent hippo, too, when these animals are out of the water.

Just how much of their lives are spent actually on the host animals is difficult to say, as one does see them perched on trees. I think that, for the most part, they roost in trees at night but on occasions they do spend the night on their hosts. I have watched thousands of buffalo and giraffe come to drink in the moonlight, but only once did I see an oxpecker on a giraffe after dark. It was perched on the shoulder and seemed as if it had settled down for the night.

Oxpeckers ride to the water on animals. When nearing the water's edge they fly off, and drink sitting on the ground, but it is not uncommon to see them run down the legs of the drinking animals which stand in the water and have their drink without leaving their perch. I have also noted them leaving their host and indulging in a dust bath but, if their host moves away, they abandon the dust bath immediately.

It frequently happens that when an animal (a giraffe in particular) starts to drink, tick birds will run down the neck and enter the animal's ear, evidently in search of ear ticks or wax. The moment the giraffe stops drinking it shakes its head and out comes the oxpecker and makes no attempt to enter the ear again until the giraffe's head is immobilised when drinking. Evidently, the inside of the ear provides some excellent food, but the birds are not welcome there. The same thing applies to buffalo.

On the whole, animals seem to tolerate the attentions of the ox-pecker rather than welcome them. Any open sore on an animal is the focus of attention by the birds, and they will peck off the scab and even pick at the raw flesh and, I suspect, eat the blood. Once I saw a flight of oxpeckers alight on a fresh lion kill as I was approaching it after the lions had been driven off. I stopped my approach to see what the birds were doing, but I was a little too close for their comfort and they took off again and disappeared.

Like starlings, they nest in holes in trees, and their favourite nesting site at Wankie is in the hollow bark of the camel thorn trees. The bark of this tree is so durable that after a tree has died – due to being ring-barked by elephant or some other cause – the sap wood rots away far quicker than the bark and this is left as a sort of sleeve sus-pended by the hard heart wood. The birds block up the lower part of this cavity, usually with dry elephant dung, and make a snug nest on it.

Game has been introduced to McIlwaine National Park from Wankie, but there were no oxpeckers there. They used to occur in this area but, no doubt, extensive cattle dipping has accounted for their disap-pearance. The game were noticeably pestered by flies and ticks so, as a corrective measure, we tried to introduce some oxpeckers from Wankie. Catching them did not prove difficult. The method used was to spread a net over a donkey and attach to the net numerous small nooses made of horse hair. When the tick birds alighted on the donkey and started moving about they became entangled in the nooses.

Oxpeckers took to life in a cage quite well and would eat grass-hoppers, flies and minced meat. We released them in sight of the game at McIlwaine and they took to the animals right away. The giraffe did not seem to mind them and, beyond shaking their heads when the birds settled, took no further notice; but the zebra were terrified and galloped off wildly and even rolled on their backs to get rid of the birds.

This experiment with oxpeckers was not a success, for eight of the nine birds released disappeared within a fortnight and the lone bird only remained a week longer.

Late in September 1935, before any artificial water supplies had been developed, I was camped about a quarter of a mile from Shapi pan, which still contained a little water, when, shortly after sunrise, I heard a commotion. On investigating, I found that the noise was being made by doves coming to drink in thousands. Every now and again they would all fly up at once with a roar of wing, which could be heard clearly at the camp.

I decided to try and estimate how many doves were concentrated on this last little water supply. To do this, I concealed myself in a tree overlooking the water, where my presence would not disturb the birds. I had hardly settled down to watch when the doves began coming in again after the disturbance I had created. First, I determined the average time a bird spent on the ground. By timing fifty individuals I arrived at a figure of fifteen seconds. Next, I counted the number of birds on the ground at any one time, and the average of fifty counts was 250 birds. There were breaks in the stream coming to drink when the appearance of a hawk scared them off but, as often as not, they scared themselves for no apparent reason.

The pressure seemed to be from shortly before sunrise at about 5.45 a.m. to about 7.45 a.m., and during that time the total of breaks amounted to about ten minutes. A mathematical calculation gave the number of 110,000 doves drinking there on that morning. How many came to the water twice (due to being scared off) is impossible to say, but there was a tendency for the pressure to be greater when they started to come in again after a scare. The pan was only deserted for about a minute after a false alarm, and longer if there was a hawk about – which occurred only twice during my observations. The doves coming to drink were all Cape ring doves (*Afropelia capicola*). Although Wankie Game Reserve has a very varied number of doves on the whole, on this particular morning only one type was present; while there were no sand grouse and only a few glossy starlings and Meyer's parrots.

Heavy concentrations of sand grouse, the double-banded variety, coming in to drink in the evenings during the hot weather at the end of the dry season, are remarkable; but I was never able to count them as, by the time they came, it was too dark to see them on the ground. They have a habit of congregating near the water and not actually drinking. They may spend as much as ten minutes or more just sitting around before they drink. During this time there is a continuous noise of soft chattering, as if they were discussing the events of their day. At a given signal, not apparent to humans, they all run down to the pan's edge, drink for a couple of seconds and then fly swiftly off in a cloud, and by this time it is difficult to see unless one sits in a position with the evening sky behind the birds. But with the doves, this is not the case. They seem more intent on having their drink and being off again out of the danger zone.

The spotted or variegated sand grouse are more like doves in their habits. They come to water about 10 a.m. and spend little time on the ground. They are not very common at Wankie, but twenty or thirty can be seen coming to drink at Nehimba or Shakawanki, if one happens to be at these pans at the correct time.

The yellow-throated sand grouse sometimes occur at Wankie, but only during the wet weather when they may be seen on the open glades, wandering about in the short grass like domestic pigeons or flying past in flights like ducks.

The birds of Wankie fall into three main groups. Those to the south of the watershed comprise birds of the Kalahari; those to the north are the birds of the Zambezi valley; then there are the migrants who spend only a short part of the year in the reserve. The Kalahari birds are at the eastern extremity of their range and the Zambezi birds at the western limit of their range. There is some overlapping among these two groups. The double-banded sand grouse and the Cape ring dove are types which occur in both areas. The yellow-throated and spotted sand grouse, do not occur generally north of the watershed.

The numerous pans attract great numbers of ducks and waders during good rainy seasons, the most notable being the knob bill duck, fulous duck, red bill teal, pochards, pygmy geese, spurwing geese, and an occasional Cape wigeon and maccoa duck.

Some of them breed in the reserve in favourable seasons, notably the knob bill duck, which breeds in hollow trees away from the water and prefers the small pans. The ducklings walk from the nest site to the water and from one pan to another, the mother bird flying above them, calling as they proceed along the elephant paths which lead from one pan to another. Teal and spurwing geese nest at the larger pans on ant-hills surrounded with water and well covered with vegetation.

My sons and I used to have great fun catching and ringing young duck, and we had one remarkable recovery, a teal ringed at Wankie was shot in Angola. It must have travelled to the western edge of its range during our dry season.

The catching and ringing of ducks was an interesting game. What we did was to seek out a brood which were well advanced but still unable to fly, and this was usually about March when the pans were full. At our approach the parent birds would take off and the young ones would dive under water. We then took up strategic positions and, whenever a bird came to the surface for air, one of us would rush at it and force it to dive again. In this way we would tire them out and, when exhausted, they would hide under water lily leaves or other weeds with only their heads above water. We could then approach close enough to make a grab at them and, together with a bunch of weeds, bring them to the surface.

This game was not without hazards. On one occasion, when accompanied by my cousin, Bill Wragg, we had got a number of young red bill teal exhausted and were watching for the heads to appear when Bill asked me to come and have a look at a duck he had stalked, as he did not like the look of it. I went over and joined him where, sure enough, the head which was partly concealed below some water weeds was that of a cobra, and a big one at that. How we had not come in contact with the snake in our dashing about the pan I do not know, for there did not seem to be a yard of the pan (a small one) which we had not covered and there was not a bunch of weeds anywhere we had not examined.

When tired out, the teal and knob bill ducklings will often leave the water and sneak away into the grass and hide. We countered this by keeping a sharp lookout on the edge of the water for any sign of a ripple as a bird left the water, and then watched for any movement in the grass. Immediately this happened, we would be after the bird. My young sons became very expert at this task and we found we could catch and ring up to one hundred birds each season.

FINALE

IT was never my intention to end my career in an executive post at the top of the tree and it came as a bit of shock and disappointment when, in 1961, after thirty-four years at Wankie and near pensionable age, I received orders to pack up and move to Salisbury.

I had never lived in a town, or even in a village for that matter, for the past thirty-eight years. My wife, too, had become a confirmed wilderness dweller after thirty years with me at Wankie in the little cottage we had come to love so well. We both dreaded the move into the city. It was a heart-rending experience to have to find homes for our dogs and cats. The Siamese, Katie Cat, whom we knew was expecting a family just about the time we were due in Salisbury, and our old parrot, a Congo grey, who was a part of the establishment, we decided we could not part with and would have to go with us.

The day of departure arrived. The pantechnicon did not look big enought to hold all the furniture and junk we wanted to take with us, and indeed it was not. We had to dispose of some, and some we just gave away. On arrival in Salisbury by car, complete with Katie Cat and Polly (fortunately our sons were away at school), we stayed for a few days with good friends of ours who, like ourselves, had spent many years in the bush under primitive conditions on tsetse fly research. Our days with them were spent flat-hunting, and when we found something more or less suitable we were ready for the pantechnicon again, which arrived three days after we did; and we set about settling ourselves in our new home.

We went about it in a very half-hearted way as we both knew it would not do, but said nothing to each other. Katie Cat relieved the tension by announcing that she wanted her sheepskin bed unpacked immediately or else she would put her babies in my wife's best hat. We settled her in a cupboard while the removal men moved things round. My wife said she found it hard to keep good tempered and I wondered if I could take it.

Never in my wildest dreams or nightmares had I thought it would come to this. It had always been my intention when I reached retiring age in five years' time to move on to a small farm, and with the herd of indicator cattle I had at Wankie, set up farming on a small scale. But this life in a flat was the last word : people on either side of us and above us; an endless stream of hawkers all day trying to gain our custom for the supply of vegetables, fruit, bread and cakes, and hundreds of other items for which we had no use. I suppose we looked like country bumpkins and were considered fair game.

Office at 8 a.m. in a collar and tie daily was a penalty indeed, for one who had owned only one town suit in twenty years, and worn khaki shorts and shirts all his life. Of course, I paid periodical visits to the various parks, including Wankie, and when I returned from one or other of these trips I noticed that my wife was even more glad to see me than in the old days when I had to leave her in our own home in the wilds for, sometimes, two weeks at a time.

I had no qualms about handing over my post at Wankie to Bruce Austin who had been with me over ten years and knew the working of the park and all its problems, as well as having sound ideas of his own. By the time I came to Salisbury, Wankie had reached the stage when I had a staff of eight to manage affairs without me, and it was my intention to spend the last five years doing research in the field and finding out something about the problems for which we had not discovered the answers; such as overstocking and its effect on the game generally and on vegetation. Indeed, these matters loomed ahead menacingly and a solution was so urgent that soon after I took up my new post at head office, trained scientific staff were recruited to study and deal with them.

Life in a flat soon got us both down. We felt forced to buy a home in the suburbs. So we spent the evenings motoring around the outskirts of Salisbury inspecting many of the houses that were for sale and, finally, settling for one which was large enough and stood on an acre of ground. When we moved into this house we felt that we had escaped from prison. I could actually walk around the garden, which was all our own, one whole acre of it. I could walk and look over every square foot of my garden in five minutes.

INDEX

REPORT ON WANKIE GAME RESERVE
October, 1928 - March, 1930

I have the honour to forward herewith my report on the Wankie Game Reserve up to the end of the year ending 31st March 1930.

WORK DONE:
I arrived and commenced duty at the end of October, 1928. The first step taken was to inspect the water supply in the Reserve. After the severe drought, there was some doubt as to whether any water existed and I proceeded at once to investigate.

Only at "Giraffe Spring" did we find water at a depth of four feet. Ngwashla, which is the largest pan in the Reserve, proved to have held water longer than any other. It still contained three feet of thick mud. Elephant had visited this pan the previous night in search of water and two Sable had been bogged in an endeavour to obtain the last drop of existing water. All other pans were tested to ascertain whether there was water below the surface, but in each case there proved to be two to three feet of black, hard silt; below this, a clay seal which, in every case, proved damp, but no water was present.

Nothing could be done in the Reserve until such time as rain had fallen and provided water.

The first patrol into the Reserve was done on foot late in November and a later patrol was done by motor in December. Further walking patrols to Ngwashla were done in January.

Two horses were provided for transport and arrived here on the 28th December but, unfortunately, could not be used until February when saddlery arrived. One horse had died in the meantime from horse-sickness, thus all provisions had to be carried by natives until the arrival of two pack mules in July. By this time, only the larger pans contained water and I have, consequently, not been able to do any patrols in the very dry parts of the Reserve.

Approximately 1,800 miles have been covered in patrols during the period.

POACHING

No extensive poaching was done in the Reserve, but petty poaching went on to an extent along the railway and at the Rhodesia Native Timber Company Stations. This proved difficult to check owing to railway farms not being included in the Reserve, and poachers were using these as a shield. Two cases were handed over to the Police, but in each the case was difficult owing to the proximity of open ground. One person was fined £3 for having shot an Eland. On the whole, however, I am pleased to state that the Reserve has been remarkably free from this menace.

GAME CATCHING

A careful check was kept on game catchers, who were authorised to capture game on private land adjoining the Reserve. Permission was also granted for the capture of game on a railway farm, but this was, however, not used.

After visiting the General Manager of the Rhodesia Railways, and obtaining his sanction to protect all game on railway farms adjoining the Reserve, the matter was handed over to my Chief, and the farms in question have now been closed.

Permission was also obtained for myself and my natives to use the railway strip for patrol purposes between Dett and Kennedy.

NATIVE RANGERS

Great difficulty has been experienced in obtaining a competent staff of native rangers. Seven are now employed and these patrol all the railway frontage and as far along the south boundary as they can travel in a day. Each native visits water supplies within his reach as often as possible. The duties of these rangers are to report any signs of poaching or persons in the Reserve and general movements of game along their respective beats.

A considerable amount of time was lost by rangers drawing rations from the main camp and arrangements have been made by which they draw 15/- per month and supply their own food. Each native has to report once a month.

LABOUR

Bushmen are employed as guides, but owing to my not being allowed to shoot any game in the Reserve, I have not been able to obtain a really competent guide. Only the older bushmen, who have actually lived in this part of the country or have accompanied hunters, are acquainted with the Reserve.

213

WATER SUPPLY

The water supply in the Reserve is far from good, and up to the present, no steps have been taken to improve it. Practically all the water supplies in the Reserve are on the fringe of the Kalahari Sand, or, in other words, on the watershed.

There are three distinct types of water supply found in the Reserve, namely :-
(a) Pans
(b) Surface waters
(c) Rivers

Of the latter, there are only two - the Dedeema and Dolilo in the north portion of the Reserve which can be termed "permanent water."

Seven surface waters are known to me, and all are permanent and do not give out during the dry season, although in some of them, the water level varies considerably, but may never actually show on the surface. Giraffe Spring, for instance, never has water on the surface, but it can be found at a depth of 2 to 4 feet. Dopi on '"Balcarris" has a little water on the surface at the end of the wet season, but this soon dries up and the level of the water recedes to approximately six feet below the surface at the end of the dry season.

The pans are entirely dependent on drainage for their supply of water and although they may hold out throughout the dry season in a normal year, they cannot be termed "permanent water". The water in these pans becomes very foul towards the end of the year.

THE RIVERS

The Dedeema and the Dolilo form good watering places for the game, but I cannot state definitely what length of water course actually exists in the Reserve, as I am not certain where these rivers cross the boundary of Deka Ranch, but I am confident that each of these rivers start in the Reserve. They appear to have been much frequented by game towards the end of 1928 and a very fair number of elephant visited this water supply during the dry months of 1929. A large portion of the water in these rivers contain salts which make it unfit for human consumption, but this appears to be an attraction to some types of game.

214

The Lukosi River is of interest, as the water is present in fairly good quantities at the source, but owing to the amount of sand in the river bed it is of little use to game. This water may be permanent, but owing to the depth of the sand it is difficult to be certain. A number of Elephant, Buffalo and Giraffe drink at this place as long as water lasts and Elephant dig considerable holes in the sand to obtain water.

The Sinamatela River contains a better supply, but it is not frequented much by game. The Inyantue River does not contain any water, other than what is held up in the railway dam. This, unfortunately, burst in January, 1929, and only holds water up to September, but nevertheless affords a drinking place for a fairly large herd of Elephant while it lasts.

THE PANS
All the pans in the Reserve are found on the watershed - being formed by water draining into depressions where, in time, a clay seal has been formed by decaying vegetable matter making these pans watertight. Game of all kinds appear to favour these drinking places so long as they last and it is only when the water becomes very low and foul that they resort to the more permanent water supplies. Some of these pans are very extensive, covering approximately one acre, and have a depth of ten feet in some cases. Not all this is lined with a clay seal, however, and the pans soon dry up after the rains until all the water is standing on the clay. After that, the water stands well and in many cases will hold water throughout the year after a rainfall of about 25 inches.

The rainfall at Dett, as registered by the Stationmaster, is 27,19 inches for this season, but I do not think that the south and west portion of the Reserve have had quite that amount. The following pans held water throughout 1929 :-

Ngwashla had four feet of water at the beginning of the rains.

Heatley's Pan, Mtoa, Tshebema, Makaclau and a pan on Balcarris named Nyamandhlovu also contained water, and I should estimate that of these only Heatley's Pan, Mtoa, Makaclau and Ngwashla will hold water throughout this year.

LEECHES IN WATER
Some of the pans are seriously affected by leeches. These are particularly numerous at Ngwashla. So much so, that elephant avoided this pan until late in the season.

215

BOUNDARIES OF THE RESERVE

The boundaries of the Reserve are, on the whole, very difficult to pick up. The south boundary from Old Ngamo runs almost entirely through waterless Sinanga and is most difficult to patrol. The western boundary or Panda-ma-tenka road is also very indistinct south of Tamatsatsa. The north boundary borders almost entirely on private land and only a very few of the boundary lines are cut, making the beacons very difficult to find. The eastern boundary was also very complicated before the railway farms were included in the protected area, and could be treated as part of the Reserve.

GAME

The Reserve is, on the whole, well stocked with game. The following animals occur :-
Elephant, Giraffe, Eland, Sable, Roan, Koodoo, Gemsbuck, Waterbuck, Bushbuck, Reedbuck, Impala, Duiker, Steinbuck, Sharpe's Steinbuck, Klipspringer, Zebra, Warthog, Ostrich, and Tsessebe.

Rhinoceros are doubtful, and so also are Wildebeest. Some signs of Rhino were seen at Dedeema and also at Masuma, (headwaters of Lukosi) in the early part of the dry season, but no trace of them could be found towards the end of the season, and it is possible they were only visitors to the Reserve during the rains. A small herd of Wildebeest were seen at Ngwashla on my first visit, but I have seen no sign of them since that time. A small herd was seen on the east of the line near Kennedy during April, and since then a number have been shot west of Intundhla, which may be the same herd.

DISTRIBUTION AND NUMBER OF GAME

It is as yet difficult to give any accurate estimate as to the numbers of the different species, but I think I shall be safe in placing Eland as the most numerous, with Sable next.

The Elephant are difficult to estimate as their numbers fluctuate considerably due to their movements across the Western border. I think 1 000 head will give a fair idea of the number present, while there are possibly more during the months of September to December.

The number of Giraffe is possibly over 1 000. They are found over practically the whole of the Reserve, but more so on the edge of the Sinanga.

216

Buffalo occur only on the Dedeema and a small herd visited the Reserve during the rains in the vicinity of Inyantue. I shall not estimate this number at more than 100.

Roan are common in the north west portion where grass is more plentiful, as they are chiefly grazers, while Sable are also common in this part. Both these species are, however, not absent from the sandveld.

Koodoo are most common in the hilly country, particularly near Dedeema, while a few are to be found near the Sinanga in the sand.

Waterbuck are limited to the Dedeema and Dolilo - being only a very few present.

Bushbuck are only found in the vicinity of the Inyantue. Reedbuck and Zebra are confined to the grass land in the north west, while a few Tsessebe are also found there, Zebra also occur in small numbers near Shapi and Mababa.

Impala and Warthog are confined to the Mopani belts, but during the early part of summer quite a number of Impala are found in the hills near Mopani. Sharpe's Steinbuck or Grey Steinbuck are found in the hilly country and Klipspringer are found in the large hills and granite kopjes near Inyantue.

Ostrich are common in the grassland and are also to be found in the vleis of Intundhla and Ngamo.

Gemsbuck occur in small numbers in most parts near the Sinanga, particularly common near Ngwashla.

NOTES OF GAME IN RESERVE

Elephant
It appears general that during the dry months, the Elephant feeds largely on trees which contain a fair amount of sap, such as Mtoa, Bloodwood, and a similar tree known by the natives as Inyanshlova. The young Mopani are also eaten to an extent, especially just before it bursts into leaf.

Gonde are perhaps destroyed more by Elephant than any other trees. Elephant do not appear to frequent Gonde or Msasa during the rains or in the cold weather, but as soon as the trees burst into leaf (early in September) hundreds of them are broken down and the young leaves eaten off. Often a large tree over a foot in diameter is pushed over and only one to two pounds of leaves are taken. I have noticed that one Elephant pushed over eleven trees in 200 yards.

During the hot weather, the patches of teak forest in the Sinanga are favourite loitering places and these animals may be seen standing in the shade for many hours at a stretch. Often they are seen lying down or leaning against a big tree.

Where water is situated near the Sinanga, as for instance Shakawanki, they very often drink in the heat of the day, and spend a good deal of time digging in the sand or bathing in the pool.

It is a strange fact that the larger water supplies are not frequented until the smaller pans have dried up. Many water supplies are ruined while they still contain a good supply of water by elephants puddling them on purpose to make a mud bath. This is done by an elephant standing in one spot and "marking time" for as much as a quarter of an hour. Four or five elephants doing this at once in a small pool about a foot deep soon reduces it to a thick slime. After this, the water soon dries up and is of no further use as a drinking place.

GAME TRACKS
Practically the whole of the Reserve is covered with elephant paths leading in all directions. It is a strange habit these animals have of making a path direct from one water hole to another.

GIRAFFE
Giraffe are most numerous on the edge of the Sinanga, but do nevertheless occur over the whole of the Reserve.

Giraffe will sometimes leave their young in charge of one or two old cows when venturing into the open. I came across a single cow with four young ones all under a year old in April. Closer examination of the spoor showed that there had been more old animals present. After following this, I came on six cows and a bull at a saltlick. Obviously these were the parents of the young animals left in the bush.

ELAND
Eland occur in very large herds throughout the sandveld and are occasionally found in the hills and Mopani, but only in small herds in the latter parts. Herds of over 200 are not uncommon and are usually found in the Gusi or Teak.

218

BUFFALO

Buffalo only occur near the Dedeema, where a herd of about 80 are permanent during the wet weather. They appear to wander a good deal, and for a time were at Masuma, and even reached Mababa; but during the dry season they appear to confine themselves to the hilly country near Dedeema. They are very shy and if disturbed will move off to some other locality at once. In recent years they have been much hunted by Sportsmen from Wankie, and even now they are subject to hunting when on Deka Ranch. There are a fair number of calves with this herd, but I have never had an opportunity of studying them carefully.

A small herd of Buffalo visited the Reserve near Inyantue. They were seen at Mtoa and also at Danga. One bull passed close to Dett and almost reached Balcarris, but returned. This herd is at present in the Reserve.

SABLE AND ROAN ANTELOPE

Sable and Roan Antelope are found in most parts of the Reserve, but are most numerous in the north west portion. Sable are often seen in herds up to as many as 100, but Roan are seldom seen in more than herds of 10. These animals feed chiefly on grass and are dependent on water, drinking every day during the hot months. They appear to be very fond of the salts found in the Dolilo and also frequent the Silica salt licks a good deal. Roan appear to have the habit of leaving very young calves, as I have seen two calves about three months old unaccompanied.

KOODOO

Koodoo are found in most parts of the Reserve, but are very numerous in the hilly country. They appear to drink regularly while water lasts, but do not move about much in search of water. Leaves appear to provide sufficient nourishment during the hot weather.

In the winter the herds are mixed, but from the end of September to April the cows are very seldom accompanied by a bull. The bulls forming small bands of their own. Both sexes are subject to attack by Wild Dogs and usually fall an easy victim. Large numbers of these animals must be killed each year by this pest.

GEMSBUCK

Gemsbuck are interesting, as many of the old hunters claim that this buck is migratory, only being found here during the dry season. This, however, is not correct today, as I have observed a pair of these animals at Tshembema in November, 1928, and have seen them or their spoor on every visit. Today there are three, the calf being over half grown. They have been seen at Balcarris at all seasons.

At Ngwashla, I was struck by the number of these animals which are reported to be so scarce in this country. Some very young ones were seen there in December, 1928, and several small herds are always present at Ngwashla.

In the western portion of the Reserve these animals are common, but they do not occur in large numbers. They are not dependent on water, and feed to a large extent on roots in the dry parts.

VERMIN
Vermin are not protected in the Reserve, and efforts are being made to reduce their numbers. Hyenas are the most common, being found in every part of the Reserve.

Lions occur in all parts of the Reserve, but are most numerous in or near the Sinanga. During the wet season they appear to wander a good deal, and do considerable damage to young buck of all kinds.

The total number of vermin destroyed was :-

Lions : 18, Leopards : 4, Hyena : 15 (known), Wild Dogs : 10, smaller carnivora : 13.

Total Sixty.

EQUIPMENT AND TRANSPORT
For purpose of transport a riding horse and two pack mules have been provided. The pack mules proved far from satisfactory, but after a good deal of time and trouble spent in patient training, they have now reached a stage when they can be more or less relied on. They are not, however, quite able to carry all my requirements, and I have therefore purchased two donkeys on my own behalf. These I have used to carry a supply of water when travelling over waterless stretches or when the country is unknown to myself or my guides, and it is doubtful whether any water can be found.

A .423 Mauser rifle was provided for protection and to destroy vermin, but this unfortunately burst. Since then I have been using my own rifle and ammunition.

A small supply of .423 ammunition was issued, but no .318 ammunition, which are the two rifles I use.

A hand auger for testing for water was supplied and has been used in many cases. This, however, will only test to a depth of 10 feet.

I trust a few suggestions regarding the work for the coming year will not be out of place.

IMPROVEMENT OF WATER SUPPLY
The most essential item is, I think, the improvement of water supply. In a very dry season game are hard put to find water, and I am sure a large majority of them will leave the Reserve at such times. Existing surface waters such as Shakawinki and Nehimba could I am sure be easily improved by the use of a dam scraper.

MAP OF RESERVE
A good detail map of the Reserve is essential.

The mapping of the Reserve will be a difficult undertaking, due to the large stretch of waterless country, but this will be overcome by working in these parts during the wet season. A prismatic compass and a cyclometer have been provided, but for mapping on a large scale, more efficient instruments will need to be provided.

POLICING THE RESERVE
A more efficient force of native rangers and a uniform for them will be of great assistance and provide a better safeguard against poachers and grassfires.

GRASS BURNING
I would recommend annual controlled burning off of grass in the north and north west portions of the Reserve where there is little or no forest of any value. This would provide new grass for the game during the latter part of the dry season. New grass is a great attraction to game of certain types such as Eland, Sable, Roan, Zebra, Tsessebe and other grass eating animals.

ERECTION OF PERMANENT QUARTERS
Two suitable sites are receiving consideration. There is the present site of my permanent camp, which is a high healthy spot 1½ miles north of Dett and Balcarris homestead.

221

REPAIRS TO SADDLERY
Owing to the unruly nature of the two pack mules, it has been necessary to forward all my saddlery for repairs. This, however, proved beyond repairs, and arrangements have been made for the renewal of this saddlery; but in the meantime the old saddles were returned, according to my wish and are being used until the arrival of the new saddles.

NATIVE HONEY HUNTING
A source of considerable amount of damage both by grassfires, and also to game. Natives are always accompanied by dogs, and while hunting honey are apt to destroy young animals whenever an opportunity arises. It is difficult to keep a check on these natives, as at present I have no authority to keep them out.

GAME CATCHING ON PRIVATE LAND ADJOINING RESERVE
I strongly recommend that no further permits be issued for the capture of game on land adjoining the Reserve.

EXCHANGE OF LAND FOR BALCARRIS
Balcarris is a great drawback to the Reserve, as it forms an ideal place for hunters wishing to capture game which exists only in the Reserve. Animals captured on Balcarris are, after all, animals from the Reserve, being only visitors to this part.

SUNNYSIDE FARM
I would suggest that no person be allowed to follow a wounded animal into the Reserve unless accompanied by myself or my representative, and only after I am satisfied that the animal in question has actually been wounded.

WORK TO BE DONE
As soon as possible patrols will be done into the dry, unpatrolled parts of the Reserve. This I hope to complete before the end of April, 1930.

> I have the honour to be,
> Sir,
> Your obedient servant.

E. DAVISON
Game Warden

OPERATION WHITE RHINO
THE IMPORTATION OF EIGHT
SQUARE-LIPPED RHINOCEROS
(CERATOTHERIUM SIMUM)

J B Condy, Veterinary Research Laboratory
and
E Davison, Department of National Parks,
Salisbury, Southern Rhodesia

The Square-lipped Rhinoceros, the largest land mammal in the world after the elephant, was to be found in Central Africa from the earliest times. A pre-historic rock painting in the Matopos National Park is almost certainly of a white rhinoceros, judging from the length and shape of its skull.

Selous (1881, 1893) Le Roux (1925) Coryndon (1894) Nicholls (1892) and others, record that white rhinoceros were common up to 1890 in Matabeleland, Mashonaland and Gazaland, but from that date there was a rapid decline in their population and by 1900 only a few stragglers remained. There is no accurate record of when the last one was shot, but was probably about 1925 (Willamson 1962).

In August, 1962 eight white rhinoceros were imported into Southern Rhodesia from the Umfolosi Game Reserve, Natal. Four of these animals (1 male and 3 females) were released in the Matopos National Park, and four (2 male and 2 females) were released in the Kyle Dam Game Reserve. This importation of a rare animal to an environment where they had occurred previously is a historic event in the annals of wild life conservation, and as it entailed a 1,200 mile journey overland, over 5 days and 4 nights, the longest land journey to which this species has ever been subjected, a report on the journey and how the animals behaved is worthy of record.

The convoy assembled at Beit Bridge at mid-day on the 3rd, August, four lorries and one Land Rover having started from Salisbury and travelled via Fort Victoria and four lorries and one Land Rover and a water trailer had started from Bulawayo.

Staff with the exercise consisted of:-

Assistant Director of National Parks, Mr E Davison, in charge.
Veterinary Surgeon, Mr J Condy, from the Veterinary Research Dept.
Senior Game Ranger, Mr R Fothergill, Wild Life Conservation Dept.
Game Ranger T Orford, Wild Life Conservation Dept.
Parks Warden J Hatton, National Parks Dept.
Mechanic Mr A Smith, C.M.E.D.

12 African drivers and 6 lorry attendants as under:-

Department of National Parks

Romigius   Sandisa   Fuyata   Simoni   Pawuli
Keyi   Nqilinqa Muliviyeli Samson   Mafinita

Department of Wild Life Conservation

Mapfumo   Albertino Langton   Muskiwa   Teguru
Tasiana   Manwere   Kusaya

Three members of the team, Mr Condy, Mr Fothergill and Mr Orford preceded the convoy by four days in order to gain more knowledge of the handling of the White Rhino before the return journey started, which was scheduled for the 9th August.

The Route chosen from Umfolosi to Rhodesia was not that originally planned. Due to heavy rains and the bad conditions of all Zululand roads, it was necessary to keep to main roads, and details of the Journey are given in Table 1.

Capture and pre-journey treatment
The animals were caught by the staff of Umfolosi Game Reserve using the technique described by Harthoorn (1962). A projectile syringe with a standard immobilising dose of 3 grammes "Themalon", (diethylthiambutane) 100 milligrams Hyoscine hydrobromide and 14 cc "Largactil" (Chlorpromazine hydrochloride) in all animals.

The white rhinoceros appears to be a very much more sensitive, and probably a more intelligent creature than the black rhinoceros. After capture a great deal of persuasion is necessary before they will eat either taff hay or lucerne in their pens, and it is often necessary for a human to

224

remain with them constantly for the first 3-4 days. Some will only eat when offered hay in the hand, and if the attendant stops talking to the animals and moves away, the rhino will stop eating. Some will not eat hay for several days, and to ensure their not starving, a gruel consisting of maize meal, glucose, condensed milk, molasses, salt and sugar has been devised by staff of the Umfolosi Game Reserve. Most of these temperamental animals take readily to this gruel, and within a few days are eating hay.

The reluctance on the part of most white rhinoceros to take readily to pen feeding is very noticeable, compared with the experiences gained on Lake Kariba with black rhinoceros. The latter have been known to eat lucerne hay within 6 hours of being captured, and no cases have occurred, that animals have refused food for more than 12 hours.

From previous experiences, in stocking other game parks and reserves in the Republic of South Africa, it has been found that white rhinoceros if captured, moved immediately to their new environment and released, will settle down to grazing natural pastures without any trouble. The long journey to Rhodesia, however, necessitated only transporting animals which had been accustomed to pen feeding, which is essential if they are to be treated for any length of time.

For at least a week before the journey commenced, the rhinoceros had been fed and watered in their crates which were tied to the entrance of the pans. They became quite accustomed to entering and even sleeping in these crates. At least twenty-four hours before leaving Umfolosi, each rhinoceros had been confined to their respective crates, and the latter were finally loaded so the animals' heads faced the rear end of the vehicle.

Method of Travel
Eleven vehicles comprised the convoy. Each rhinoceros was carried on a five ton diesel truck, and three Land Rovers equipped with two-way radio, transported the staff of veterinary surgeon, game rangers and mechanic.

The rhinoceros were transported in stout wooden crates reinforced by metal bands. These crates were of two different patterns. The most recent and best design by the Umfolosi Game Reserve staff was a crate with three doors at each end. These comprised, in addition to the common type of stable door, another door one foot high which gave access to

225

the bottom of the crate. Through this, feeding, watering and cleaning were carried out with ease.

Canvas sails were secured over the entire front and half on the top of the crates, an opening of 42" x 30" over each animal's head being left open at all times.

From the commencement of the journey a careful watch was kept on all animals. After having travelled the first 20 miles, some were noticed to be lying down and some were standing and eating, obviously quite at ease.

At various times of both day and night the animals were observed while the trucks were in motion. At no time did they appear restless, and various individuals were often to be seen standing and eating, even at midday.

Adequate ventilation of the crates was ensured all the time, and during the hard frost in Pietermaritzburg, the open portion on the top of the crate over each rhinoceros's head was not covered over. At one stage the tarpaulin of one crate was rolled forward to leave an opening on the top of the crate at the end near the cab of the truck. There appeared to be no advantage in doing this, dust particles were noticed to be almost stationary in this opening while the vehicle was in motion.

Feeding
During daylight travel the convoy stopped at least once per day for refuelling and other business. At all stops, an attendant saw that there was fodder available to the animals. By this time individual preferences were known, some only ate taff hay, some ate taff and lucerne hay.

Table II shows records of feeding habits of two males and two females, while the trucks were actually in motion. It will be seen that three ate both during morning and afternoon travel, while one, Ngazana, never ate while the trucks were in motion in day time. He was seen once, at 8.30 pm on the 3rd day of travel, to be eating oat hay while laying down.

Watering was carried out in plastic baths, and although they were given access to water both morning and evening, it was observed that most animals drank more in the evening, some not consuming any water in the morning. One animal, Mashayezonke, had taken an intense dislike to the plastic bath, and would only drink water off the floor of its crate.

Weather conditions varied from a frost during the first night at Pietermaritzburg, to very warm weather while crossing the Northern Transvaal. During the night of frost, it appeared from observations on the respirations and general behaviour, that no time were they distressed. No rain occurred during the journey, and the change in altitude from sea level to ± 6,000 feet appeared to have no effect on the animals.

Veterinary Treatments

Tranquillisation was carefully considered. Two animals Mashayazonke and Chianna were nervous and had fought their pens, the former breaking her anterior horn off. The two were therefore given 300 mgms each of Chlorpromasine an hour before the journey commenced. As they appeared settled later in the day, no further tranquillisers were administered. It was decided to interfere with nature as little as possible, and only treat when necessary. All the remaining six animals appeared at ease throughout the journey and no further tranquillisation was necessary.

Nyoni and Mashayazonke both had large suppurating lesions due to a previous infection on the skin. Both had courses of Penicillin before the journey. Nyoni was therefore given 2.5 gms oxytetracycline daily for the first two days of travel, and Mashayazonke was given the same treatment during the last two days of travel. Their skin lesions were dressed twice daily, with a Sulphanilamide-iodoform powder.

The serum of one female (the only animal it was possible to obtain serum from) was subjected to the routine agglutination test for Brucellosis, and found to be negative. Recently two Black Rhinoceros from Lake Kariba have shown positive reactions to this test.

On arriving at the Kyle Game Reserve the 4 rhinoceros had abrasions on the backs which were treated with wound dressing powder. These abrasions were apparently due to a shortage of bedding.

Examination of the faeces of all animals, revealed moderate to heavy infestations of nematodes. Bot fly larvae of the genus Gyrostigma are known to occur in White Rhinoceros at Umfolosi. As these eight rhinoceros being imported to Rhodesia were to be released in an area where rhino (and their parasites) had not occurred for many years, an opportunity arose to try to reduce their parasite burden to below the critical level necessary for their survival.

227

Accordingly they were all dosed with an anthelmintic very successfully, the detailed results of which are being published elsewhere.

All eight animals received 1000 units of vitamin B12 before being released.

The Umfolosi Game Reserve and surrounding country had been a Trypanosomiasis area up to 1950. As all the eight rhinoceros concerned were under four years old, it was considered unnecessary to use a trypanocidal drug.

Release
After having been in their crates for eight days, journey's end arrived on 3rd September. The trucks carrying the crates were reversed into pits at the entrance to the pans, and after securing the crates to these entrances, the sores and abrasions on all animals were treated before release.

The reactions of most of the animals was to enter the pens after a preliminary sniff. Umfaan, however, refused to leave his crate for nine hours after the door was removed.

At varying times after arrival in Rhodesia they were treated with an anthelmintic, and on 21st September the four at the Matopos National Park were the first group to be finally released from their pens into an enclosure of 250 acres in the 2,000 acre Game Park section. Within an hour of release they were grazing the natural pastures. They established their "territory" which was a relatively small one of their own choice, not extending more than half a mile from the pens, and returned daily to the pens to feed on taff hay, sleeping in the same place every day. They made no attempt to wander until the first rains brought on a flush of new grass. When this happened they explored the whole area of the fenced game camp.

At the Kyle Dam Game Reserve an usually dense and dry mat of natural pasture, in places four foot high, constituted a fire hazard which endangered the lives of all animals. The rainy season was not far off, so the four rhinoceros were retained in their pens until the first rain fell.

Conclusion - From the success of Operation White Rhino - Southern Rhodesia, it must be concluded that with reasonable care, these animals can be transported over very long distances by land. Apart from supplying ample bedding to prevent abrasions, it is difficult to recommend any improvements on the method of crating, feeding, watering and transport.

In view of the apparently fairly high level of internal parasitism of white rhinoceros in their natural habitat at Umfolosi, it would be a wise precaution to treat all rhinoceros that are captured in this reserve, against internal and external parasites, before they are removed to other areas.

The white rhinoceros was to be found in most areas of Southern Rhodesia during the last century, and was even very common in some parts up till 1890. There is no reason to believe why they should not do very well in the two game parks where the eight were released in September 1962.

Acknowledgements
The authors wish to acknowledge the considerable assistance and advice of Ian Player and members of the staff of Umfolosi Game Reserve.

The Natal Parks, Game and Fish Preservation Board, the Durban City Police, Natal Provincial Police, Royal Agricultural Society of Natal, Andrews Motel Fort Mistake, the Immigration and Customs Officials of both Republic of South Africa and Southern Rhodesia, they were most helpful and it took the whole convoy only a little over an hour to pass both Immigration posts, and the B.S.A. Police are to be thanked for their assistance in helping to make a smooth passage for the convoy.

The C.M.E.D. who supplied the vehicles and made available Mr A Smith a mechanic with a light service vehicle. Mr Smith did very valuable work and thanks to his services not one of the lorries with a rhino on board experienced mechanical trouble.

R Fothergill, T Orford and J Hatton are thanked for assisting in collecting information en route.

The costs of capturing the animals and the transport were defrayed by Public subscription.

Caltex (Africa) Ltd., are to be thanked for supplying all fuel for the convoy, and Pfizer Central Africa (Pvt) Ltd;, for supplies of Terramycin.

References

Coryndon, R.T. (1894)   The African Review
Harthoorn, A.   (1962) Jl. Natal Parks, Game and Fish. Pres.
Board   Vol. II No. 2 P. 1.
Le Roux, S. (1925)   Brit. South Afr. Annual.
Nicholls, J.A. (1892)   The Sportsman in S. Africa P. 63.
Selous, F.C. (1881)   A Hunters Wanderings in Africa.
Selous, F.C. (1893)   Travel and Adventure in S.E. Africa.
Williamson, T.W. (1962) Personal Communication.

27th November 1962

BUSHMEN OF WANKIE NATIONAL PARK

by Ted Davison

Over the last 50 years the activities of poachers in the Wankie National Park have changed dramatically. When I took up the post as Warden there in 1928 one of my first tasks was to find out as much as possible about the place. So little was known and so few people had ever been there that it was natural that I looked to the Bushmen "Poachers" for information.

There being no permanent water in the Reserve there was little or no human occupation except for some Bushmen families who lived in the area for most of the year. These people fell into two classes, the "wild" Bushmen and the "tame" Bushmen. The tame ones were those who had drifted into the settled areas and taken up occupations with farmers or Railway Employees. A few of these acted as guides and trackers to hunters, and it was from them that I recruited a few members of my staff. To start with I obtained the services of some very good guides but once they realised that I was not there to hunt and shot only a limited amount for the pot they left. They were afraid too that if their services resulted in a relative being jailed they would suffer some reprisals. These tame Bushmen had acquired a knowledge of the use of firearms and wire snares. They tended to kill more than they needed and carted it into the Tribal Trust Lands for sale or barter. They were dangerous too, for they would not hesitate to shoot if cornered. One of our tame Bushmen was shot in cold blood after a party had been captured by our Rangers. One of the party who had escaped when their camp was rushed at dawn crept back and shot our Bushman guide as he was standing near those who had been caught.

The "tame" Bushmen were mostly of the Sili Tribe and they had occupied the Eastern and Northern parts of the area before the White man arrived. Some of the old men knew the area well. It was their grandchildren who I employed. Some of them joined my staff and these invariably consulted their elders about the area before and after a patrol into any unknown part.

It frequently happened on patrol that a pan with good water was discovered but our Bushmen guides were unable to put a name to it. After consultation with their elders on their return home they would come up with a name, in some cases two different names would be advanced by different families. It was difficult to know if the two families were talking about the same pan.

It was not always pans that we were searching for as there were rumours of some stone ruins said to exist in the Reserve. It took some years before anyone who had actually seen them could be located. Finally an old Bushman Chief named Maboma agreed to guide me to these ruins if I would pay his tax for one year. (£1,00).

We spent a fruitless two days wandering about in some hilly country and finally Maboma admitted that he had visited the ruins only once when he was a small boy and that it had then been during the rains when all the trees were in full leaf. As it was now the dry season he could not recognise the area.

Maboma agreed to have another try when the trees were in full leaf. On the advice of my Guides I did not accompany the party as the old man felt he could recognise the area better if he did not fear meeting up with other Bushmen who might be in the area. This was done and Maboma went straight to the ruins. It is quite possible that on the first visit he wandered about looking for signs that other Bushmen were in the area, and finding something decided it was safer not to meet up with them in the company with "The Police" as they called me.

The ruins were named Mtoa after a good pan which was only a mile or so away. They were soon after declared an Ancient Relic and protected. Our party was not the first to have visited the ruins as someone had dug a fairly large hole in the centre of the enclosure evidently looking for relics or treasure. It seems possible that when Maboma visited the place with his father the ruins were quite well known.

The Western and Southern parts of the Reserve were less well known. When the old Panda-ma-Tenga road which formed the Western boundary of the Reserve fell into disuse after the Railway was built through to the Victoria Falls few people ever visited these parts. It was in these dry semi-desert areas that we encountered what I like to think of as the Wild Bushmen. These people were of the Masarwa Tribe and spent all their life in the Reserve and did not move out when the

232

pans dried up. They knew of sand covered pans, (which we now call Seeps) where the water covered by sand was held up by a clay seam. The water could be obtained by digging down some five or six feet and it was here that these Bushmen survived during the dry season.

These "wild" Bushmen recognised only one "crime". This was the possession of a firearm. It was surprising how many of them did have guns. Almost all of these were Tower Muskets, a muzzle loading weapon manufactured about the middle of the 19th century and brought to the area by early hunters and traders such as Selous. The presence in the Reserve of these "wild" Bushmen did no more harm to the wild life than a pride of lions did, except on the odd occasion when some chance powder and caps were in good supply.

Catching these interesting little people was not a very difficult undertaking as they were of the opinion that as long as they were not in possession of a firearm they could have done no wrong. The greater part of their food was provided for them by lions and it was the regular thing to hunt for meat simply by watching the Vultures. They were surprisingly clever at determining from the flight of the birds how far away the kill was and if it was a fresh kill.

We did not entirely turn a blind eye to the presence of these little camps. When we located one the occupants seldom ran away. At least the women and children would stay put and almost welcome us. If after a search of the camp we found traces of firearms, such as a mould for making lead slugs or a pouch with traces of powder in it we would arrest the owner of the hut in which it was found. The men usually returned at dusk but without their guns.

The practice was to take the arrested man, with the evidence of firearms with us. After a couple of days by arrangement with my "wild" Bushmen Guides the arrested "wild" Bushman would be allowed to escape after being informed that we now knew his spoor and even his smell and that we could easily catch him again if he came back.

During the first few years in the Reserve I collected up several muskets and in a few cases the owner was jailed for a month or two. On release they showed no animosity and would come to my main camp (where Main Camp now stands) and ask to purchase food to get them back to their families. Some of them had been paid a small sum on being released from prison and this was the first money they had ever owned. We invariably gave them some food, a utensil to carry and cook it in, some matches and we parted good friends. But the most treasured possession, the muzzle loader was not returned.

A patrol by horse and pack mules into areas where Bushmen were known to be located were usually enough to put them to flight. The spoor of a horse or two was a sure sign that the Police were about.

Compare this state of affairs with the poacher of today. The Bushmen are still about and they do no more harm than they did 30 years ago. Now however the Reserve has been invaded by people from the tribal areas who are well supplied with modern rifles obtained from the guerrillas. They also find a ready supply of good plain steel wire, ideal for making snares, which they take with impunity from the Foot and Mouth fences erected by the Veterinary Department to control the spread of Food and Mouth from the game to cattle and vice versa. Once inside the Reserve these modern poachers find a ready supply of water at the pumps erected for the benefit of the game. These places and game paths leading to the water make ideal sites for wire snares.

The amount of game that has been destroyed in the last few years is very considerable. Most of it has been attributed to the use of wire snares and has affected chiefly Wildebeest, Eland, Kudu, Sable, Roan, Giraffe and Buffalo. Elephant too suffer by getting a noose around their trunk or foot. They invariably break loose taking the wire with them and suffer for weeks before losing a part of the trunk or die from gangrene in the foot.

10 May 1982

Colony of Southern Rhodesia

Government Gazette

PUBLISHED BY AUTHORITY

Vol. VIII. No. 13.   Salisbury, Friday, March 28, 1930   *Price Sixpence*

No. 8 of 1930.]

PROCLAMATION
by

His Excellency Sir Cecil Hunter Rodwell, Knight Commander of the Most Distinguished Order of Saint Michael and Saint George, Governor and Commander-in-Chief in and over the colony of Southern Rhodesia.

WHEREAS by section 2 of the "Game and Fish Preservation Act, 1929," certain powers may be exercised by the Governor by Proclamation:

Now, therefore, I, the Governor aforesaid, in the exercise of the said powers, do hereby proclaim and make known:

I.   The First Schedule to the said Act shall be amended to read as follows:

Part "A" - Ordinary Game

Duiker, steinbuck, Sharpe's steinbuck (locally known as grysbok), oribi, klipspringer, warthog, francolin (including pheasant and partridge), sand grouse (Namaqua partridge), guinea-fowl, dikkop.

Part "B" - Special Game

Buffalo, zebra, reedbuck, bushbuck, koodoo, sable, waterbuck, lechwe, pookoo, impala, tsessabe (in the native districts of Sebungwe, Lomagundi, Wankie, Insiza, Belingwe, Chibi and Gwanda only), Lichtenstein's hartebeest (in the native districts of Ndanga and Bikita only), gnu or wildebeest.

Part "C" - Royal Game

Elephant, rhinoceros, hippopotamus, giraffe, eland, roan, gemsbuck, inyala, sitatunga, Lichtenstein's hartebeest (in all native districts except Ndanga and Bikita), tsessabe (in all native districts except Sebungwe, Lomagundi, Wankie, Belingwe, Insiza, Chibi and Gwanda), ostrich.

II.   The following close seasons for game shall be observed:-

I.   Ordinary game - Mashonaland :
    (a) birds, from 1st October to 30th April;
    (b) antelope, from 1st November to 30th April.
    Matabeleland : birds and antelope, from 1st November to 30th April.

2.   Special game - throughout the Colony, from the 1st December to the 30th June.

III.   Oribi shall be protected throughout the Colony, except in the native districts of Melsetter and Lomagundi, for a period of five years,

IV.   The following birds and animals shall be protected throughout the Colony:-

    (1)   All species of storks *(Plataledae, Ciconiidae* and *Scopidae).*
    (2)   Nordmann's pratincole *(Glareola melanoptera).*
    (3)   Small white heron and cattle egret *(Bubulcus ibis).* •

    (4)   Wattled starling *(Dilophus carunculatus).*
    (5)   All species of plovers *(Charadriidae).*
    (6)   All species of cranes *(Gruidae).*
    (7)   All species of owls *(Strigidae).*
    (8)   The standard-winged nightjar *(Cosmetornis vexillarius).*
    (9)   All species of bee eaters *(Meropidae).*
    (10)   All species of rollers *(Coraciidae).*
    (11)   The narina trogon *(Hapaloderma narina).*
    (12)   All species of flamingoes *(Phoenicopteridae).*
    (13)   All species of ibis *(Ibidae).*
    (14)   All species of orioles *(Oriolidae).*
    (15)   All species of sunbirds *(Nectariniidae).*
    (16)   All species of bustard *(Pauuw* and *Koorhaan).*
    (17)   All species of lovebirds *(Agapornis).*
    (18)   Lemur *(Gelago crassicaudatus).*

V.   The skins and plumage of all birds described in the last preceding list shall not be sold or exported otherwise than under special permit issued in terms of section (8) (d) of the said Act.

VI.   The areas herein defined shall be game reserves, and it shall not be lawful to hunt game therein without the special permission in writing of the Minister:-

Wankie Game Reserve

All Crown lands in the Wankie native district lying west of the railway line and south of the following line:- From the beacon No. 153 on the western border of the Wankie native district, eastwards following the boundaries on the southern side of the following farms, namely, Deka, Mahohoma, Nantwich South, Tom's Extension and Deka Ranch to the easternmost beacon of the latter; thence in a direct line to the north-west beacon of Sinamatela Ranch; thence southward following the boundaries of that ranch to the Sinamatela River; thence down the Sinamatela River to the south-west boundary of the Wankie Concession; thence southward along the boundaries of that Concession and Railway Farms No. 47 to the railway line.

GOD SAVE THE KING

Given under my hand and the public seal of the Colony of Southern Rhodesia, at Salisbury, this twentieth day of March, one thousand nine hundred and thirty.

C. H. RODWELL,
Governor.

By command of His Excellency the Governor.

H. U. MOFFAT

AFTERWORD

Ted Davison died on June 10th, 1982 in Harare, many miles away from the beloved wilderness of which he was chief guardian for so long. His ashes rest in the same grave as his parents, in the small town known today as Chegutu – referred to below in a letter written to the headmaster of Hartley Primary School in April 1980.

"When I was born there was no church at all, and as I was registered when one or two days old, I was registered as Edward. There was some lapse of time before I was Christened and as I was the first white baby boy born in the village, I was Christened Edward Hartley. I am sorry to say I have never had this mistake corrected, so I am officially Edward Davison.
What is now Hartley School was at that time the hospital under Dr MacKenzie and it was by far the biggest building in the village. When passing Hartley now I frequently call in at the old cemetery (which is now full), as both my parents are buried there, and there is not even room for me. The new cemetery is nearby but it is not such a nice site."

One of his sons remembers a flight of green pigeons erupting out of a nearby tree, the birds flashing in brief, bright, noisy garrulity above the silent humans below watching the ashes being laid to rest.

Sunshine and storm aplenty there has been in this fair land in the last seventy years, since a young Ted Davison stepped down off the train in Dete late one summer's night to take up his duties as first custodian of Wankie Game Reserve. If he saw changes in the region during his long association with the Park, both during and after his tenure, he would have seen a whole lot more were he still alive today.

Sixteen years after his death Hwange National Park continues to rate as one of the premier wildlife destinations in Africa, and is generally regarded as the country's flagship game sanctuary, attracting tourists increasingly – especially those of particular importance to Zimbabwe's exchequer, the foreign visitor. Sadly, Hwange, like most of the Parks

Estate in the country, is decidedly ragged around the edges these days, in need of a lot of tender loving care. There is too much being taken and not enough being given back. A habitué of the region, especially a purist, may be excused for viewing a Hwange sojourn with mixed feelings. On the one hand there is a huge stretch of semi Kalahari wilderness hosting a great diversity of animal, bird and plant species. On the other there is the largest national park in Zimbabwe falling apart at the seams. Hwange, for this writer, is rather like a much loved friend who is struggling to recover from some debilitating illness, whom one visits often, hoping against hope that the next visit will see the friend up and running, the malaise a thing of the past.

Today Hwange survives in spite of a lacklustre commitment by its managing body, despite increasingly depleted budgets; it struggles along in the face of frequent staff turnover, insufficiently trained staff, minimal upkeep of vital machinery, little in the way of veld management, and a serious lack of tourist management. The animals are there of course (and there are details of their exact status today elsewhere herein), seen by the visitors on the platforms and plying the ever-deteriorating roads. Elephant, giraffe, zebra, buffalo, lion, kudu, steinbuck, warthog – they are all out there on show. The animals are doing their bit. The keepers of the kingdom are not.

Outside of the miserable government allocated budget there has been, arguably, in current times, more funds available to the national parks research and management team than ever before, via agencies such as USAID, WWF, NORAD, CIRAD, the Beit Trust, Ford Foundation, Wildlife Conservation International, WISDOM and many other bodies. This is not readily evident, to anyone perusing Hwange today, or over the last decade or so. In this context tribute should be paid to the constant efforts made by such organisations as the Matabeleland Branch of the Wildlife Society of Zimbabwe, the Hwange Conservation Society, Wankie Colliery, many other commercial businesses, and the various safari companies located around the fringe of the Park – keeping pumps working, re-building bridges, repairing dam walls and spillways, sinking boreholes, building and repairing water troughs, supplying fuel – the list goes on. Hwange and its wild inhabitants would be in an even sorrier state without them.

But, nevertheless, having said all this, whether one is staying in one of the plethora of luxury camps/lodges dotted around the fringe of the Park, or in the more budget-friendly national parks accommodation found at the three principal access points, Hwange still offers a fine wildlife viewing experience. And, for the average tourist, who will usually be met with a smile at the entrance gate, who will be welcomed at, perhaps, Mandavu Dam, by an ever cheerful gentleman called Bala, with his kettle at the ready, there will not be much that is readily evident of the malaise. Plus, if one is to be positive, to keep the candle in the dark alight, one has to hope that the funds generated by wildlife tourism - for so long disappearing every year into the bottomless pit of government treasury, now at long last being channelled back into the Department – will herald a new beginning. The animals, and their custodians, deserve a break.

WATER IN HWANGE

From day one the water situation in Hwange has always been cause for concern. This was evidenced by Ted Davison's feedback in his first reports to headquarters in March 1930. The water factor is the reason why the area was punted for wildlife usage in the first place – it was no good for agriculture. So the spectre of drought and the effect of successive poor rainy seasons has always been present, and there have been times when the game has suffered badly. **It could be happening as you read this.** As time and progress marches on, it would not be unreasonable to hope that an antidote for this particular malady would have been discovered. After all, man has walked on the moon, hydroponics has turned desert into super-productive land, computers evolve almost weekly, there is talk that the quagga is set for a come-back. Ergo, why has there not evolved a long term

efficient solution to the water problem in Hwange National Park?
Ahh, yes, well, no, fine...

In early 1995 a strategic management workshop held in Hwange,
attended by 45 concerned, clear-thinking, like-minded folk, agreed
that a crisis indeed existed with regard to the supply of water for
wildlife in the Park. During the four-day think tank, the reasons for
the crisis were distilled down to three basic levels.
1. Water management problems, including declining borehole yields
    coupled with old and frequently breaking down equipment.
2. Disagreement on animal densities and their ranges.
3. Inadequate funding for the Park.

Ummm, yes, nothing new there, methinks. In fact, it is almost a re-
play of an impassioned detailed, blow-by-blow 17-page report done
six months earlier in July 1994, compiled by the Matabeleland Branch
of The Wildlife Society of Zimbabwe, handed to (and discussed with)
the then Minister Responsible for Environment and Tourism,
expounding on precisely these issues – to which the Minister
expressed surprise, nay, shock. And here we are, with 1998 sliding
away behind us...

To give you, dear reader, an idea of some of the pressures a game
warden is under these days, trying to run a national park, here are
some extracts from a report presented at the above workshop by the
then Warden of Main Camp.

CURRENT MANAGEMENT PROBLEMS
PROVISION OF ARTIFICIAL WATER FOR GAME IN HWANGE NATIONAL PARK
JANUARY 1995

The provision and management of artificial water supplies in
Hwange National Park (HNP) is an extremely important management
activity. To keep viable game populations within the Park, it is

essential that water is pumped for them. The old dry season migration route taken by water dependent species to the Gwaai river, has long been cut off by the commercial farms on the Gwaai (which are usually enclosed by strong game (fences) and the Veterinary fence for the control of foot and mouth disease.

Since the early 1930's, when the first boreholes were pumped in Hwange National Park, the provision of water to animals in the dry season (which lasts almost seven months of the year) has resulted in the increase in number of all species. If water is not provided, animals will die in large numbers and this could inflict irreversible damage to the most diverse wildlife population in the country. Throughout the park, there are fifty operational boreholes with thirty-five of these situated in the Main Camp sub-region which is the largest chunk of the park covering approximately 10 000 square km in extent and is mainly the sandveld area (Kalahari sands).

Without the usual large concentration of game in Hwange during the dry season when the bush is more open, there would be no peak tourist season. Obviously when a pan dries up, no animals can be viewed there with any certainty. The absence of water in the Park would thus be catastrophic for the tourism industry (which is probably the third largest foreign currency generator in Zimbabwe). It is bad publicity for Hwange when normally busy pans are deserted and devoid of game. The image of Hwange as a premier national park and tourist destination would thus be negated.

During the past four years the provision of water for game in the Park has gradually become worse and in fact, every year since 1990 the Park has faced a major water crisis. During the 1994 pumping season, game water supply operations fell into a total state of collapse. Existing boreholes are presently running unpredictably because of ageing equipment which cannot be replaced from a shoestring budget. Mechanical breakdowns are encountered almost on a daily basis. Certain boreholes considered not strategic by the Park Wardens have had to be shut down to cannibalize spares to maintain others, particularly on the tourist routes. This has resulted in the 'unnatural' concentrations of animals around key water points and the associated degradation of the ecosystem. Only about 6% of the Park is savanna grassland and most of this area is being subjected to extreme hoof pressure, over-grazing and destruction of trees, mainly around the water points

Other ecological problems which also come into play because of the water shortages in the park are:
1. The increase in the number of mortalities, particularly of water dependent species which are unable to walk long distances in search of water.

2. The exclusion of other animals drinking at pans by elephant which dominate scarce water reserves, to the detriment of specially protected and rare species.

Current Management Problems
The main reasons and factors causing the game water supplies predicament in HNP are:
i. inadequate funding
ii. late authorization to begin pumping
iii. ageing and obsolete equipment
iv. erratic rainfall
v. depletion of underground water reserves
vi. overpopulation of large wild herbivores.

The predicament has been made worse because of a long history of inadequate funding and the failure to replace ageing equipment such as diesel engines and borehole pumping equipment. It has also not been possible to repair or re-case collapsed boreholes or to sink new holes at sites where the original ones have dried up.

Inadequate funding. Unworkable annual monetary allocations are granted by central government, although realistic financial bids are submitted to Head Office each year. Over a period of eight years, between 11,7% - 72,64% of the financial bids have been allocated to stations. HNP and the Department of National Parks and Wildlife Management (DNPWLM) has had to rely on arbitrary donations from non-governmental organisations and well-wishers for financial and material support to sustain game water supply operations. Wardens in the Park have now developed a begging syndrome in order to keep the system alive. To maintain thirty-five pumped pans, the Warden in charge of the Main Camp sub-region was allocated a measly Z$283 220 for the 1993/1994 financial year against a realistic financial estimate of over

241

Z$680 000.   Z$203 220 of that allocation came from the United States Agency for International Development (USAID).

Financial allocations are further weakened by the devaluation of the Zimbabwe dollar and the ever increasing cost of spare parts and components.

Operating on a shoestring budget has further hampered Wardens from carrying out essential management functions such as pan dredging, major trough repairs, control of soil erosion around troughs and maintenance of engine shelters.   Pan dredging or scooping was last done some thirty years ago at a few pans like Caterpillar, Dopi and Mabuyamabema.   Today most of the pumped pans have accumulated tons of mud and silt and require dredging. A large number of animals become trapped in the mud when the level of water in the pans is low; dredging of the pans may help reduce the number of mortalities each year and also increase the holding capacity of pans.

For the past five years, major trough repairs could not be done because of the lack of funds, despite their importance as water storage facilities.   The only major works done recently was by Raleigh International teams who reconstructed four troughs, one each at Josivanini, Mbazu, Beaver and Manga II.   This was accomplished during their two expeditions in 1993 and 1994.

Soil erosion control around the troughs and pans should be an ongoing exercise, but this can not be done without sufficient funds.

It has also been difficult to maintain the few remaining engine shelters without money: the result is dilapidated and shanty looking structures, which are an eyesore.   In addition, it has also not been possible to erect new shelters, thus exposing engines to the natural elements, a factor which also greatly reduces their working life and efficiency.

Late authorization to begin pumping.   Spending cannot take place until the official notification of annual allocations is received.   This comes as late as September, ie four months after the pumping season should begin, by which time most pans will be dry.   The government financial year runs from July in one year to

June the next year. Although spending can take place by way of a Presidential warrant, the bureaucracy involved is stifling.

Pumping needs to begin as soon as possible after the rainy season to maintain the levels of water in pans. When they are permitted to dry up completely (which has been the case these past four years) their recovery rate is slow and in some cases the pans never reach more than 20% full, despite pumping twenty hours each day.

Ageing and obsolete equipment. The diesel engines currently used to pump water for game were donated to HNP by the Indian government in 1986 as part of the government to government aid programme. A wide range of essential spare parts was also donated to maintain the engines. The engines have now exceeded their life expectancy (which is normally five years) and the stock of spares was depleted in 1990, hence the critical problem of constant mechanical breakdowns. At the end of 1990, cannibalizing engines for used spares became the order of the day. At that time thirty-nine engines were in fair running condition compared to 1988 when forty-one engines were in mint condition. Today thirty-five are operational, albeit in poor condition. All engines except for one require major overhauls.

Most of the down-hole equipment, ie pipes, rods and pump elements have also exceeded their life expectancy, and using such equipment in its present state is straining all other working parts. Most borehole casings are corroded and have not been replaced since their installation, resulting in the caving-in of holes.

Erratic rainfall. Erratic rainfall and long periods of drought, in past years, has also been a contributory factor to the game water supplies predicament. Average annual rainfall for the Park is 620 mm, but in recent years, way below average rainfall has been received. Table 3 shows a comparison of rainfall figures between 1985 and 1990. It also shows the number of months pumped in each year.

Depletion of underground water reserves. The water table has been declining noticeably (borehole yield tests done regularly reveal this trend) and some boreholes have dried up completely. Since the early 1930's when the first boreholes were pumped in the Park, no major repair or maintenance work was done to boreholes. A few holes were cleaned and deepened in the early 1970's, but since then no further work was carried out despite some boreholes having caved in, resulting in significant yield drops.

Over-population of large wild herbivores. Large herds of game, particularly elephant and buffalo drinking at the pans during the dry season, coupled with high rates of evaporation and seepage only serve to exacerbate all the problems already outlined. Elephants are destructive by nature and have a tendency to destroy water installations, eg if a pump is not running, but they can smell water in the pipes underground, they will dig and rip out pipes to get at the water.

Personnel/general problems. The lack of technically trained staff to repair and maintain engines and borehole equipment is also a major problem. There are insufficient tools and inadequate workshop facilities to carry out repairs. Furthermore, the Park does not have reliable transport with which to conduct this major operation efficiently. The one and only heavy duty truck used for game water supply operations has been plagued by constant mechanical problems for the past three pumping seasons.

A general lack of motivation is evident, particularly amongst the pump attendants, because very little incentive is offered to them. They survive for up to seven months of the year on dry rations consisting of 25 kg of mealie meal, 1 kg of dried kapenta fish, 1 kg of sugar beans and 500 g of coarse salt per month, but do not receive fresh rations of any sort. Clearly, this is not a very healthy diet. Their working conditions, accommodation and remuneration is poor and they are not issued any form of protective clothing or camping equipment.

Possible solutions. An immediate short-term solution to the game water supplies problem would be a huge injection of funds to remedy the immediate crisis situation, before it gets even worse. A long-term rehabilitation programme also needs to be implemented and new, innovative ideas to conserve underground water reserves, fuel and funds needs to be developed. More research is also required to investigate the effects of the current method of artificial water provision and effects in totality.

244

Alas, at the risk of being repetitive, as I write this and check the date in my diary, I note that May 1998 is about gone. And nothing yet has happened. It would seem, sadly, that all the king's horses and all the king's men are not about to put Hwange together again.

THE MANAGEMENT UNIT

Shapi Pan at midday, March almost over, with late season thunderheads building up impressively in the distance way beyond the pan. The smell of rain strong in the air even though it is very still, with not a breath of wind. The waterhole itself full, the surrounding vegetation looking wonderful. Not a sign of life. Not even a frog or a cicada for background music as I sit listening to the silence, forking my way slowly through a tin of beans and viennas. The perfect balanced diet. My eyes drift back time and again to the pan itself, looking at all the water in there. Looking so, so good, even if there's nothing much going on. Shapi is one of those pans that offers either feast or famine, in terms of game viewing. There's either every giraffe in the Park meeting there for a convention, or even the francolins are calling in hushed whispers. My mind wombles back over sights I've seen across the years ... the one-eyed giraffe with healed scar tissue covering one side of its face, elephants, the two sable bulls in a no-quarter duel, more elephants, the bullfrogs out en masse after the first rains of the season, their chorus deafening, almost, *almost*, reaching my ears just after turning off the tar road. And there is history at Shapi Pan. And, as always, my thoughts ghost back to that time in April 1972, to that terrible midnight of the lioness. It killed veteran game ranger Len Harvey and mauled three other people, including fellow Parks stalwart Willie de Beer. I never knew Harvey, and I'm not especially religious, but I always mentally light a small candle when I visit Shapi.

In those days the Culling Unit had its base at Shapi. Shortly after the lion incident the unit was moved to Waterloop Siding, closer to Main Camp, and in time Waterloop was re-named Umtshibi, after one of the dominant tree species of the area. It has been hard to pinpoint when the Management Unit as such came into being. At the time of his death, Len Harvey was head of the culling and capture unit in Wankie, and it was at Shapi that the first ever contractor's camp was established. Contractors tendered annually to national parks headquarters to harvest the meat and hides coming from elephant culling operations, with parks keeping the ivory. Paul Grobler was the first successful cull contract tenderer. Alongside Harvey and de Beer there were other names well known in the wildlife fraternity who were involved in the first culls in Wankie and, later, in Mana Pools. Ron van Heerden, Tinkey Haslam, the Coetsee brothers, Robin Hughes ... alive or gone, their names still crop up in campfire conversations on occasion.

The Management Unit, though associated primarily with culling operations both within Wankie and elsewhere in the country, has always had a much wider mandate than the emotive issue of animal population management control, and what follows is a small history of this vital part of the Wankie story.

The Unit incorporated three separate, individually headed divisions, these being:-
1. culling and capture unit
2. fire management unit
3. conservation unit
The latter section was, in its time, the busiest, being responsible for land and soil management, and considerable logistical and material support was channelled into its operations. Erosion control, particularly in the Robins and Sinamatella regions, along with gully reclamation, brushwork establishment, fencing enclosures, deflection fences, and the re-routing of roads was the principal raison d'être of the conservation unit. After a life span of about six years, during

246

which time the objectives of the day were all achieved, this responsibility was absorbed into the first two units.

In terms of fire management, in an area like Hwange where the bush is tinder dry for months, the creation and maintenance of fire breaks, along with the seasonal monitoring of controlled burns were, *are*, a vital part of wilderness management. At the time that Len Harvey headed the culling unit, the fire unit was managed by Henry Pringle out of Main Camp, whilst the conservation aspect was headed by 'young' Norman Payne. With Harvey's death and the move to Umtshibi, the culling unit came successively under the leadership of Willie Koen and Cliff Freeman. In later years, from 1979 until 1987 Clem Coetsee became head of the Management Unit, and in time his name would become as synonymous with wildlife as those early doyens, Davison and Fothergill.

Along with culling work, the Management Unit was also responsible for capture and relocation exercises, and over the years a variety of species were moved. These included buffalo, giraffe, roan antelope, sable antelope, zebra, waterbuck, tsessebe, wildebeest, and of course, both species of rhino. In recent times, now out of the Parks system and running his own wildlife management service, Coetsee has pioneered the translocation of elephants, moving entire breeding units. At this time of writing over 1400 elephants have been translocated.

CULLING

Sit around a campfire in the African bush for long enough of an evening and, sooner or later, the 'elephant problem' surfaces; along with those other perennials, malaria and snakebite treatment. To cull or not to cull – such a hotly debated subject, and one so often shrouded with misinformation – sown by both pro-cull and anti-cull human proponents. In the meantime the human animal continues to do three things well. These are to procreate, and, subsequently, to put immense pressure on the space and food sources of our planet. We are literally eating ourselves out of house and home. Then, what we don't devour or debase, we manage very competently to ruin or destroy. However, we are also very adroit at pointing fingers, and this is where the elephant comes in for more than its fair share of condemnation. Sadly, the very problems that the human species causes for itself are also visited upon the elephant populations of Africa. The animals retreat before an ever expanding human population invading their range, a population that is only too ready to cry 'foul' should elephants trespass upon their newly won territory in any way. In turn, the displaced elephants are compressed into a few small areas, 'islands' of protection that have been set aside for them. Here, in time, their breeding and feeding habits begin to outgrow their havens, and consideration has to be given to culling, population reduction. By humans. Then there is the ivory trade, with its networks all over the globe, with, really, little control over it. Because the numbers of elephants, overall, are diminishing. But still you will read, on occasion, that there are too many elephants. *Too many elephants?* Not really. There are too many humans. But any suggestion that humans need culling, could do with a little scientific population reduction, would be met with considerable brouhaha, of course. There would be much wringing of hands. So, let us look at some facts, and try for a little perspective.

Zimbabwe is one of the very few countries in Africa where the elephant population, to date, has thrived and increased. Indeed, there are more elephants now than there were at the turn of the century, and it is worth mention here that when Selous realised his dream and arrived in the African hinterland to hunt big game in and round the region now known as Hwange National Park, the elephants were already in retreat from the hunters' guns coming from the south.

In 1960 it was estimated by the then Department of National Parks and the Game Department of Rhodesia that there were 32 000

248

elephants in the country. In 1989 the Department of Wildlife and National Parks Management of Zimbabwe estimated there were between 40 000 and 60 000 elephants, and in 1996 it was judged that their numbers had increased to between 60 000 and 73 000. At this time of writing (mid 1998) the Department estimates that there are 80 000 elephants in Zimbabwe.

Elephant populations increase at between 4% and 5% per year, with a calving interval of 4.3 years (in Hwange / B R Williamson 1976). In 1997, by way of an aerial survey carried out for the Department of National Parks and Wildlife Management by World Wildlife Fund, paid for by USAID, it was estimated that Hwange National Park carried an elephant population of 31 613 animals (in fact between 24 651 and 38 575 with a confidence limit of 22%). In 1987 it was estimated that there were 19 264 elephants, whilst a decade earlier it was estimated that there were 10 563 (*Bulawayo Chronicle*, 23 December 1979, quoting the late Basil Williamson, Wankie N P ecologist). Researchers and biologists judge that Hwange can hold, in terms of vegetation food source and destruction, and water supplies, about 14 000 elephants. At this time of writing, 45% of the country's elephant population is within the Hwange and neighbouring Matetsi region, this also taking into account the cross-border movement with Botswana.
The 'islands' of protection show signs of bursting at the seams.

The first organised culls of family breeding units took place in Wankie National Park in 1966, whilst sporadic population reduction had already been taking place, focusing essentially on bulls, since 1960.
After the Wankie '66 operation, other culls followed, in Mana Pools in 1969, 1970 and 1972, and subsequently in the Sebungwe and Gona re Zhou areas. Since 1960 culling, together with elephants killed in the course of day to day business for a variety of reasons, notably via tsetse control, sport hunting, problem animal control, crop protection, ration provisions, etc, some 50 000 have been killed

within Zimbabwe. 20 322 of that figure were killed within Hwange and its environs.

There has been no culling since 1987. This is because the relevant Management Unit had its hands full with the capture and translocation of black rhino out of poacher-threatened areas, for almost five years, and then, from 1992 up until this time of writing the Department of National Parks and Wildlife Management has simply not had the funds, leadership or infrastructure to continue with culling tasks, along with many other duties.

And so, the $64 000 question.

Do Zimbabwe's elephants, Hwange's elephants, have to be, *need to be*, culled?

Elephants … water … the two go hand in glove: do we know *enough* about that equation and the elephant *densities* in the different vegetation zones? *If* we do, and given that elephant poaching, drought or disease does not inflict massive mortalities, and that population estimates are, *in fact*, correct, then, regrettably, the answer has to be 'Yes'.

Why? Because of the way of the world in which we live. Because Rhodesia, and then Zimbabwe, protected her elephant populations so well, whilst in most of the rest of elephant-populated Africa this was not the case. Because the human animal, being so smart, has managed to do rather more successfully that which the elephant is no longer allowed to do. Breed prolifically. And, by way of fire, the wheel, firearms, landing men on the moon, super-drugs and a few other improvisations, man has got himself firmly ensconced at the top of the food chain. And, with the best will in the world, he has put things out of balance. The scales have been tilted. He, or she, is the world's master fixer, the super-predator, the one with the finger on the button, who decides which way the pendulum shall swing. Even if it is thrown off kilter on occasion by Mother Nature's rearguard action – El Nino, the occasional earthquake, a flood here or there, Vesuvius waiting for the right moment.

Aesthetics don't come into it any more. Gone are the days when wildlife could be preserved, conserved, simply because it appealed to some inner feeling. Because a giraffe, say, looked so good, walking across a sunset. It is a sad fact of life that wildlife, what there is left, has to pay for itself. Whether it is via camera tourism in reserves and parks, whether it is as a trophy smacked up on a wall in some far-off den, or whether it is as a farmed product. Wildlife that does not pay for itself has to move along, because there are people out there who covet its space. And for the elephant, pushed into its tiny 'island', and increasing to the degree that the 'island' can no longer accommodate it and the vegetation and the water resource and the other wildlife surviving in the same small area, there has to come a time when it has to make way. The luxury of waiting for nature to take its course, for elephant dynamics to adjust, eventually, of their own accord to conditions and geographics, is no longer an option. There is nowhere for it to go. If it leaves its 'island', it is immediately a trespasser, and we know what happens to trespassers. And within the 'island', if the elephant and its co-inhabitants are to live an anywhere normal existence, the bush and water factors have to be monitored. Managed. As do the elephants themselves. And culling has become a part of management. If there is any consolation to be had in this aspect of wildlife management it is that in Rhodesia (as with Zambia, Uganda and South Africa) the whole business, once introduced, was carried out efficiently and with minimum possible stress to the elephant populations. Further, much was learned by biologists from destroyed elephants, and the 'product' from the culled animals was not left to waste, which in itself would be a crime, unforgivable decadence. The meat, protein, has been harvested and used to feed hungry tribespeople, whilst skin, tusks and other parts of the animal have proved to be a considerable source of income to various fringe bodies, for example via CAMPFIRE (Communal Area Management Programme for Indigenous Resources). For anyone who has come to love and respect the elephant, the foregoing makes for some sombre reflection. But it is where we are today. Wildlife, now a luxury and not a right anymore, has to pay for itself.

251

Still and all, questions creep up on me, now and again. Vegetation destruction and canopy loss are usually amongst the main factors put forward in any knowledgeable argument where culling is advocated. On my wanderings around this beautiful country of ours, I see the destruction of the environment becoming increasingly evident – for tourist carvings around Victoria Falls, slash and burn cultivation where trees have grown for centuries, endless bundles of firewood for sale on any main road in the country, mature teak trees cut and piled within the precincts of Hwange National Park itself – a handful of examples of the uncontrolled hand of man. Who has the status of Royal Game.

And something else ... Governments come and go. In a week a country can have a new government. Ailing economies can be put back on track in a few years. Corruption can be purged in a few months. But the effects of out-of-control population growths are irreversible, become catastrophic, on man and animal alike. Zimbabwe, whose human population increase is one of the highest in the world, has a population which has doubled in twenty years.
What to do?

TOURISM

Tourism is the life-blood of any national park, with, however, an essential weather eye having to be kept on the impact of visitors to any such facility. Keeping that fine balance is not an easy task, even without the inhibiting factors mentioned at the beginning of this Afterword. The following few figures showing how tourism has progressed in Hwange may be of interest.

By the end of 1949, twenty years after Ted Davison's arrival in the area, the number of visitors in Wankie for that year was 2771. These made their way around on a limited amount of roads, with the Main Camp access only open to visitors from June to November, the dry season (See Ch 12 pg 120). Almost twenty years after that, in 1968, a record number of visitors had been recorded using the Park, this having leapt to 27 236 people, providing a revenue of £50 302.

In 1971, via the Main Camp access, 38 373 visitors had enjoyed Wankie's increasingly beckoning spaces, providing a revenue of R$119 701. (19 019 visitors entered through Sinamatella, whilst a further 8 917 used the Robins Camp gate – giving a total of 66 399 tourists.) Interestingly, this year saw the opening of the new Wankie Safari Lodge, situated on the Dett vlei, together with the completion of the nearby Wankie National Park aerodrome. It was another record year, but there was early concern developing over visitor pressure, highlighted by a note in that year's annual report that – *"Already there have been instances of up to 40 vehicles crowded around the same pride of lion".* Food for thought perhaps, today, when one sees the madding crowd perusing Ten-Mile-Drive on a busy afternoon.

Twenty years further on, the 1991 access through Main Camp was 68 048, this being made up of day visitors together with accommodated visitors. A visitor high occurred in 1994 (89 504 tourists), whilst 1996 saw a considerable drop, indicated by a figure of 46 871. What this indicates is hard to say. Perhaps the tourist boom in the neighbouring states of South Africa and Namibia had something to do with it, for they have some excellent well-managed wildlife destinations. Perhaps Zimbabwe could be marketing its tourist product more energetically. There again, maybe our value-for-money reputation has taken a knock or two. Probably it is a combination of all that and more, but whatever the case, as we make the turn into the last lap of this century, we need more than ever to nurture our tourist viability. Because, when one considers that in 1995 alone, from tourists coming through its gates, Hwange National Park earned Z$30 million for the country – quite apart from other indirect revenue – then surely the 'gift horse' should be given more oats.

POACHING

There has always been poaching. There always *will* be. Snares are being set around some waterhole as you read this. The trick is to try and keep it within manageable proportions. Poverty in Africa does not look like being a reversible trend, and, whilst there is that situation, there will be poaching. People get desperate. People have to eat. So, what is called 'subsistence poaching' will always be a factor for game wardens, now and forever. This in itself is hard enough to contain, let alone prevent, particularly with the constraints influencing today's conservation. To stop poaching, to slow it down even, there has to be control, human presence in the affected areas. Anti-poaching patrols have to be vigorously maintained, with the relevant staff motivated. A patrol has to do just that. It serves no purpose for an anti-poaching patrol to sit under an ebony tree for a week, fudging it, for whatever reason. Tourists, be they of the camera or gun-toting type, should be encouraged to foray out into the wide blue yonder – suitably chaperoned, of course. It is no good having vast closed areas with no men on the ground. Because the wildlife will go. Once gone, it will be awfully hard to get it back again. The snares, traps, dog packs and weapons have to be kept in check. I know of areas within national parks in Zimbabwe that are already bare, where wildlife, in fact any sign of wildlife, has disappeared.

As hard as subsistence poaching is to keep from spiralling out of control, it is the commercial poaching that takes an even greater toll of our wildlife heritage. Whether it is in the demise of the tiger for its sought-after anatomical parts by the Chinese, the boatloads of bush meat coming endlessly out of the African rainforests on the myriad of waterways, or the illegal bird trade throughout the world – second only in blood money to drugs – the commercial poaching responsible, yet another arm of organised crime, is a cancer that is long ago out of control. And whilst attentions tend to become focused on the 'dramatic' animals; rhinos, gorillas, whales etc – the flagship species – the toll on countless smaller creatures mounts virtually unnoticed.

In Zimbabwe the most catalogued object of the commercial poachers' attention has been our rhino populations (dealt with in detail under Wildlife – Then and Now), with devastating results. With the rhino down, the anticipated onslaught against our elephant population has been slow in coming, with some scattered incidents in the Zambezi Valley and Sebungwe areas being the only evidence so far. But it will come. Do not doubt it.

Hwange has been subjected to little commercial poaching pressure in the last four years, fortunately. There is a train of thought in some circles that, given our healthy elephant population, some poaching of these animals would not be too much of a dilemma. Once it starts, however, who knows how easy it is to halt. The white rhino demise in Hwange is an example. The poaching only stopped when there were no more rhino left to kill. I personally would like to see the role of Honorary Wardens reinstated, drawn from the ranks of the Professional Hunters of the country. Whilst there are certainly a few 'smash and grab' types lurking in this fraternity, by and large they constitute a dedicated body of men and women, with collective fingers on the wildlife pulse and, most of all, a vested interest in the future of wildlife. As it is, many are ex-national parks staff, so it would make sense to bring them in and use their knowledge.

There is a military adage that says a patrol is as fast as its slowest man, by inference meaning that the patrol is as *effective* as its weakest link. There is no doubt that the Zimbabwean government, through its past continuing lack of support for its Department of National Parks & Wildlife Management, both in a moral and financial sense, despite the millions of dollars earned via tourism, must have a large portion of the blame for the rhinos' demise laid firmly at its door. Peter Beard, in an interview with *Newsweek* (December 2 1996) puts the commitment to current conservation efforts at its simple best:

> *"If we really wanted wildlife, we'd do a lot of things differently. But we don't. We want air conditioning."*

There is also this. It is no use declaring a dramatic headline snatching 'shoot to kill' policy against poachers decimating wildlife if the staff of the relevant department are underpaid, uncared for, unmotivated and subjected to permanent crisis management. It has been the rule, rather than the exception, that the efforts of any staff in the field who *are* prepared to grasp the nettle and stand in the door of meaningful conservation – and there are precious few such individuals left – are very soon subject to suspicion and mistrust by the higher armchair-bound echelons, with transfers, suspensions and witch hunts being the order of the day.

The work and management ethic established by the early wildlife custodians like Ted Davison and Rupert Fothergill, maintained by the stalwarts who came after them – men like Austen, Reece, Gregory and the redoubtable Clem Coetsee – has, sadly, been diluted of late. True, there are workshops, seminars, conferences, discussions, talks – too much talk and perhaps too much time spent in front of computers, with not enough being done on the ground. Emancipation is a fact of life in Zimbabwe, Africa for that matter. Fine, no problem ... progress is progress, and it is long overdue that some of the wrongs committed in the scramble for Africa are righted. But along with progress has come a huge unwieldy bureaucracy, stifling meaningful decision making and eroding much of what *is* occasionally being done.

If Hwange National Park, or any other wildlife 'refuge' in Zimbabwe, is to go into the new millennium with any kind of hope, there has to be a major sea change in the attitude of the government and, in tandem, the Department of National Parks & Wildlife Management.

WILDLIFE – THEN AND NOW

In an area as vast and wild as Hwange how does one estimate the wildlife numbers? That is, with any degree of precision upon which a management policy can be instigated? It is no easy task. The elephant scenario is probably the best example of how different sets of numbers are arrived at. On the one hand there is a figure achieved via aerial census. Then there is the annual game count undertaken over a 24-hour period at water points throughout the Park that, if not providing exact figures, certainly helps establish trends in animal watering behaviour. And then, along with restricted road counts, there are the 'feelings' and observations made by various people 'on the ground' in the Park on a regular basis. Seldom are the elephant numbers obtained by these different sources the same, and there has been, is still, much debate.

However, we have talked about Africa's mega-herbivore, the elephant, elsewhere in this Afterword, so let us have a look at its larger co-inhabitants that can be seen in the Park.

Prior to 1996 the last in-depth survey of Hwange's wildlife was carried out between August 1969 and June 1971, with the figures published by the Trustees of the National Museums and Monuments of Rhodesia in their Museum Memoir No 5 of 1975. Viv Wilson headed the survey, assisted by fellow museum personnel and a variety of National Parks and Wildlife Management staff. A perusal of the Acknowledgements of this literature will bring to light the names of several of Wankie's colonial-era wildlife guardians, men whose contributions then helped make Hwange the enduring sanctuary it has remained to this day. Austen, Williamson, Rushworth, Mitchell, Fynn, Williams, de Beer, Harvey, Braybrooke, Herbert ... names that are threads in the tapestry of wildlife conservation that has had more than its share of rips and tears in its fabric throughout Africa over the last years.

The estimated numbers of larger game species then in the Wankie National Park were recorded thus: -

APPENDIX B.   Estimated numbers of larger game species (Nov 1973) in the Wankie National Park.

	c. 300	
Spotted hyaena	c. 500	
Brown hyaena	fairly rare	
Leopard	c. 300	
Lion	c. 500	
Cheetah	c. 80	maximum
Elephant	c. 10 500	
Black rhino	c. 30	
Square-lipped rhino	c. 40	
Zebra	c. 4 000	
Warthog	c. 3 000	
Hippopotamus	5	
Reedbuck	c. 250	
Waterbuck	c. 800	
Impala	c. 8 000	
Gemsbok	c. 120	
Roan	c. 600	
Sable	c. 1 800	
Tsessebe	c. 100	
Wildebeest	c. 1 800	
Kudu	c. 3 500	
Eland	c. 1 600	
Buffalo	c. 10 000	

Today, 25 years later, the latest estimates are out, gathered during 1997 and again put together with Department and researcher assistance, by the indefatigable Viv Wilson. The figures reflect mixed fortunes amidst the wildlife denizens, and themselves raise a whole new gamut of questions and conjecture.

Lions are usually near the top of any tourist's spot-list and Hwange has always been a good destination for people wanting to see Africa's largest carnivore. It is worth noting that, in Wankie's earliest formative years, lion – along with hyena, leopard, cheetah and wild dog – were destroyed by the Department in order to give the thinly spread herbivores in the embryonic Park a chance to multiply. At this time of writing it is judged that the lion population has increased to at least 1000 animals, and that they are well entrenched. Of concern, however, is the status of male lions in certain areas that abut neighbouring safari and farmland regions outside the Park. It is local knowledge that a considerable amount of male lions, on leaving the boundary of Hwange, are shot in the adjacent safari areas every year. And there is a strong-held belief in some circles that, on occasion, the lions are lured out of their Hwange sanctuary by baits and recorded calls by safari operators not overly concerned with hunting ethics or the effect that this may have on lion pride society.

The spotted hyena, it seems, has done well over the years, with their numbers up and estimated to be between 1000 and 1500 animals. Both the foregoing statistics are good news for the bush lover fond of the night music of these two predators. The status of its cousin, the brown hyena, is rare.

The leopard, that most secretive of loners, also seems to be more than holding its own – and will probably be around long after its more obvious carnivore neighbours have retreated. How one establishes just how many of these cats who walk by themselves *are* out and about has to be a headache-provoking task, and their numbers are estimated as having increased to 1 000.

The cheetah population, again difficult to gauge because of its wide-ranging habits, is in debit, with an estimate that there are *perhaps* 50 of these long-shanked predators present at this time.

The wild dog, subject to considerable monitoring by researchers of late, is also not holding its own, when its present day estimate of 100 animals *maximum* are compared to the circa 300 figure of 25 years ago.

Once widespread over most of Africa, today only four countries support stronghold populations (Zimbabwe, Botswana, Tanzania and the Kruger National Park only in South Africa), with perhaps some holdout groups in Zambia, Ethiopia and Senegal. The painted hunting dog (which is the recommended terminology these days) has, compliments of the human animal, had more than its share of persecution over the years. Cast as a villain in the popular press since the turn of the century, it is only in recent times that its reputation is losing some of the tarnish, with its role in the wilderness fabric being properly interpreted. Still, though, even today, their very large home ranges frequently results in packs moving outside the boundaries of protection afforded by national parks, whereby shooting and road deaths continue to exact a high toll.

Food for thought is that whilst cheetah and wild dog are decreasing, one of their important prey species, impala, has increased dramatically. One may wonder how much the considerably increased lion and hyena populations have affected the dynamics of the smaller predators. A long overdue carnivore study is about to be initiated, which hopefully will begin to shed some light on the habits and carnivore interaction in the Park.

Moving on to herbivores, the survey has estimated that there are some 25 000 elephant in Hwange.

After the elephant, the largest herbivore is the rhinoceros, and a short history of its decline and fall would not be amiss here.

Both species of African rhino have fared poorly in the Wankie region, with the white or square-lipped at this time of writing to all extent and purpose being once again extinct, represented by perhaps three or four scared and scattered individuals – too few and far between to sustain a population.

Its first wipe-out came towards the end of the last century, compliments of the early European hunters and explorers. Selous recorded the presence of probably the last square-lipped rhino in 1896, in that area that gave him so much good sport, the Dett vlei, about which he had earlier written:

"A herd of nine giraffe stalked slowly and majestically from the forest, and, making their way to a pool of water commenced to drink ... one or other of them from time to time, straddling out its forelegs in a most extraordinary manner in order to get its mouth down to the water ... One after another, great herds of buffalo emerged from the forest on either side of the valley and fed slowly down to the water. One of these herds was preceded by about fifty zebras, and another by a large herd of sable antelopes. Presently two other herds of sable antelopes appeared on the scene, a second herd of zebras, and five magnificently horned old kudu bulls, whilst rhinoceroses both of the black and white species were scattered amongst the other game, singly or in twos or threes all down the valley."

Thereafter, for some 66 years, the second largest African land mammal no longer roamed the sun-washed spaces it had inhabited since the earth first formed.

After the successful re-introduction of white rhino back into the territory in 1962, with the eight animals being released at Kyle and Matopos thriving (see Ch 15 pg 154 and the report on Operation White Rhino) the way appeared clear to further bolster this new Rhodesian population. Consequently, between November 1966 and March 1967, 35 more white rhino were introduced, this time into Wankie, and again translocated up from the lush coastal vales of Zululand in South Africa. This new nucleus was made up of 16 males and 19 females, which bred up slowly but successfully to a peak of, maximum, 150 animals by late 1990.

Then, as the last decade of this century evolved, disaster struck again. This time the plunderers did not carry Rigby or Gibbs sporting rifles, did not weigh in with Hollis muzzle loaders. For this time around the weapon of destruction was the brainchild of one Mikhail Kalashnikov, a weapon much vaunted in military circles and so ubiquitous in the trouble spots of the world – the AK 47 Assault Rifle. If any one weapon has contributed to the misery and demise of wildlife on the African continent it is this favourite of global guerrilla movements (the armament now carried, paradoxically, by most field staff of the Department of National Parks and Wildlife Management of Zimbabwe).

The new onslaught against the white rhino occurred between 1991 and 1993, and only ceased when that animal was, essentially, no longer represented in Hwange National Park. Animals that lived within gunshot range of the Main Camp headquarters were killed as easily as those whose territories were more far flung. An expensive de-horning exercise, initiated at the eleventh hour and largely funded by outside concerned agencies, did nothing to save the species. The dedication and hard work carried out in the middle 60's and nurtured thereafter was wiped off the slate in one prolonged hit and run, barely challenged exercise. Interesting, and incorrect, are the rhino poaching figures quoted in a table on page 24 of ELEPHANT MANAGEMENT IN ZIMBABWE, a report handed out at the 1997 CITES conference in Harare. It states that 43 black or white rhinos were killed illegally between 1990 and 1995. If this figure were correct, a bit of simple arithmetic begs the question – why are we not seeing any rhinos in the Park today?

Black rhino, perhaps helped by the inhospitable terrain which they favoured, were still in limited evidence (see Ch 15 pg 146) long after the last white rhino had gone down in 1896, but even so also became locally extinct. This state of affairs was reversed in October 1962 by the introduction of eight black rhino (six females, two males) rescued from the rising waters of the new lake, Kariba, on the Zambezi River and translocated to Wankie. Four more (one male, three females), coming from the same source, were introduced in March 1963. During the following month one of the females was killed in a fight with another rhino at Mandavu Dam. The carcass of a male rhino was found in the same area in May, showing signs of battle damage, and it was deduced that this had been the female's protagonist. Forty more, bringing the total to 48 (because of the aforementioned and other fatalities), came into Wankie in October 1965. These had been driven up via the Hostess Nichol Trail from the Sengwa area abutting the now fully spread Lake Kariba, where they had been under severe human pressure, and, together with the previous new arrivals ex Operation Noah, they heralded a new era of black rhino population in Wankie. The re-introduced nucleus of animals thrived and gradually moved back into territories once inhabited by their predecessors in the hard country that hugs the vast expanse of the Kalahari.

However, at the same time as the white rhino were being wiped out, so too were the guns turned on the black rhino. First in the Zambezi Valley, where next door Zambia provided a safe haven for the poachers sent by the commercial fat cats in Lusaka, with their connections in Johannesburg, Harare, the Far East and Yemen. As the 80's went by it became apparent that anti-poaching operations, notably Operation Stronghold, were not saving the species. This, despite much financial assistance coming from sympathetic external and internal organisations, as well as a lot of materiél, together with, at the time, a dedicated, blood-sweat-and-tears nucleus of field staff. With the rhino war in the Valley being lost, it was decided to translocate as many of the animals as possible into national parks and selected private sanctuaries where they could be better monitored. Thus, in 1984, 1987 and 1993 more black rhino were translocated from the Dande, Mana/Chewore and Chizarira areas respectively, boosting by 91 animals (after capture mortalities) the earlier new arrivals of the 60's. This step, in the context of Wankie at least, did not stop the poachers from continuing with their destruction, and the numbers dwindled. As the last white rhino were being gunned down, with, again the black rhino holding on a little longer, the concept of Intensive Protection Zones evolved, and at last a flicker of light winked, if albeit intermittently, for the future of the remaining black rhinos.

Created in late 1993, there are today four IPZ's in Zimbabwe, areas patrolled and monitored by both national parks staff and elements of the Zimbabwe National Army. Only two of these, at Matusadona and Hwange, can be considered as successful black rhino recovery zones. It is no coincidence that the relevant wardens at both localities are men who have, under extremely difficult circumstances, shown supreme dedication. The zones, together with the private refuges, are working, at this time of writing, and so, once again, the species is showing signs of a comeback. The IPZ within the Hwange precincts in the northern rugged part of the Park has in trust the new nucleus of yet a third generation of black rhinos. One can only hope that this time their future is more secure.

The buffalo population within Zimbabwe as a whole has decreased in the last dozen years, with the Middle Zambezi Valley, Gona re Zhou and Hwange National Parks recording the most significant down-trend. In Hwange their numbers have dropped by more than half, with their population estimated as being around 5 000 animals. Any reasons offered by this writer would only be conjecture, but, as the buffalo is water-dependent, needing to drink in a 24 hour cycle, water has to fit into the equation somewhere.

The Hwange environment looks to be treating the giraffe well, with its figures judged as being up to 3 000 animals. Sometime in the remainder of this year it is proposed that some 50 giraffe will be captured by the Management Unit and translocated to the lowveld.

Impala, with its catholic feeding habits and ability to adapt to different vegetation zones, is the most numerous animal in the Park, after the elephant, and has now colonised its way from Sinamatella to Main Camp area. Sometimes passed by for the more 'dramatic' Hwange residents, these graceful medium-sized antelope, the colour of "newly minted copper pennies" are estimated as being some 15 000 strong.

The population estimates for the other main herbivores in the Park are as follows:-

Sable	circa	2 600
Roan*........................	perhaps	300
Tsessebe*	perhaps	20
Reedbuck*	perhaps	200
Waterbuck...................	circa	600
Zebra	circa	3 500
Wildebeest	circa	1 800
Eland	circa	500
Warthog	circa	4 500
Hippopotamus.............	circa	30

* indicates a radical decline

CONCLUSION

As we knock on the door of the new millennium, what does the future hold for Hwange National Park? Is there any light at the end of the tunnel for it or other national parks of the country whose stars have dimmed in the last twelve years or so? In recent times the wildlife cause has broken more than a few hearts, and it is easy to become a cynic. Certainly, whenever I ruminate about wildlife and the future, about conservation past and present, it is hard to stop the depression creeping in. So, as to the future, well ... maybe, perhaps ... yes.

Only very recently, in early June 1998, I dared to feel that there may be a match poised, ready to re-light the candle that might again push back the darkness. What caused this was my introduction to a 145-page, blue-covered tome labelled –

HWANGE NATIONAL PARK MANAGEMENT PLAN 1999 – 2003
at a workshop held at Main Camp. Yes, another workshop, this one attended by over 50 people, made up of Department personnel and a variety of 'Stakeholders' whose livelihoods are deeply affected by the fortunes or misfortunes of Hwange. Perhaps the most important people present were the two Swedish gentlemen representing Jaakko Pöyry Consulting – facilitators who chaired the two-day session and monitored the wide-ranging discussions about the new management plan.

There are, at last, major changes in the Park Management System, not the least of them being millions of dollars being made available, and negotiations between Zimbabwe, the World Bank and the Global Environmental Facility well under way for a soft loan to implement the Park Rehabilitation and Conservation Project (PARC). The acting director let it be known that 30 million Zimdollars were earmarked for soon release to Hwange National Park. All stirring stuff, indeed. There did occur a fair amount of re-inventing the wheel, evident in 'new' formulations and strategies advocated, but if one were to join in the spirit and rapport of the occasion it was certainly a landmark event in that Park management and stakeholders, for so long locked in to that 'them against us' syndrome, had re-focused their energies and grasped the nettle to jointly administer the antidote for the malaise so long afflicting Hwange.

The Hwange National Park Vision Statement reads thus:-
"Make Hwange National Park acknowledged world wide as a leading place in a friendly Africa for a life-time experience of wildlife at any time of the year. A conservation and customer oriented management will, in co-operation with Park stakeholders offer a unique biodiversity in flora and fauna."

Fine words, this clarion call, and the people on the ground would appear poised to make it work. As long as their efforts are not negated by the higher echelon bureaucracy or sleight-of-hand governmental machinations, Hwange National Park looks set for a

Z A

Livingstone

Victoria
Falls
National
Park

Victoria Falls

N
W   E
S

Scale
1: 1,000,000. 14.78 miles = 1 inch

Matetsi

ZAMBEZI - MUTENGA

Baobab

Hunters
camp

Robins
camp

o Baobab Pan

Deteman

Deteman

Shu

Dandan
Pan

Shumba
Pan

B O T S W A N A

PANDA MA-TENGA

Hehimba
Pan

Irriga-vile

"Shakwan"

Shubeshube pa

KONU

Damtchetchi

Kywushia

Burn
liark

comeback, and this plan could, indeed, *"... be the cornerstone of a dynamic, transparent and representative national wildlife and resource management policy."*

If however, the stumbling blocks of the past are to remain as the cornerstones that will take the Park into the new century, Hwange will go down. To quote from the Management Plan ...

"Failure to implement the plan may send wrong signals to all who devoted their time and effort in coming out with this plan. The old operation system characterised by lack of identity with the park, suspicion and imposition of some policies is likely to prevail which might be detrimental to wildlife utilisation particularly in the communal areas. Park staff are also likely to be demoralised and will see the planning process just another assignment for Head Office, another piece of paper to add to the shelves and wastage of resources and funds."

With optimism and cynicism jousting for the upper hand in my mind, I took my leave of the workshop, coming out into the hot dry winter sunshine, pausing, listening to the ever-cheerful sparrow weavers and plaintive-sounding hornbills. From the direction of the airstrip a zebra stallion shrilled, with, closer, the strident call of a red-billed francolin competing with the querulous mutter of grey louries. They were sounds that Ted Davison would have cocked an ear at, so long ago. I wondered if his spirit was around, had dropped in to eavesdrop on the proceedings. Had a fair idea of how *he* would read the signs.

Keith Meadows – Bulawayo – July 1998